THE WHOLE BODY OF COOKERY DISSECTED

William Rabisha

THE WHOLE BODY OF COOKERY DISSECTED,

Taught, and fully manifested, Methodically, Artificially, and according to the best Tradition of the *English*, *French*, *Italian*, *Dutch*, &c.

OR,

A Sympathy of all Varieties in Natural Compounds in that Mystery.

A FACSIMILE OF THE EDITION
PUBLISHED IN 1682

PROSPECT BOOKS
2003

This edition first published in Great Britain in 2003 by Prospect Books, Allaleigh House, Blackawton, Totnes, Devon TQ9 7DL.

© 2003, Prospect Books.

A CIP record for this book is available from the British Library.
ISBN 1-903018-11-0

Designed and typeset by Tom Jaine.

Printed and bound in Great Britain by the Cromwell Press, Trowbridge, Wiltshire.

CONTENTS

Foreword	7
Table of Contents	9
The Text	27
Glossary	363

FOREWORD

The first issue of William Rabisha's *The Whole Body of Cookery Dissected* was in 1661, the publisher being Giles Calvert, at the West End of St Paul's. There were subsequent editions in 1673 and 1675, as well as that of 1682, which is the text here reproduced. The publishers of this last edition were George Calvert and Ralph Simpson.

For this present edition, the text has been digitally scanned, cleaned up as far as possible, and reproduced at the same size as the original. A new table of contents has been provided, as well as a glossary. There are certain infelicities in the original ordering of the text, as well as in the page numbering, which mean that Rabisha's own table of contents is misleading. The text has therefore been given a single, modern pagination.

The importance of Rabisha's work has long been recognized. This foreword does not explore that beyond the obvious statement that the book was a celebration of the return to normality after the Civil War and Interregnum (Rabisha had followed the King to foreign parts during the 1650s), and that it served as propaganda for the old ways of hospitality. Parallels may here be drawn with Robert May's *The Accomplisht Cook*, first published in 1660. This conservative aspect is particularly marked by the recycling of *Certain old useful Traditions of Carving, and Sewing*, a text that originated in the fifteenth century before going through several versions culminating in that written by John Murrell and incorporated in *Murrels Two Bookes of Cookerie and Carving* of 1631. Parts of this text were also reprinted by Robert May. In addition, Rabisha reprinted, he says from the records in the Tower of London, the order of service of a feast given by George Neville, Archbishop of York in 1468. Rabisha's self-avowed intent was 'that thou maist see what Liberality and Hospitality there was in Antient times amongst our Progenitors: … Thus hoping to see Liberality flourish amongst us once more, as in old time'. This is the same as the feast for the enthronization of the Archbishop more properly dated 1465 which is reproduced by Richard Warner in *Antiquitates Culinariae* (1791), taken in that instance from Leland's collections. The first public record of the feast, as far as early-modern England was concerned, had been extracted by Matthew Parker, Elizabeth's first Archbishop of Canterbury (see Felicity Heal, *Hospitality in Early Modern England*). As with his reproducing *Traditions of Carving, and Sewing,* Rabisha occupied well-trodden ground.

The printing of this book is not of the most uniform. Different fonts of type have been deployed, and the impression on the page is often very uneven.

I am grateful to Alan Davidson for the copy of Rabisha that was used here, and to Ben Morrow for assistance in scanning.

Tom Jaine

TABLE OF CONTENTS

This list of headings and recipe titles is copied from the text itself, with all errors included. The page numbers are to the modern pagination, in square brackets at the foot of each page.

The Epistle Dedicatory	[29]
To the READER	[31]
In Commendation of the Author.	[36]
A Bill of Fare for an Extraordinary Feast,	
on a Flesh-day in the Spring.	[38]
A Bill of Fare for a Fish-Dinner in the Spring.	[39]
A Bill of Fare on a Flesh-day for the Summer Season.	[41]
A Bill of Fare on a Fish-day, for the Summer season.	[43]
A Bill of Fare for a Flesh-dinner in Autumn.	[44]
A Bill of Fare for the Winter Quarter, for a Flesh day at Dinner.	[45]
A Bill of Fare for three Courses for the Winter-season,	
of Fish and Flesh, in February and March.	[46]
THE TABLE.	[47]
THE TABLE. Rare Receipts in Cookery.	[59]
THE TABLE. Very rare and most choice Receipts for	
all manner of Preserving, Conserving and Candying &c,	[62]
Certain Old useful Traditions of Carving and Sewing, &c.	[65]
The whole Body of COOKERY DISSECTED.	[67]
BOOK I.	[67]
How to pickle Cowcumbers.	[67]
How to pickle Mushroms.	[68]
To pickle the tops of Elder.	[68]
To pickle Elder buds in March, before the Tree leaves.	[68]
To pickle Clove-gilly-flowers.	[68]
To pickle Pursland stalks.	[69]
To pickle Artichokes.	[69]
To pickle the tops of Turnips.	[69]
To pickle green Figgs.	[70]
To pickle Barbaries red.	[70]
To pickle Sampier green.	[70]
To pickle stalks of Thessel or Sherdowns.	[70]
To pickle Reddish tops.	[71]

To pickle Taragon.	[71]
To pickle Cowslips.	[71]
To Pickle Fennel or Dill.	[71]
To pickle Red Cabbage.	[71]
To pickle Burdock Roots.	[71]
To pickle Lemmon and Orange Pill.	[72]
To pickle Ashen Keys.	[72]
To pickle curled Endive.	[72]
To pickle Charnel.	[72]
To pickle Quinces.	[72]
To pickle Bramble-Fruit.	[73]
To pickle Broom-buds.	[73]
To pickle Bog-berries.	[73]
To pickle Grapes.	[73]
To pickle Red and White Currans.	[73]
To pickle Elder, or many other buds of trees in the Spring, that useth to serve for Spring-sallets.	[74]
To pickle Cabbage-stalks.	[74]
To pickle Shampinnions.	[74]
To pickle Sleep-at-noon.	[74]
To pickle the stalks of March-Mallows.	[74]
To pickle Alexander-Buds.	[75]
To pickle Mallagatoons.	[75]
BOOK II.	[76]
How to Sowce, Pickle and Coller all manner of Flesh.	[76]
To Coller and Sowce Brawn.	[76]
To Coller Venison.	[77]
To Coller Beef Red.	[78]
To Coller Veal.	[79]
To Coller Pig.	[79]
To Coller Pork.	[80]
To Coller Mutton.	[81]
To Coller Goats-flesh.	[81]
To Coller Geese.	[82]
To Coller Swan.	[82]
To Coller Brand Geese or Wiggens.	[82]
BOOK III.	[83]
To Sowce, Pickle or Marble Fish.	[83]
To Coller Eels.	[83]
To Sowce a Tench, to be served in Jelly.	[83]

To pickle Smelts white or red.	[84]
To Marble Sowls, Plaice, Flounders, Smelts, or any other Fish that is fitting to Marble.	[84]
To pickle Lobsters, and to preserve them.	[85]
To pickle a Conger Eel.	[85]
To Pickle and Sowce Sturgeon.	[85]
To pickle Caveer.	[86]
To Coller Sowls.	[87]
To Coller Salmon.	[87]
To Sowce Lumps.	[88]
BOOK X.	[88]
Cold baked Meats of Flesh.	[88]
To make Paste of Rye-Flower.	[88]
To Bake Venison in Crust, or in Pots.	[89]
To bake a Fillet of Veal to be eaten cold.	[90]
To bake a Calves-head to be eaten cold.	[91]
To bake a Fawn or Kid to be eaten cold.	[91]
To bake a Hare.	[91]
Another way to bake a Hare.	[92]
To bake Pork to be eaten cold.	[93]
To bake Brawn to be eaten cold.	[93]
To bake Rabbets to be Eaten cold.	[94]
To bake Pigeons to be Eaten cold.	[94]
To bake Bran-Geese, or Wild-Geese.	[94]
To bake a Turkey.	[94]
To bake Herns.	[94]
To bake a Swan.	[95]
How to bake a Goose.	[95]
Cold Baked Meats of Fish.	[95]
To bake a Lamprey Eel Pye.	[95]
To bake a Turbert.	[96]
To bake a Salmon.	[96]
To bake an Eel to be Eaten cold.	[97]
To bake a Pike.	[97]
BOOK V.	[97]
How to make several sorts of Jellies, Leaches, and Creams.	[97]
To make Jellies.	[97]
How to season and run Chrystal Jellies.	[98]
How to run Colours.	[99]
To make Jellies of Oranges.	[99]

To make Harts-horn Jelly.	[99]
How to make Leach.	[100]
How to run your Leach into colours.	[101]
The use of your Jelly and Leach.	[101]
To make divers sorts of creams.	[102]
To make Cheese and Cream.	[102]
Another way.	[102]
To make Apple Cream.	[102]
To make Quince-Cream.	[103]
To make a Cream called Sack and Pottage.	[103]
To make a Sack-Posset the best way.	[104]
To coddle Codlings green, to serve up with Cream.	[104]
To make Barly Cream.	[104]
To make Rasberry Cream.	[105]
To make Red Currans Cream.	[105]
To make Cabbage Cream.	[105]
To make Snow Cream.	[106]
To make Almond Leach Cream.	[106]
To make Goosberry Cream.	[107]
To make Rice Milk or Cream to be eaten hot.	[107]
To boyl Milk or Cream with French Bread, to be eaten hot.	[108]
To make Spring Pottage.	[108]
To make a Water-Grewel.	[108]
To make Punnado.	[109]
To make Barley-Grewel.	[109]
To make a Pearmane Cawdle.	[110]
To make a Lemmon Cawdle.	[110]
To make a Florendine, or Made-dish of Rice.	[110]
To Butter Rice.	[111]
To make a Florendine or made-dish of Apples.	[111]
To make a Florendine or Made-dish of Spinage.	[112]
To make Pasties to fry.	[112]
To make a Florendine or Made-dish of Kidney of Veal.	[112]
To make toasts of a Kidney of Veal, called Marrow toasts.	[113]
To make a Florendine or a Made-dish of a Calves-Chaldron.	[113]
To make a Made-dish of Apples and Red Currans.	[114]
To make a Made-dish of Artichokes.	[114]
To make forced Meats.	[115]
To make part of the said forced meats green for your use.	[115]
Another forced Meat.	[116]

BOOK VI. [116]
Containing strong Broths, and Pottages,
with other preparations of Cookery. [116]
To make Strong Broth for your use in dressing of Meat. [116]
An excellent Cordial Broth. [117]
To make Pottage of broth, to serve up with a Bisk,
or grand boyled Meat. [117]
Another way. [118]
To make a Broth or Pottage, called Skinck. [118]
To make white Broth. [119]
To make Stewed Broth. [120]
Another, a Consumption Broth. [120]
To make Red Pottage. [121]
Another Broth. [122]
How to draw Gravie. [122]
How to draw Butter. [122]
How to Recover it. [123]
How to make Barley Broth. [123]
BOOK VII. [124]
Which teacheth to make all manner of hot
boyled meats of Flesh. [124]
How to make a Bisk. [124]
To make a brown Bisk. [126]
To make an Olue. [126]
How to force all manner of Meats. [127]
Your Leare for your sweet forced meats. [128]
How to make a forced boyled meat. [128]
Your Leare and garnish for sweet forced boyled
meat of the same kind of Fowl. [129]
To boyl Capons or Chickens in white Broth. [129]
To boyl a Hanch of Venison. [130]
To boyl Legs, Necks, or Chines of Mutton, four wayes. [130]
Another way. [131]
Another way. [131]
Another way to make a Lear for the said meat. [131]
To boyl a Leg of Veal and Beacon. [132]
To make your green sauce two ways [132]
To boyl a Breast of Veal. [132]
To boyl a Knuckle of Veal with the Neck cut in five pieces
to be skrved in Broth. [133]

To boyl a Leg of Pork.	[133]
To boyl Capons or Hens for the Winter-season.	[134]
Another way with Mushrooms.	[134]
To Boyl Chickens.	[135]
Another way.	[135]
Another way.	[135]
Another way	[136]
Another way to Boyl Pullets and Chickens for the Winter.	[136]
Another way.	[137]
To Boyl Wild-Ducks, Wigeons or Teal.	[138]
Another way.	[138]
To Boyl Rabbets.	[138]
How to boyl Pigeons.	[139]
To boyl Plovers.	[140]
To boyl Caponets or Pullets.	[140]
To make a forced boyled Meat.	[141]
To Boyl Udders and Tongues.	[142]
A boyled meat after the French fashion.	[143]
Another way according to the French fashion.	[143]
BOOK VIII.	[144]
Containing how to make several sorts of Puddings.	[144]
How to make a Quaking Pudding.	[144]
Another way.	[145]
To make a dish of Puddings of several Coulours.	[145]
To make Marrow Puddings to boyl in Skins.	[146]
To make black-Puddings to be kept.	[147]
To make Polony Sassages to keep all the year.	[148]
Another way for Sassages.	[149]
To make a Pudding of Hogs-Liver.	[149]
To make a baked Marrow Pudding.	[150]
To make an Oatmeal Pudding.	[150]
To make a Pudding of Rice flower.	[151]
To make a hasty Pudding.	[151]
To make Andolians.	[152]
BOOK IX.	[153]
Contains Hash, Stewed, Broyled and Carbonadoed meats.	[153]
To farce a Fillet of Beef.	[153]
To stew a Breast of Mutton.	[154]
To farce a Fillet of Veal.	[154]
To stew Venison.	[155]

How to stew Calves Feet.	[155]
To hash a Shoulder or Leg of Mutton.	[155]
How to make a raw Hash of a more excellent way, new invented.	[156]
To Hash a Calves head.	[156]
To Hash Hens or Pullets with Eggs.	[157]
To make a Hash of Capons.	[158]
To Hash Partridges.	[158]
To Hash Ducks, or other water-fowl.	[158]
To Hash a Rabbet.	[159]
Carbonadoes and Broyled meats.	[159]
To Carbonado a Goose.	[159]
To Carbonedo Turkies.	[160]
To Carbonado Henns.	[160]
To Carbonado Veal.	[160]
To Carbonado Mutton.	[160]
A dish of Collops of Mutton, Broyld.	[161]
Steaks of Pork Broyled.	[161]
To Carbonado a Calves head.	[162]
To Broyl a Chine of Park.	[162]
BOOK X.	[163]
Containing Frigasies and Frying.	[163]
How to fry all manner of Garnishing.	[163]
How to fry Oysters in Batter.	[163]
A Frigacy of a Hen or Capon.	[164]
To make a Frigacy of Chicken brown.	[165]
Another way for Chicken or Rabbets.	[165]
To smear Collops of Veal.	[166]
To fry a dish of Lamb-stones and Sweet breads.	[166]
How to make a Frigacy of Lamb.	[167]
A Frigacy of Veal.	[167]
A dish of Collops of Mutton with a savoury hogo.	[168]
To fry Coller'd Pork.	[168]
Another way.	[168]
A Frigacy of Partridge or Woodcocks.	[169]
A Frigacy of Ducks or Widgeons.	[169]
A fryed meat of Bacon.	[169]
To make a fryed meat, called an Amlett.	[170]
Another way.	[170]
To fry Primrose-leaves in March with Eggs.	[171]

To fry Clary.	[171]
To fry Apples.	[171]
How to make an Orangado Phraise.	[172]
A Tanzie of Cowslips or Violets.	[172]
A Tanzie of Spinage.	[173]
To fry Artichokes, or Spanish Potatoes.	[173]
To make Fritters.	[173]
To make Pancakes.	[174]
Another way to dress a dish of Collops of Veal.	[174]
To fry Calves Feet, or Sheeps Trotters.	[175]
How to Frigacy Neats Tongues and Udders.	[176]
To potch a dish of Eggs for a weak stomach.	[176]
Another way rich and strengthening.	[177]
Another way.	[177]
How to Butter Eggs.	[177]
Another way.	[178]
To fry Collops and Eggs.	[178]
BOOK XI.	[179]
Containing all manner of Sallets and Roast-meats, with their several Sauces.	[179]
To make Sallets.	[179]
To make a Grand Sallet for the Spring.	[179]
The Flesh Sallet of a Capon or Turkey.	[180]
A made dish of Parmizant.	[181]
A Sallet of a dryed Neats-Tongue.	[181]
A Sallet of Fennel.	[182]
A Sallet of green Pease.	[182]
A Sallet of boiled Spinnage.	[182]
Rules how to roast Meats, with their several Sauces.	[183]
To roast a Hanch of Venison.	[183]
To roast a Jegget of Mutton.	[183]
To roast a Shoulder of Mutton with Oysters.	[183]
To roast a Chine or Neck of Veal.	[184]
To roast a Breast of Veal.	[184]
A Fillet or Leg of Veal Farced.	[185]
To roast Olives of Veal.	[185]
To roast a whole Lamb or Kid.	[185]
To make a Kid of a Pig, and a Pig to be roasted.	[186]
Te roast a Calves-head.	[186]
To roast Leverets, and Rabbets.	[187]

To roast a Lambs Head.	[188]
To roast Venison.	[188]
Several Sauces for your Fowl in general.	[189]
For Capons.	[189]
For Hens.	[189]
For Turkie.	[189]
For Chickens.	[189]
A sauce for roast Pigeons.	[190]
Sauce for Rabbets.	[190]
Sauce for Pheasants, Heath-Poots, or Cocks of the wood.	[190]
Sauce for Woodcocks.	[190]
Sauce for Quails.	[190]
Sauce for Ducks, Wigeons, Teal, or Plover.	[191]
BOOK XII.	[191]
Treats how to boil or stew Fish to be eaten hot with Compositions.	[191]
How to boil, or stew Fish, to be eaten hot.	[191]
To boil a Pike.	[191]
To stew a Carp.	[192]
Another way to boil Carps.	[193]
To stew a dish of Flounders.	[193]
Another way.	[194]
To boil Perches.	[194]
How to make a Bisk of Fish.	[194]
To dress a Codds head the best way.	[196]
To make an Olive of Fish	[197]
To boyl Mullet or Base to he eaten hot.	[198]
To stew or make broth, with Whitings or Smellts.	[198]
How to stew or boyl Eeles.	[199]
Another way.	[199]
To dress a dish of smalls Jacks.	[199]
To stew a dish of Breams.	[200]
BOOK XIII.	[201]
Containing how to bake, Fry, Broyl, Rost, and Frigacy certain sorts of Fish.	[200]
How to make Sawce or Lear without Butter, or thickning with Eggs.	[201]
To fry Fish, and all manner of Garnishing with Oyl.	[201]
Another way, how to thicken your lear for fish without eggs.	[202]
To stew a dish of Trouts.	[202]

To boyl and serve a whole Salmon.	[203]
To Roast a Pike.	[203]
To roast Eeles.	[204]
To roast Porpus.	[205]
To roast a Carp.	[205]
To Roast a Salmon whole.	[206]
How to Spitchoock an Eele.	[206]
For Boylnig.	[207]
To broyl Flownders or Plaice.	[207]
How to fry a dish of Maids.	[208]
To fry a dish of Ling for first course.	[208]
How to Frigacy or Butter Crabs or Lobstors.	[209]
How to Frigacy Shrimps, Perriwinkles, Pranes, Crawfish, &c.	[209]
A Phraise of Cockles.	[209]
How to broyl Oysters.	[210]
To Broyl Scollups.	[210]
How to bake certain Fish.	[211]
To bake a Carp two ways.	[211]
To make an Eele Pie.	[211]
To bake Turbet.	[212]
To bake a Salmon Pie to be eaten Hot.	[213]
To bake a Joll of Ling in a Pie.	[213]
Another way.	[214]
To bake a Pike in a Coffin.	[214]
To bake a Lump in a Coffin.	[215]
To bake Flounders or Plaice.	[215]
To bake an Oyster Pie.	[216]
To make a Batylle of Pye of Fish.	[216]
To make Peteets of Shrimps or Pranes.	[217]
To Marrinate a Carp, to be eaten hot or cold.	[217]
To Hash a Carp.	[218]
A Frigacy of fresh Salmon.	[218]
To Frigacy great Plaice or Flounders	[219]
To make Chewits of Salmon.	[220]
To broyl a Carp.	[220]
To force an Eele.	[221]
BOOK XIV.	[222]
Contains several sorts of hot baked Meats of flesh.	[222]
To bake a Gammon of Bacon, to be eaten hot, with the Ingredients.	[222]

To make a Pye of Mutton	[223]
Another way.	[223]
For a sweet Lamb Pie.	[223]
Another way for a savoury.	[224]
Another way.	[224]
To bake a Hen to be eaten Hot.	[225]
How to bake an Hen another way.	[225]
Another way to bake a Hen in a Patty Pan.	[226]
To bake a Capon or Turky in a Patty pan.	[226]
How to season and bake a Pasty of Venison.	[227]
Another way to bake Venison, to be eaten hot.	[228]
To make a Battley, or Bisk Pyes in the Spring.	[228]
To make a Sherdoon Pye in the Spring.	[230]
To make a Lumber Pye.	[230]
To make a dish of Chewits.	[231]
To make an Ox cheek Pye.	[231]
To make a Calves head Pye.	[231]
To make a Neats-Tongue Pye, to be eaten hot.	[232]
To make a Chicken Pye for the Winter.	[233]
Another way.	[233]
Another way.	[233]
To make a Calves head Pye.	[234]
To make an Olive Pye.	[234]
To make an Artichoke Pye.	[235]
To make a Skerret Pye.	[236]
To make a Potato Pye.	[236]
To make Marrow Pasties to fry.	[236]
To make egg Pyes.	[237]
To make a Trotter Pie, and Taffaty-Tarts.	[238]
To make an Orangado Pye.	[239]
Another way.	[240]
A hot baked meat of compounds.	[240]
To make Pigeon Pye.	[241]
Another way.	[242]
To make a Kid Pye.	[242]
Another way.	[243]
Two other wayes.	[243]
To make a Pasty of an old Goat.	[244]
To make a Lamb-Pasty.	[244]
To bake a Fawn, or young Roe.	[245]

To make Pasties of Pies [sic, rice] to fry.	[245]
BOOK XV.	[246]
Contains all manner of Tarts, and made Dishes.	[246]
How to make a Bacon Tart.	[246]
To make an Almond-Tart.	[246]
To make a Pine-apple Tart.	[247]
Another Tart of Pistaches.	[247]
To make a Spring Tart.	[247]
To make a Cowslip Tart.	[248]
To make a Cheese Tart.	[248]
To make a Prewen Tart.	[249]
To make Cheese Cakes.	[249]
To make a dish of Puffs.	[250]
To bake a set Custard.	[251]
To make Tarts of the Jelly of Pippins.	[251]
To make a Goosberry Tart green, and clear as Christal.	[252]
To make Puff-Paste.	[252]
To make a laid Tart for Preserves.	[253]
To make a Warden or Pear-Pye.	[254]
To Bake a Quince Pye.	[254]
To make a Pye with whole Pippins.	[254]
A set Tart.	[255]
RARE RECEIPTS IN COOKERY	[257]
To make a Bisk divers wayes.	[257]
To boyl a Capon in Rice.	[259]
A Bisk another way.	[259]
To boyl a Leg of Mutton the French fashion.	[260]
To boyl Partridges.	[261]
Capons in Pottage in the French fashion.	[261]
To make a boyled meat, much like a Bisk.	[262]
To boyl a Neck, Loyn, or Chine of Mutton, or a Neck, Leg, Fillet, Knuckle of Veal, Leg, or Loyn of Lamb.	[263]
To boyl a Chine of Veal whole, or in pieces,	[263]
To bake a Pig to be eaten cold, called a Mare-maid Pye.	[264]
Another way.	[264]
To bake Steaks the French way.	[264]
A Pudding stewed between two dishes.	[265]
To make French Puffs with green herbs.	[265]
To Bake all manner of Land-fowl; as Turkey, Bustard, Peacock, Crane, &c. to be eaten cold.	[266]

TABLE OF CONTENTS

To fry Sheeps-tongues, Deers-tongues, or Calves-tongues.	[266]
To bake a Pig to be eaten hot.	[267]
To bake all manner of Sea-fowl, as Swan, Whopper, to be eaten cold.	[267]
To Harsh a Carp.	[268]
For the Stock for Jelly.	[268]
To make a Jelly as white a Snow, with Jordan Almonds.	[269]
To make some Kick-shaws in Paste, to fry or bake in what form you please.	[269]
To make a Pottage.	[270]
To make a small Bisk of flesh roasted.	[270]
A Jelly for service of several colours.	[272]
To bake Apricocks green.	[273]
To make an Oatmeal Pudding.	[273]
To make an Oatmeal Pudding boyled.	[273]
Oatmeal Puddings, otherwise of fish or flesh blood.	[274]
To make white Puddings an excellent way.	[274]
To make an Italian Pudding.	[274]
To make Metheglin.	[275]
How to make Ipocras.	[275]
To Jelly Lobsters, Crawfish, or Prawnes.	[276]
To Stew Crabs.	[276]
To force Crabs.	[277]
To make water Leach.	[277]
To make a boyled Pudding.	[278]
Another way.	[278]
A baked Pudding after the Italion fashion, corrected.	[279]
To blanch Manchet in a frying-Pan.	[279]
Another way.	[279]
To boyl Pidgeons the French Fashion.	[280]
To boyl Mullet, or Pike with Oysters.	[280]
To boyl Carps an honourable way.	[281]
Another way to boyl a dish of great Flownders.	[281]
To make a Hash of Partridges or Capons.	[282]
A rare Frigasy.	[282]
To make a Bisk of Carps and other several Fish.	[283]
To dress Eggs in the Spanish fashion.	[285]
To dress Eggs in the Portugal fashion.	[285]
To dress Eggs called in French Ala Augenotte, or the Protestant way.	[286]

To dress Eggs in fashion of a Tansey.	[286]
To dress Poacht Eggs.	[286]
To butter Eggs upon Toasts.	[287]
An excellent way to Butter Eggs.	[287]
To make Cheese-cakes.	[288]
To make Dowsets.	[288]
How to make a congealed meat, to be eaten cold.	[289]
How to congeal a Turkey or Capon.	[289]
How to make small Pindents to fry for first Course.	[290]
How to make rich Pancakes.	[291]
Another way to make them crisp.	[291]
How to fry a leg, breast, or neck of Lamb.	[291]
How to make a green Frigasy of Chickens.	[292]
A fryed meat in haste for the second course.	[292]
How to make a Pudding with Whey.	[292]
How to make Apple-pyes to fry.	[293]
How to make a boyled meat, a forced meat, a dish of Collops, and a roast meat, and a baked meat, of a leg of Veal, with some other small ingredients.	[293]
A Fridayes dish made with Barley.	[295]
For a Friday, to make a dish of fryed toasts.	[296]
Another Friday, or Lent dish.	[296]
A second course-dish in the beginning of the Spring.	[296]
To make a made dish.	[297]
An excellent way how to broyl Eeles.	[297]
How to butter a dish of eggs with Anchovies.	[297]
How to fry a dish of Cheese.	[298]
How to broyl a leg of Pork.	[298]
How to roast the said Collops.	[298]
How no make a Palate Pye.	[299]
Very rare and most choice RECEIPTS For all manner of Preserving, Conserving, and Candying, &c.	[301]
To Preserve Pippins.	[301]
Another way.	[301]
Another way to Preserve them Green.	[302]
To Preserve Apricocks.	[302]
Another way.	[302]
Another way to Preserve them Ripe.	[303]

To Preserve Pippins Red.	[303]
To Preserve Pears.	[304]
Another way for white Pippins.	[304]
To Preserve Medlars.	[304]
To Preserve Peaches.	[305]
Another way.	[305]
Another way.	[305]
To Preserve Quinces.	[306]
Another way to preserve them white or red.	[306]
To perserve Goosberries.	[306]
Another way.	[307]
Another way.	[307]
To preserve Mellacatons.	[308]
To preserve Damsins.	[308]
Another way.	[308]
To preserve Grapes.	[309]
Another way.	[309]
To preserve Cherries.	[309]
Another way.	[310]
Another way.	[310]
To preserve Barberries.	[311]
To preserve Raspberries.	[311]
Another way.	[312]
To preserve your Pomcitrons.	[312]
To preserve Oranges and Lemons.	[312]
To preserve Saterion Roots.	[313]
To preserve red Rose-leaves.	[313]
To preserve Enula Campana Roots.	[314]
To preserve Currans.	[314]
To preserve Mulberries.	[314]
To preserve Eringo Roots	[315]
To preserve green Walnuts.	[315]
To preserve Angelica Roots.	[315]
The time to preserve green Fruits, according to other Authors.	[316]
Here begins your Conserves.	[317]
Conserve of Barberries.	[317]
Another way.	[317]
To make Conserve of Violets.	[317]
To make a Marmalade of Quinces.	[318]
To make Conserve of Borage flowers.	[318]

To make Conserve of Rosemary flowers.	[318]
To make Conserve of Bugloss-flowers.	[318]
To make Pectoral rolls for the Cough.	[319]
To make Conserve of Strawberries.	[319]
To make Conserve of Prunes or Damsins.	[319]
To make Conserve of Red and Damask Roses.	[320]
To Conserve Couslips, Marigolds, Violets, Scabions, Sage and Roses, &c.	[320]
To make a Pomander.	[320]
Another way to Conserve Strawberries.	[320]
To make Conserve of Cichory-flowers.	[321]
Here follows the Sirrups.	[321]
To make sirrup of Pomcitrons.	[321]
To make sirrup of Liquorish.	[322]
To make sirrup of Hore-hound.	[322]
To make sirrup of Hyssop.	[322]
To make sirrup of Violets.	[323]
Another rare way.	[323]
To make sirrup of Mulberries.	[323]
To make sirrup of Clove-Gillyflowers.	[323]
To make sirrup of Roses solutive.	[324]
Another way to make sirrup of Damask-Roses.	[324]
To keep your liquor of Roses all the year.	[325]
To make sirrup of Cowslips.	[325]
To make sirrup of Lemons.	[325]
To make sirrup of Maiden-hair.	[325]
To make sirrup of dry Roses.	[326]
To keep Cherries all the year, and to have them at Christmas.	[326]
Candying.	[326]
To Candy Violet-Flowers.	[326]
To Candy Pears, Plumbs, Apricocks, to look clear, &c.	[327]
To Candy Borage-Flowers.	[327]
To Candy Rosemary-Flowers.	[327]
To Candy all sorts of flowers after the Spanish way.	[328]
To make Manus Christi.	[328]
To Candy Goos-berries.	[328]
To dry Apricocks.	[329]
To Candy Enula-Campana.	[329]
To Candy Eringo-roots.	[329]
Another way.	[330]

To dry Pippins.	[330]
To candy Rose-leaves as natural, as if they grew on trees.	[330]
To Candy all sorts of Flowers, Fruits and Spices, the clear Rock-Candy.	[331]
To Candy Marigolds in Wedges, the Spanish Fashion.	[331]
To Candy all manner of Flowers in their Natural colours.	[331]
To Candy Ginger.	[331]
PASTES.	[332]
To make a Paste of Pippins the Genova fashion, some with leaves, some like Plumbs with stalks, and stones in them.	[332]
To make Paste of Orenges and Lemons.	[332]
To make Paste of Goos-berries.	[333]
Certain old useful Traditions of CARVING, and SEWING &c.	[334]
Terms of a Carver.	[334]
The Office of the Butler, Pantler, Yeoman of the Seller, and Eury.	[334]
Of the Sewing of Fish.	[338]
Service.	[338]
Of Carving of Flesh.	[338]
Service.	[338]
Sauce for many sorts of Fowls and Flesh.	[341]
Of the Feasts and Service from Easter unto Whitsuntide.	[341]
General Directions for the Carving up of Fowl.	[342]
Lift that Swan.	[342]
Rear that Goose.	[342]
To cut up a Turkey or Bustard.	[343]
Dismember that Heron.	[344]
Unbrace that Mallard.	[344]
Unlace that Coney.	[344]
Sauce the Capon.	[345]
Allay that Pheasant.	[345]
Wing that Partridge.	[345]
Wing that Quail.	[345]
Display that Crane.	[345]
Dismember that Heron.	[346]
Unjoynt that Bittern.	[346]
Break that Egript.	[346]
Untach that Curlew.	[346]
Untach that Brew.	[346]

Break that Sarcel.	[346]
Mince that Plover.	[346]
A Snite.	[346]
Thigh that Woodcock.	[347]
From the Feast of Whitsuntide unto Midsummer.	[347]
From the Feast of Saint John the Baptist, unto Michaelmas.	[348]
From the Feast of Saint Michaelmas, unto the Feast of Christmas.	[348]
Sewing of Fish.	[349]
First Course.	[349]
Second Course.	[350]
Third Course.	[350]
Of Carving of Fish.	[350]
Sauces of all Fish.	[351]
An excellent way for making Ipocras.	[352]
An approved Receipt for a Consumption, that hath long remained.	[352]
To coller Flounders.	[353]
To roast a shoulder of Mutton in Blood.	[353]
To make a Portugal Pie.	[353]
To stew a carp.	[354]
To make a Bacon Tart.	[354]
To make Vever Ollie, or Cheese-Pottage.	[355]
Reader	[357]
A great FEAST made by George Nevil Chancellor of England, and Arch-Bishop of York, in the days of EDWARD the FOURTH, 1468.	[359]

The whole Body of
COOKERY
DISSECTED,

Taught, and fully manifested, Methodically, Artificially, and according to the best Tradition of the *English, French, Italian, Dutch*, &c.

OR,

A Sympathy of all Varieties in Natural Compounds in that Mystery.

Wherein is contained certain Bills of Fare for the Seasons of the Year, for Feasts and Common Diets.

Whereunto is annexed a Second Part of Rare Receipts of Cookery : With certain useful Traditions.

With a Book of Preserving, Conserving and Candying, after the most Exquisite and Newest manner : Delectable for Ladies and Gentlewomen.

LONDON,
Printed for *George Calvert* at the *Half-moon*, and *Ralph Simpson* at the *Harp*, in St. *Paul*'s Church-yard, 1 6 8 2.

✧✧✧✧✧✧✧✧✧✧✧✧✧✧✧✧✧✧✧✧✧✧✧✧✧✧✧✧✧:✧
✧✧✧✧✧✧✧✧✧✧✧✧✧✧✧ ✧✧ ✧✧✧ ✧✧✧ ✧: ✧✧✧

To Her Highneſs the Illuſtrious Dutcheſs Dowager of *Richmond* and *Lynox* her Grace.

To Her Highneſs the Dutcheſs of *Buckingham* her Grace.

To the moſt honourable, renowned and ſingular good Lady, the Lady *Jane Lane*.

To the right honourable and ſingular good and vertuous Lady, the Lady *Mary Tufton*.

To the honourable the vertuous good Lady, the Lady *Agnes Walker*.

May it pleaſe your Graces and Ladiſhips,

Hoſe boundleſs unſpeakable *Vertues* dwelling in you, which have been daily manifeſt (even in thoſe late covetous deſtructive *Times* under the cloak of *Frugality*) in your *Liberality* and *Hoſpitality*, by which you have been upholders and nouriſhers of all ingenuous Arts and Sciences, and in particular that of the ſaid Myſtery of *Cookery*, who have not only entertained thoſe of the Arts as Domeſtick Servants in your Houſes, but have conferred many high favours on them beſides : And thus according to your various Roots of Goodneſs, you have

A 2   ſprung

The Epistle Dedicatory.

sprung forth, and born fruit for the nourishment of all that came under your shadow, but differently, according to your noble worth, which I shall more particularly set forth in several Dedications to your Graces and Ladiships; and since my small ability can give no symptom of a thankful acknowledgement, save this small Tract of my Practical Experimental labours in my long Travels in several Kingdoms, if admitted into your Treasury of Volumes, I question not but upon perusal, it may, as the Widows Mite, find acceptance. I humbly crave your favourable construction thereof, that thereby it may receive further strength under the shadow of that gracious Canopy, which is the height of his ambition, who desires to be devoted,

Your Graces and Ladiships

poor unworthy

Servant till death,

Will. Rabisha.

To

To the READER.

Impartial Reader,

Any reasons have at last induced me to present the World with this small Tract of my many Years study and practice in the Art and Mystery of Cookery.

First, In that I was brought up in the Family of an honourable Lady, who spared for no cost nor charge, for my instruction in the said Art, not only at home in her House, but also abroad in the late Kings Court, of ever blessed memory, and in the Houses of certain honourable Persons, and at the entertainment of Embassadors, besides many other Feasts: Since which time, I have served as Master Cook to many honourable Families before and since the Wars began, both in this my Native Countrey, and with Embassadors and other Nobles in certain forreign Parts: Thus having through Traditions, and my constant practical experience in this the long progress of my life, received knowledge herein, and considering the World is a Body, and every individual and rational Soul a Member thereof, and that Man was not born for himself, but for the good of the whole, it is but just to pay Tribute unto her, from whom I received all, which I do account but a very small compensation, to return this my Mite into the same Treasury from whence I first received it.

Secondly, It hath been the practice of most of the ingenuous Men of all Arts and Sciences, to hold forth to Posterity

To the Reader.

Posterity, what light or knowledge they understood to be obscure in their said Art : And the wisest of Philosophers, learned and pious Men of old, have highly extolled these principles, who went not out like the snuff of a Candle, but have left their Volumes to after-ages, to be their School-master in what they have a mind to practise; which calls back time and gives life to the dead.

Thirdly, I was further encouraged to this work, by seeing that happy and blessed restauration of our long-exiled Royal Luminaries; and the hopes of the benevolent Influence of Liberality and Hospitality, which is in part the Life of Arts and Sciences. It is indeed like the Sun in the Firmament, which keeps not his light and heat for himself, but in his Gradual revolution, freely bestows himself to the giving of life, feeding and cloathing the whole Universe : And doth not his Representation and Production, even our Sun, or King, and his Nobles do the like ? Do not thousands live by their benevolence? What have they more than others, but honourable respect and attendance ? As for Food and Rayment, they pay for, by which all Men live ; for all that they have comes to the Purse, Pocket, Back and Belly of all Men Yearly; they are like a great Wheel that moves the next ; and so they move one the other, that none stands idle; the removing of which, is the destruction of the whole, which we have lately found by woful experience, occasioned by *Solomons* fools, even Men to whom God hath given riches, so that they want nothing for their Soul of all that they can desire, yet God giveth them not power to eat thereof ; but a Stranger eateth it, but this hath been their vanity, and their evil disease ; notwithstanding they had as good pretences as *Judas*, who said, Wherefore serves this waste, it might have been sold for much Money and given to the Poor.

Fourthly, Being desired by many young Practitioners in this Art, and others, for Receipts and assistance therein,

To the Reader.

in, I was the more willing to prefent thefe my fmall endeavours to publick view, for the fatisfaction of all thofe that are ingenuous, and defirous to be inftructed in the faid Practice. I do not queftion but divers Brethren of my own Fraternity may open their Mouths againft me, for publifhing this Treatife, pretending that thereby it may teach every Kitchen wench, and fuch as never ferved their times, and fo be prejudicial to the Fraternity of Cooks; but thefe are to let them know, the fame may as truly be faid of all other Arts and Sciences, the Aftronomer, Mathematician, Navigator, Phyfitian, Chirurgion, Farrier, and many hundred more. And what Artifts amongft them, make not themfelves perfect, as well by ftudying their Volumes, as by practice. Yet there is an evil amongft moft Men, when they have learned themfelves by other Mens light, they would extinguifh that light, that none might follow them; and fo Men monopolize all knowledge therein to themfelves, and condemn all thofe that are a guide and light to the ignorant; there is none other but fuch will condemn me in what I have done. Again, they are miftaken that think a Tract of this kind can be very beneficial unto any, but fuch as have been in fome meafure Practitioners, and underftand the nature of the ingredients propofed for the performances of any one thing; for experience fhall tell all my Brethren, that it is an hard thing to teach a young Practitioner to drefs many hundred of the faid Difhes, after the compofition is made; nay, although they look on them, and give them direction, yet will they fpoyl it in the doing, therefore I hope it will anfwer my end and no more; which is for the inftruction of young Practitioners, that give their minds to the ftudy thereof; and to the end that it may, I here prefent unto the Reader this fmall Tract in a methodical form, as Cookery lyes in its order and Workmanfhip, containing in the firft part therof, fifteen Books, the firft fix of

A 4   which

To the Reader.

which may be called Cookery in its preparations to Feasts or Common Diets, and in that regard they are to be performed Months, Weeks, or Dayes before hand, for the greatest part thereof; the first contains Pickles, the second how to sowce, pickle, and coller all manner of fish; so through all your preparations of cold Meats of all kinds, Jelly, Leaches, Creams, and many other useful and necessary things for your Feast on all occasions; and in the seventh Book you begin to see your Cookery in its heat, running through all the rest of the Books in all kinds of Cookery, in a methodical manner. I have also for thy further instruction composed certain Bills of Fare for the four seasons; and a second Book, called, Rare Receipts in Cookery, with some usefull old Traditions and new Instructions, which will be very necessary and advantagious for the Fraternity of Cooks; together with a Book of Preserving, Conserving and Candying: I would desire the Reader in all these, for his further benefit, to observe these few particulars.

1. First, that whereas the Dishes of Meat may seem too big in most, or all the Receipts to some; that makes no matter to the teaching of them that have occasion to have them less; it is remedied in taking an equal proportion of each ingredient, according to the quantity as you intend to dress, whether half, or a quarter, or so much as the Receipt. Again, if you would augment, you must take a bigger quantity of each simple in your general compound.

2. If Salt be left out where it ought to be, as it is possible it may, correct that fault; also take out your faggot of sweet herbs, Onions, Garlick, or whole Spices from your Meats, when you go to dish your Meats; for I have omitted to mention this in every Receipt, because once done, will serve for all.

3. That the Reader would take notice, that the second Part, called Receipts, was intended to be placed in the

first

To the Reader.

firſt Part, in order and form, every ſort by it ſelf, as the firſt Part is compoſed; but the Author being abſent in the Countrey, that and many things more intended were neglected: only I deſire the Reader to correct it in his own thoughts, and enlarge it by what is done, until the Author gets further opportunity to add thereto.

4. Let not the Reader think that the Bills of Fare be too big, but conſider, if he intends to have fewer diſhes, what an advantage he hath to have his choice out of ſo many.

5. Whereas there are ſome Bills of Fleſh, only for Fleſh-dayes, and others of Fiſh, for Fiſh-dayes, in caſe you would have both Fiſh and Fleſn, you may make a mixture at your pleaſure.

6. Obſerve that ſome things propoſed are not in ſeaſon the whole Seaſon, or three Months, but part thereof; for example, in *March* and *April* Oyſters are in ſeaſon, but not in *May*; in which time Trouts and many other ſorts of Fiſh and ſome Fleſh, as Bucks, are not in ſeaſon, but they are in ſeaſon in *May*; ſo the like in all the other Seaſons of many things. You muſt correct your Bills of Fare for theſe things, and take that which comes in, for that which went out: So minding the four Seaſons, the ingenuous Practitioner will be able to make a Bill of Fare of himſelf, without the help of any. I have in the whole Matter uſed my uttermoſt endeavour to inſtruct the ingenuous Practitioner. If any thing therein be omitted or profuſe, I ſhall deſire thy charitable conſtruction thereof; if it be worthy of thy acceptance, it anſwereth my expectation, and will further encourage him to ſerve thee in the like matter, who ſubſcribes himſelf, thine in the Art and Myſtery of Cookery,

Will. Rabiſha.

In Commendation of the Author.

Ooks burn your Books, and vail your empty brains;
Put off your feigned Aprons, view the strains
Of this new piece, whose Author doth display
The bravest dish, and shew the nearest way
T'inform the lowest Cook how he may dress,
And make the meanest meat the highest mess:
To please the Fancy of the daintiest Dame,
And sute her Palate that she praise the same;
Give him return of worth, (besides due wages)
And recommend his Book to future Ages.
Let it be known Rabisha here hath hit
The fairest passage that hath dared it.
   But read his Book, and judge his pains,
   His is the labour, yours the gains.
Of vacant Herbs and Roots he maketh Sallets,
And Pickle for your use, to please all Pallats.
To coller, sowce, and pickle Flesh so rare,
None that is extant can with him compare.
To Marinate, to Sowce, and pickle Fish,
So rich, so high, as any Heart could wish.
See how he baketh Flesh and Fish, for cold
Varieties, of each both young and old.
Jellies and Leaches fit for Royal Courts,
And Creams for Ladies choice of divers sorts.
His Broths, Pottages, to the taste and sight,
Would Esau-like, make some to sell their right.
Preparatives great store he doth compound,
For boyl'd and bak'd, so rare and so profound.
Next boyled meats rehearseth in such order,
As doth become so skilful a Recorder.

For

For Puddings, like to his have not been seen,
Fit for the Royal Table of a Queen.
To Carbonado, and to Hash and Stew,
He all correcteth, by his Art more new.
To Fry and Frigasie, his way's most neat ;
How he compounds a Thousand sorts of Meat!
His Sallets are prepar'd each in their Season,
Dished in form, by Arts admired reason ;
To roast and sauce your Flesh of every kind,
Forc'd, Fearst, with Pallats hogo to each mind.
Next how to stew, and boyl all sorts of Fish,
With rich ingredients to every Dish.
Learn here to bake, broyl, frigasie and roast :
Nay more, collered fish, fry'd, fearst, and forst.
Flesh bak'd Meats hot, so rich and excellent,
Whose savoury taste would give to all content.
With Tarts so delicate, 's new invention,
Doth far surpass my apprehension.
Besides, he hath set forth two Bills of Fare,
For every Season within the Year.
A second Book he hath of rare Receipts,
Affecting freedom, more than avarice baits.
In these his works the noble will delight,
For he can make and marr an appetite.
Therefore brave Book, into the World be gone,
Thou vindicat'st thy Author ; fearing none
That ever was, or is, or e're shall be,
Able to find the Parallel of thee.

A

A Bill of Fare for an Extraordinary Feast, on a Flesh-day in the Spring.

First Course.

1. A Bisk or grand boyled Meat.
2. A Chine of Mutton or Veal, with Oysters.
3. A Grand Sallet.
4. A dish of boyled Carps.
5. A dish of Pheasants.
6. A grand Pattee of Chickens.
7. A Pottage or Skink.
8. A Turkey.
9. A Carbonado.
10. A Sallet of Capon.
11. A Calves head hashed.
12. A Chine of Beef.
13. A Lumber Pye.
14. A dish of boyled Puddings.
15. A dish of larded Collops smeered.
16. A boyled meat of Hens, with a Gammon of Westphalie Bacon.
17. A Grand Sallet.
18. A Jigget of Mutton with Oysters.
19. A Pike with small fish fryed.
20. A Hare larded.
21. A Frigasie of Chickens.
22. A Lam-Pye.
23. Marrow Puddings.
24. A Kid larded & forced.
25. A dish of Heath-Poults larded.
26. A forced Meat boyled.
27. A dish of Olives of Veal roasted.
28. A made dish.
29. A soused Pigg.
30. A boyled Sallet of Spinage, &c.
31. A rump of Beef.
32. A dish of Hens roasted
33. A dish of cold Meats of several sorts.
34. A Cold baked Meat.
35. A dish of coller'd Veal, soused and sliced.

Second

Second Courſe.

1. A diſh of Quails.
2. A diſh of tame Pigeons.
3. A diſh of young Turkeys larded.
4. A diſh of great Sowls fryed.
5. A diſh of Anchovies.
6. A diſh of rich Tarts.
7. A diſh of Tanzies of ſeveral colours.
8. A diſh of Cowſlip Cream.
9. An Orangado Pye.
10. A diſh of Jellies.
11. A diſh of Chickens.
12. A diſh of Leveretts.
13. A diſh of Prewen Tarts.
14. An Almond Cream.
15. A diſh of Peaſe in *March* or *April*.
16. A diſh of Ruffs.
17. A diſh of young Ducklins.
18. A Potatoe Pye.
19. A diſh of Sturgeon.
20. A Sallet of Neats-tongue.
21. A diſh of pickled Smelts.
22. A diſh of laid Tarts.
23. A Frigaſie of Apples.
24. A Chine of Salmon broyled.
25. A diſh of Caveer and Potargo.
26. A diſh of young Rabbets.
27. A ſet Cuſtard.
28. A cold baked meat of Veniſon.
29. A diſh of roaſted Pigeons wild, larded.
30. A diſh of Leach.
31. A Trotter Pye, with Taffatee Tarts.
32. A diſh of broyled Oyſters.
33. A diſh of coller'd ſouſed Eel.
34. A diſh of collered Beef, as red as Anchovies.
35. A diſh of Pranes, Shrimps, or Oyſters.

A Bill of Fare for a Fiſh-Dinner in the Spring.

Firſt Courſe.

1. A Bisk of Fiſh.
2. A diſh of rich Puddings boyled.
3. A Sallet of Spinage or Peaſe.

4 A Carp Pye.
5 A Rock of Butter.
6 A diſh of fryed Ling, with poached Eggs.
7 A Salmon boyled whole.
8 A diſh of Maids in green.
9 An Eel Pye.
10 A diſh of buttered rolls.
11 A Pike roaſted.
12 A Joll of Ling.
13 A diſh of Toaſts.
14 A diſh of Perches boyled.
15 A diſh of buttered eggs.
16 A diſh of Mullets or Bace, with ſmall Fiſh.
17 A diſh of Puffs.
18 A diſh of Barrel-cod.
19 A ſtewed Carp.
20 A Salmon Pye.

Second Courſe.

1 A diſh of Sowls fryed.
2 A Spitchcock Eel with Shrimps buttered.
3 A diſh of broyled Oyſters.
4 A diſh of fryed Smelts.
5 A Spinage Tart.
6 An Eel Pye.
7 A diſh of buttered Crabs.
8 A diſh of Skerrets fryed green.
9 A diſh of broyl'd Breams.
10 A diſh of Anchovies.
11 A diſh of roaſted Eels.
12 A diſh of Tarts of ſeveral ſorts.
13 A chine of Salmon broyled.
14 A diſh of Trouts fry'd
15 A Fraiſe of Shrimps.
16 Collered Eels fouſed.
17 A Lampry Eel Pye.
18 A diſh of broyl'd Whitings.
19 A diſh of Crafiſh buttered.
20 A diſh of Cheeſe-cakes.

In this Bill of Fare, I have altogether omitted Fleſh, becauſe there is enough mentioned in the other Bill, you may but add three diſhes of Fleſh (of either boyled, baked, roaſted, haſhed, carbonadoed, frigaſied, ſtewed, or broyled) to every Five diſhes of the Firſt or Second Courſe of Fiſh here preſcribed ; which will make it up thirty two diſhes to each Courſe, (if you pleaſe you may ſubſtract them to a ſmaller number, or common diet.) Again you muſt obſerve, that a Bill of Fare cannot

not be made for any one of the Seasons; because they vary; for in some Months many things are in season, that are not in others; as for example, Lobsters, Crafish, Crabs, Salmon, Trouts, besides certain herbs and flowers, these are not fully in season in the beginning of *March*, but they are in *May*; As also Oysters and certain other Fish, and Wild-fowl, are in season the beginning of *March*, but out in *May*; therefore according to the time of your Feast, you must take what is in season in the place of that which is gone out, notwithstanding specified in the Bills of Fare: And as in this Quarter, so in all the other.

A Bill of Fare on a Flesh-day for the Summer Season.

First Course.

1 A Boyled meat of Pullets or Caponets bred in *March*.
2 A dish of rich Puddings of several colours.
3 A chine of Veal larded, and Mutton drawn with Time and Lemon-pill.
4 A Grand sallet in plates.
5 A dish of young Turkies half larded.
6 A dish of stewed Carps.
7 A Bisk Pye of flesh.
8 A hanch of Venison boyled with Colliflowers.
9 A Frigasie of Chickens, green.
10 A dish of large Leveretts larded.
11 A forced boyled meat of a Leg of Lamb, and other ingredients.
12 A Venison Pasty.
13 A dish of Capons roasted.
14 A Marrow Pudding, or some other, boyled or baked.
15 A boyled Sallet with toast.
16 A boyled meat of a Calves-head.
17 A chine of Beef roasted.

18 A larded Bace, with small shell-fish, and other or Salmon.
19 A Lamb Pye.
20 Two Geese roasted.
21 A raw hash as a boyled Meat.
22 A shoulder of Mutton roasted in blood, or else a hanch of Venison.
23 A carbonadoed Lamb.
24 A Pig & a Kid in a Pye.
25 A dish of Pullets roasted.
26 A piece of boyled Beef, or Udders and Tongues with Cabbage.
27 A cold Hash.
28 A dish of cold Meat.
29 A dish of collered Beef or Veal.
30 A set Custard.

Second Course.

1 A dish of Quailes half larded small with Vine leaves.
2 A dish of young Heronsews larded.
3 A dish of young Pease.
4 A dish of Sowls.
5 A Sallet of Anchovies.
6 An Artichoke Pye,
7 A dish of Cream.
8 A dish of tame Pigeons.
9 A dish of Ruffs.
10 A made dish.
11 A cold baked meat.
12 A dish of forced or buttered Crabs.
13 A dish of green Codlings and Cream.
14 A dish of Chickens.
15 A young Kid roasted whole.
16 A dish of rich Tarts.
17 A soused Turbet.
18 A dish of Artichokes.
19 A chine of Salmon broyled.
20 A dish of Knotts.
21 A dish of Partridges; or at the upper end,
22 A Joll of Sturgeon.
23 A dish of Goos-berry and Cherry Tarts.
24 A dish of Spitchcock Eels.
25 A dish of Rabbets larded.
26 A dish of Caveer and Potargo.
27 A cold baked Meat.
28 A dish of young Ducks.
29 A dish of potted Venison.
30 A Gammon of Westphaly Bacon.
31 A dish of dryed Tongues.   *A*

A Bill of Fare on a Fiſh-day, *for the Summer ſeaſon.*

Firſt Courſe.

1. A Bisk or Olue of Fiſh, with ſmall Fiſh.
2. A Diſh of Barley Cream hot.
3. A Sallet, with a Rock of Butter in the middle.
4. A Carp Pie.
5. A diſh of Rice on toaſts with Wafers.
6. A Pike roaſted.
7. A diſh of Buttered Eggs.
8. A diſh of great Flounders ſtewed.
9. Souced Mullets and Bace.
10. A boyled Sallet.
11. An Eel Pie.
12. A Joll of Ling.
13. A Diſh of buttered Loaves.
14. A Diſh of Whitings.
15. A Diſh of ſhuets of Ling
16. A Diſh of quaking Pudding buttered.
17. A diſh of Perches or Plaice.
18. A diſh of Rice milk hot.
19. A Diſh of Barrel-Cod buttered with Eggs.
20. Sallet and Butter.

Second Courſe.

1. A diſh of fair Sowls fryed
2. A Diſh of Cra-fiſh buttered.
3. An Artichoke Pie.
4. A Diſh of Strawberry Cream.
5. A Diſh of Anchovies.
6. A Diſh or Chine of Salmon broyled.
7. A ſouſed Eel in collers.
8. A Diſh of fryed Smelts.
9. A Diſh of rich Tarts.
10. A Diſh of Potargo and Caveere.
11. A diſh of Trouts or Salmon-peels boyled or fryed.
12. A Diſh of Tenches in Jelly.
13. Tanzy of certain colours, on Plates in a voider.
14. A Diſh of Dowſets or ſet Cuſtard.
15. A diſh of buttered Crabs
16. A Joll of Sturgeon.
17. A Diſh of Lobſters.
18. A Spitchcock Eel.
19. A made diſh, or Egg-pies
20. A Diſh of Leach.

Theſe and many other ſorts of Fiſh, and other Varieties, are in ſeaſon in the Summer, which you may make uſe of at your pleaſure,   a   *A*

A Bill of Fare for a Flesh-dinner in Autumn.

First Course.

1. A Dish of Fowl with ingredients, for a grand boyled Meat.
2. Chines of Mutton and Veal in pieces, roasted with Oysters, and larded
3. A grand Sallet in Plates on a Charger.
4. An Olue of Puddings.
5. A Dish of Pheasants.
6. A Pattee, or Pie of ingredients.
7. Hares larded.
8. A chine of Pork boyled and carbonadoed with Turnips.
9. A Venison pasty of a Doe
10. Two hen Turkies larded
11. A Hash.
12. A chine of roast Beef.
13. A Marrow Pudding.
14. A Frigasie of Chickens,
15. A Dish of Collops of Veal larded.
16. A Dish of collered Pork.
17. A Dish of Capons.
18. A made Dish.
19. A stewed Meat with Pottage.
20. A baked Meat of Rabbets.
21. Two Geese in a Dish.
22. A Leg or Fillets of Veal farced and larded.

Second Course.

1. Partridges.
2. Quails.
3. An Amalet of preserved Lemon.
4. A Dish of rich Taffatee Tarts.
5. A Sallet of Lemmon, Caveer, Anchovies, and other of that Nature, to corroborate the Palate, and cause Appetite.
6. A Dish of Curlews.
7. Godwithes.
8. Warden Pie.
9. A dish of Rabbets larded
10. A dish of Leach and Jelly
11. A Dish of cram'd Chickens.
12. A dish of tame Pigeons.
13. A laid Tart of preserves.
14. A dish of Skeerits fryed
15. Stewed Peaches.
16. A Dish of red Shanks.
17. A Dish of Teal if good, or other wild Fowl.
18. A dish of collered Geese
19. Of Westphalie Bacon and Tongues.
20. A cold baked Meat of red Dear.
21. A set Custard.
22. Of baked Apples with Orangado. *A*

A Bill of Fare for the Winter Quarter, for a Flesh day at Dinner.

First Course.

1. A Coller of Brawn
2. A brown Bisk or Olue.
3. A Chine of Mutton or Veal in a dish larded.
4. A grand Sallet of Pickles
5. A baked Meat of small wild Fowl, with ingredients.
6. Pheasants larded.
7. A frigasie of great Chickens, or Rabbets larded.
8. An Almond Pudding baked in a Dish, with a garnish of Puff-paste.
9. A dish of stewed Broth, if at *Christmas*.
10. A dish of Hens with eggs
11. A Pasty of Venison.
12. A Hash.
13. A Chine of Beef.
14. A forced baked Meat with artificial Fowl.
15. A dish of minced Pies.
16. A Swan, or Geese.
17. Capons and white Broth.
18. Chines of Pork roasted.
19. Olives of Veal roasted.
20. A Brawns head soused.

Second Course.

1. Six Cocks.
2. Twelve Snites.
3. A dish of Anchovies.
4. A Bacon Tart.
5. A dish of Jelly.
6. A Potatoe Pie.
7. Six Plovers.
8. Six Teal.
9. Two dozen of Larks with Lard.
10. A dish of rich Tarts, in Puff-paste.
11. A Lamb in joints.
12. A Dish of Leach and Blamaing.
13. Wild Goose Pie cold.
14. Wild Ducks roasted.
15. A dish of tame Pigeons.
16. An Orangado Pie.
17. A Frigasie of Pistaches and Pine-apple Curnels.
18. A Dish of Wigeons larded.
19. A set Custard.
20. A cold baked Meat of Venison.

A Bill of Fare for three Courses for the Winter-season, of Fish and Flesh, in February *and* March.

First Course.

A Dish of Collops and Eggs.
A boyled Meat of many small ingredients, with a Pottage.
A Grand Sallet.
A Jigget of Mutton with Oysters.
Two Carps boyled.
A Lamb Pie.

A Pasty of a barren Doe.
A Hash of a Calves-head.
Olives of a Leg of Pork roasted.
A boyled Meat of Hens, with Eggs, Saffages and Oysters.
A Dish of stewed Flounders.
Geese roasted.

Second Course.

Pheasants larded.
A Dish of young Rabbets.
A Dish of Curlews.
Sowls marrinated.
A Skirret Pie.
Lamb in joints.
Broyled Oysters.
A Dish of Tarts.

A Dish of Jelly.
A Frigasie of Cra-fish,
A dish of young Hens with Eggs.
A Dish of Fritters.
A Tanzy.
A Dish of Pancakes.

Third Course.

A Dish of Scollops broyled
Westphaly Bacon.
A Dish of Anchovies.
A Dish of Tongues.
A Dish of Caveere and Potargo.

A Dish of Sturgeon.
A Dish of pickled Mushromes.
A Lamprey Pie.
A Frigasie of Pistaches.
A Made Dish of Parmisant.

The

THE TABLE.

BOOK I.

For all manner of Pickles.

How to pickle Cowcumbers, pag. 1.
How to pickle Mushrooms, 2
How to pickle the tops of Elder, ibid.
How to pickle Elder buds in March, ib.
To pickle Clove Gillyflowers, ib.
To pickle Purslan stalks, ib.
To pickle Artichokes, 3
To pickle the tops of Turnips, ib.
To pickle green Figgs, ib.
To pickle Barberries, ib.
To pickle Sampier green. ib.
To pickle stalks of Thistles or Sherdowns, 4
To pickle Reddish tops, ib.
To pickle Taragon, ib.
To pickle Cowslips, ib.
To pickle Fennel or Dill, ib.
To pickle red Cabbage, ib.
To pickle Burdock roots, 5
To pickle Ashen Keys, ib.
To pickle Lemon and Orange-pill, ib.
To pickle curled Endive, ib.
To pickle Charnel, ib.
To pickle Quinces, ib.
To pickle Bramble Fruit, 6
To pickle Broom-buds, ib.
To pickle Bogberries, ib.
To pickle Grapes ib.
To pickle red and white Currans, ib.
To pickle Elder, or many other buds in the Spring, that useth to serve for Sallets, ib.
To pickle Cabbage stalks, 7
To pickle Shampinnions, ib.
To pickle Sleep at Noon, ib.
To pickle the stalks of March-mallows, ib.
To pickle Alexander-buds. 8
To pickle Malagatoons, ib.

BOOK II.

THE TABLE.

BOOK II.

How to souse, pickle and coller all manner of Flesh.

How to coller and souce Brawn,	pag. 8	To coller Pork,	ib.
How to coller Venison,	9	To coller Mutton,	12
How to coller Beef red,	10	To coller Goats-flesh,	ib.
To coller Veal,	ib.	To coller Geese,	ib.
To coller Pig,	11	To coller Swans,	13
		To coller wild Geese,	ib.

BOOK III.

How to souse, Pickle and Marinate Fish.

TO coller Eels,	pag. 13	To pickle Lobsters	15
To souce a Tench, to be served up in Jelly,	14	To pickle Conger Eel,	ib.
		To pickle Sturgeon,	ib.
To pickle Smelts White or Red,	ib.	To pickle Caveer,	16
		To coller Sowls,	ib.
To marble Sowls, Plaice, Flounders, or any fish that is fitting to marble,	ib.	To coller Salmon,	17
		To souce Lumps,	ib.

BOOK IV.

Of cold baked Meats of Flesh.

TO make Paste of Rye flower,	pag. 17	To bake a Fillet of Veal to be eaten cold,	19
To bake Venison in crust or pots,	18	To bake a Calves head to be eaten cold,	ib.

To

THE TABLE.

To bake a Fawn or Kid to be eaten cold, ib.	*To bake Pigeons to be eaten cold,* ib.
To bake a Hare to be eaten cold, 20	*To bake Bran-Geese, or other Wild-Geese to be eaten cold,* ib.
Another way to bake a Hare, ib.	*To bake a Turkey to be eaten cold,* 22
To bake Pork to be eaten cold, ib.	*To bake Herons to be eaten cold,* ib.
To bake Brawn to be eaten cold, 21	*To bake a Swan,* ib.
To bake Rabbets to be eaten cold, ib.	*To bake a Goose,* ib.

For cold baked Meats of Fish.

To bake a Lamprey Eel Pye, 23	*To bake an Eel to be eaten cold,* 24
To bake a Turbert, ib.	*To bake a Pike to be eaten cold,* ib.
To bake a Salmon, ib.	

BOOK V.

How to make several sorts of Jellies, Leaches, and Creams.

How to make Jellies, pag. 24.	*Leach,* 27
How to season and run Chrystal Jelly, 25	*To make divers sorts of Creams,* ib.
How to run Colours, ib.	*How to make Cheese and Cream,* ib.
To make Jelly of Oranges, ib.	*Another way,* 28
To make Harts-horn Jelly, 26	*To make Apple Cream,* ib.
	To make Quince-Cream, ib.
How to make Leach, ib.	*To make a Cream call'd Sack and Pottage.* 29
How to run your Leach in colours, 27	*To make a Sack Posset the best way,* ib.
The use of the Jelly and	

a 4 *To*

THE TABLE.

To fry Clary, 88
To fry Apples, ib.
How to make an Orangado Fraise, ib.
A Tanzie of Cowslips or Violets, 89
A Tanzie of Spinage, ib.
To fry Artichokes or Spanish Potatoes, ib.
To make Fritters, 90
To make Pancakes, ib.
Another way to dress a dish of collops of Veal, 91
To fry Calves feet, or Sheeps trotters, ib.
How to Frigasie Neats-tongues and Udders, 92
How to poach a dish of Eggs for a weak Stomack, ib.
Another way, rich and strengthening, 93
Another way, ib.
How to butter Eggs, ib.
Another way, 94
To fry Collops and Eggs, ib.

BOOK VI.

Divers Sallets and Roast-meats, with their several Sauces.

TO make Sallets, pag. 95
To make a Grand Sallet, ib.
The flesh Sallet of a Capon or Turkie, 96
A Made-dish of Parmizant, 97
A Sallet of dryed Neats-tongues, ib.
A Sallet of Fennel, ib.
A Sallet of green Pease, ib.
A Sallet of boyled Spinage, 98

Rules how to roast Meat, with their several Sauces.

How to roast a Hanch of Venison, 99
To roast a Jigget of Mutton, ib.
To roast a Shoulder of Mutton with Oysters, ib.
To roast a Chine or Neck of Veal, 100
To roast a breast of Veal, ib.
A Fillet or Leg of Veal farced, 101
To roast Olives of Veal, ib.
To roast a whole Lamb or Kid. ib.

To

THE TABLE

To make a Kid of a Pig, and a Pig to be roasted, 102
To roast a Calves Head, ib.
To roast Leverets and Rabbets, 103
To roast Lambs-heads, ib.
To roast Venison other ways, 104

Several Sauces for your Fowl in general.

For Capons, 105
For Hens, ib.
For Turkies, ib.
For Chickens, ib.
For Pigeons roasted, ib.
For Rabbets, 106
For Pheasants, Heath-poots, or Cocks of the Wood, ib.
For Woodcocks, ib.
For Quailes, ib.
For Ducks, Wigeons, Teal, or Plover, ib.

BOOK VII.

Treats how to boyl or stew Fish to be eaten hot.

How to boyl a Turbert, pag. 107.
To boyl a Pike, ib.
To stew a Carp, 108
Another way to boyl Carps, 109
To stew a dish of Flounders, ib.
Another way, ib.
To boyl Pearches, 110
How to make a Bisk of Fish, ib.
To dress a Cods-head the best way, 112
To make an Olue of Fish, ib.
To boyl Mullets or Bace to be eaten hot, 113
To stew or make broth with Whitings or Smelts, 114
How to stew or boyl Eels, ib.
Another way, 115
To dress a dish of small Jacks, ib.
To stew a dish of Breams, ib.

BOOK VIII.

THE TABLE.

Winter,	ib.	To make a forced boyled meat,	60
Another way,	56	To boyl Udders and Tongues	61
To boyl Ducks, Wigeons, or Teal,	ib.	A boyled Meat after the French *fashion,*	ib.
Another way,	57	Another way, according to the French *fashion,*	62
To boyl Rabbets,	ib.		
To boyl Pigeons,	58		
To boyl Plovers,	59		
To boyl Capons or Pullets,	ib.		

BOOK VIII.

Containing how to make several sorts of Puddings.

How to make a quaking Pudding,	pag. 63	To make a Pudding of Hogs Liver,	ibid.
Another way,	ib.	To make a baked Marrow Pudding,	68
To make a dish of Pudding of several colours,	64	To make an Oatmeal Pudding,	ib.
To make Marrow Puddings to be boyled in skins,	ib.	To make a Pudding of Rice-floure,	69
To make black Puddings to be kept,	65	To make a hasty Pudding,	ib.
To make Polony Sassages to be kept all the Year,	66	To make Andolians,	70
Another way for Sassag.	67		

BOOK IX.

Containing Hashes, Stewed, Broyled and Carbonadoed Meats.

TO farce a Fillet of Beef,	p. 71	To farce a Fillet of Veal,	ib.
To stew a breast of Mutton,	72	To stew Venison,	73
		How to stew Calves feet,	ib.
			To

THE TABLE.

To haſh a ſhoulder or Leg of Mutton, ib.
How to make a Haſh of a more excellent way, new invented, 74
To haſh a Calves head, ib.
To haſh Hens or Pullets with Eggs, 75
To make a haſh of Capons, ib.
To haſh Partridges, 76
To haſh Ducks or other wild Fowl, ib.
To haſh Rabbets, ib.

For Carbonadoes and broyled Meats.

To Carbonado a Gooſe, 77
To Carbonado Turkies, ib.
To Carbonado Hens, ib.
To Carbonado Veal, 78
To Carbonado Mutton, ib.
A diſh of collops of Mutton broyled, ib.
Steaks of Pork broyled, 79
To Carbonado a Calves head, ib.
To broyl a chine of Pork, ib.

BOOK X.

Of Frigaſies and Frying.

How to fry all manner of garniſhing, p. 80
How to fry Oyſters in batter, ib.
A Frigaſie of a Hen or Capon, 81
To make a Frigaſie of Chickens brown, 82
Another way for Chickens or Rabbets, ib.
To ſmeer collops of Veal, 83
To fry a diſh of Lamb-ſtones and Sweet-breads, ib.
How to make a Frigaſie of Lamb, ib.
A Frigaſie of Veal, 84
A diſh of collops of Mutton, with a ſavory hogo, ib.
To fry collered Pork, 85
Another way, ib.
A Frigaſie of Partridges or Woodcocks, ib.
A Frigaſie of Ducks or Wigeons, 86
A fryed meat of Bacon, ib.
To make a fryed meat, called an Amlet, 87
Another way, ib.
To fry Primroſe leaves in March with Eggs, ib.

To

THE TABLE.

To *coddle Codlings green, to serve up with Cream,* ib.
To make *Barley Cream,* ib.
To make *Rasberry Cream,* 30
To make *red Currans Cream,* ib.
To make *Cabbage Cream,* ib.
To make *Snow Cream,* 31
To make *Almond Leach Cream,* ib.
To make *Goosberry Cream,* ib.
To make *Rice Milk or Cream to be eaten hot,* 32
To *boyl Milk or Cream to be eaten hot with Bread,* ib.
To make *Spring Pottage,* ib.
To make *water Gruel,* 33
To make *Punnado,* ib.
To make *Barley Gruel,* ib.
To make a *Pairmane Caudle,* 34
To make a *Lemmon Caudle,* ib.
To make a *Florendine or made dish of Rice,* ib.
To *Butter Rice,* 35
To make a *Florendine or Made-dish of Apples,* ib.
To make a *Florendine or Made-dish of Spinage,* ib.
To make *Pasties to fry,* 36
To make a *Florendine or Made-dish of a Kidney of Veal,* ib.
To make *toasts of a Kidney of Veal to fry,* ib.
To make a *Florendine of a Calves Chaldron,* ib.
To make a *Made dish of Apples and red Currans,* 37
To make a *Made dish of Artichokes,* ib.
To make *forced Meat,* 38
To make *part of the forced Meat green for your use,* ib.
Another forced Meat, ib.

BOOK XI.

Containing strong Broths and Pottages, with other Preparations of Cookery.

To make *strong Broth for your use in dressing of Meat,* p. 39
To make an *excellent Cordial Broth,* ib.
To make a *Pottage or Broth to serve up with a Bisk or grand boyled Meat,* ib.
Another

THE TABLE.

Another way, 40
To make Broth or Pottage, called Skinck, ib.
To make white Broth, 41
To make stewed Broth, ib.
Another, a Consumption Broth, 42
To make a red Pottage, ib.
Another Broth, 43
How to draw Gravy, ib.
How to draw Butter. ib.
How to recover butter when it is oyled, 44
How to make Barly Broth, ib.

BOOK XII.

Which teacheth how make all manner of hot boyled Meats of Flesh.

How to make a Bisk, pag. 45.
To make a brown Bisk, 46
To make an Olue, ib.
How to force all manner of Meats, 47
To make your Lear for your sweet forced Meat, 48
How to make a forced boyled Meat, ib.
How to make your Lear and garnish for your sweet forced boyled Meat of the same Fowl, 49
To boyl Capons or Chickens in white Broth, ib.
To boyl a hanch of Venison, ib.
To boyl Legs, Neck, or Chines of Mutton, four wayes, 50
Another way, ib.
Another way, ib.
Another way to make a Lear for the said Meat, 51
To boyl a Leg of Veal and Bacon, ib.
To make your green Sauce two ways, ib.
To boyl a breast of Veal, 52
To boyl a Knuckle of Veal with a Neck cut in five pieces, in Broth, ib.
To boyl a Leg of Pork, ib.
To boyl Capons or Hens for the Winter season, 53
Another with Sherdowns, ib.
To boyl Chickens, 54
Another way, ib.
Another way, ib.
Another way, 55
Another way to boyl Chickens or Pullets for the Winter,

THE TABLE.

BOOK XIII.

Containing how to Bake, Broyl, and Frigasie certain sorts of Fish.

How to make sauce or lear without Butter or Eggs, pag. 116
To fry Fish and all manner of garnishing with Oyl, 117
Another way for your Lear without Eggs, ib.
To stew a dish of Trouts, ib.
To boyl and serve Salmon whole, 118
To roast a Pike, ib.
To roast Eels, 119
How to roast a Porpus, 120
To roast a Carp, ib.
To roast a Salmon whole, 121
How to Spitchcock an Eel, ib.
For broyling, 122
To broyl Flounders or Plaice, ib.
To fry a dish of Maids, 123
To Frigasie or butter Crabs or Lobsters, ib.
To fry a dish of Ling for first Course, ib.
To Frigacy Shrimps, Pranes, Perewinckles, or Cra-fish, 124
A Fraise of Cockles, ibid.
To broyl Oysters, 125
To broyl Scollops, ib.
To bake certain Fish, 126
To bake a Carp two ways, ib.
To bake an Eel Pie, ib.
To bake a Turbet, 127
A Salmon Pie to be eaten hot, ib.
To bake a Joll of Ling in a Pie, 128
Another way, ib.
To bake a Pike in a Coffin, 129
To bake a Lump in a Coffin, ib.
To bake Flounders or Plaice, 130
To bake an Oyster Pie, ib.
To make a Batillye Pye of Fish, 131
To make Petteets of Shrimps or Pranes, ib.
To marinate a Carp to be eaten cold, 132
To hash a Carp, ib.
A Frigacy of Fresh Salmon, 133
To

THE TABLE

To *Frigacy great Plaice or Flounders,* ibid.
To *make Chuets of Salmon,* 134
To *boyl a Carp another way,* ibid.
To *force an Eel,* 135

BOOK XIV.

Containing several sorts of hot baked Meats.

TO bake a Gammon of Bacon to be eaten hot, with ingredients, p. 136
To make a Steak Pie of Mutton, 137
Another way, ib.
For a sweet Lamb Pie, 138
Another way for a savory, ib.
Another way, ib.
To bake an Hen to be eaten hot, 139
To bake a Hen another way, ib.
Another way to bake a Hen in a Patie-pan, 140
To bake a Capon or Turkey in a Patie-pan, ib.
How to season and bake a Pasty of Venison, 141
Another way to bake Venison to be eaten hot, 142
To make a Battally or Bisk-Pie in the Spring, ib.
To make a Sherdoon Pie in the Spring, 143
To make a Lumbard pie, 144

To make a dish of Chuets, ib.
To make an Ox-cheek Pie, 145
To make a Calves-head Pie, ib.
To make a Neats-tongue Pie to be eaten hot, 146
To make a Chicken Pie for the Winter season, ib.
Another way, 147
Another way, ib.
To make a Calves-feet Pie, 148
To make an Olive Pie, ib.
To make an Artichoke Pie, 149
To make a Skerrit Pie, ib.
To make a Potato Pie, 150
To make Marrow Pasties to fry, ib.
To make an Egg-pie, 151
To make a Trotter pie, and Taffatee Tarts, 152
To make an Orangado pie 153
Another way, ib.

A

THE TABLE.

A hot baked Meat of Compounds,	154	To make a Pasty of an old Goat,	ib.
To make a Pigeon Pie,	155	To make a Lamb Pasty,	158
Another way,	ib.	To bake a Fawn or young Roe,	ib.
To make a Kid Pie,	156		
Another way,	ib.	To make Pasties of Rice to fry,	159
Two other ways.	157		

BOOK XV.

Containing divers Tarts and Made-dishes.

TO make a Bacon Tart,	pag. 160	To make Tarts of the Jelly of Pippins.	165
To make an Almond Tart,	ib.	To make Goosberr Tarts green, and clear as Crystal,	166
To make a Pine Apple Tart,	161	To make Puff-past,	ib.
Another Tart of Pistaches,	ib.	To make a laid Tart for Preserves,	167
To make a Spring Tart,	ib.	To make a Warden or Pear Pie,	ib.
To make a Cowslip Tart,	162		
To make a Cheese Tart,	ib.	To make a Quince Pie,	ib.
To make a Pruen Tart,	163	To make a Pie with whole Pippins,	168
To make a Cheese Cake,	ib.		
To make a dish of Puffs,	164	A set Tart,	ib.
To make a set Custard,	ib.		

THE

THE TABLE.

Rare Receipts in Cookery.

The Second Part.

To make a Bisk divers ways, pag. 169.
To boyl a Capon in Rice, 171
To boyl a Leg of Mutton the French fashion, 179
To boyl a Neck, Leg, or Chine of Mutton, or a Neck, Leg, Fillet, or Knuckle of Veal, Leg or Loyn of Lamb, 174
To boyl a Chine whole or in pieces, ib.
To bake a Pigg to be eaten cold, called a Maremaid Pie, 175
Another way, ib.
To bake Steaks the French way, ib.
A Pudding stewed between two dishes, 176
To make French Puffs with green Herbs, ib.

To bake all manner of Land Fowl, 177
To fry Sheeps-tongues, ib.
To bake a Pigg to be eaten hot, ib.
To bake all manner of Sea-Fowl to be eaten cold, 178
To hash a Carp, ib.
For the Stock for Jelly, 179
To make Jelly exceeding white with Almons, ib.
To make some Kickshaws to fry or bake, 180
To make a Pottage, ib.
To make a small Bisk of flesh roasted, 181
A Jelly of several colours, 182
To bake Apricocks green, 183
To make an Oatmeal Pudding, ib

b   To

THE TABLE.

To make an Oatmeal Pudding boyled, ib.
To make Oatmeal Puddings otherwise, of Fish or Flesh blood, 184
To make white Puddings an excellent way, ib.
To make an Italian Pudding ib.
To make Metheglin, 185
How to make Ipocras, ib.
To Jelly Lobsters, Cra-fish, or Pranes, 186
To stew Crabs, ib.
To force Crabs, ib.
To make water Leach, 187
To make a boyled Pudding another way, 188
Another way, ib.
A baked Pudding after the Italian fashion, ib.
To blanch Manchet in a Frying-pan, 189
Another way, ib.
To boyl Pidgeons the French fashion, 190
To boyl Mullet or Pike with Oysters, ib.
To boyl Carps an honourable way, ib.
Another way to boyl a dish of great Flounders, 191
To make a Hash of Partridges or Capons, ib.
A rare Frigasie, 192
To make a Bisk of Carps and other several fish, 193
To dress Eggs in the Spanish fashion, 194
To dress Eggs in the Portugal fashion, ib.
To dress Eggs called in French A la Hugenota, or the Protestant way, 195
To dress Eggs in fashion of a Tansey, ib.
To dress Poacht Eggs, 196
To butter eggs upon toasts, ibid.
An excellent way to butter Eggs, ib.
To make Cheese-cakes, 197
To make Dowsets, ib.
How to make a congealed meat, to be eaten cold, 198
How to congeal a Turkey or Capon, ib.
How to make small Pindents to fry for first course, 199
How to make rich Pancakes, ibid.
Another way to make them crisp, 200
How to fry a leg, breast or neck of Lamb, ibid.
How to make a green Frigasie of Chickens, ib.
A fryed meat in haste for the second corse, 201
How to make a Pudding with Whey, ib.

How

THE TABLE.

How to make Apple-pies *to fry,* ib.
How to make a boyled meat, a forced meat, a dish of Collops, and a roast meat, and a baked meat, of a leg of Veal with some other small ingredients, 202
A Fridays *dish made with Barley,* 204
For Friday, *to make a dish of fryed Toasts,* ib.
Another Fryday *or* Lent *dish,* ib.
A second course dish in the beginning of the Spring, 205
To make a made dish, ib.
An excellent way how to broyl Eels, ib.
How to butter a dish of eggs with Anchovies, 206
How to fry a dish of Cheese, ibid.
How to broyl a leg of Pork, ibid.
How to roast the said Collops, ibid.
How to make a Palate Pie, 207

THE TABLE.

Very rare and moſt choice Receipts for all manner of Preſerving, Conſerving and Candying &c,

TO Preſerve Pippins, pag. 209	Anoher way, 216
Another way, ib.	To preſerve Grapes, ib.
Another way to preſerve them green, 210	Another way, 217
	To preſerve Cherries, ib.
To preſerve Apricocks, ib.	Another way, ib.
Another way, ib.	Another way 218
Another way to preſerve them ripe, 211	To preſerve Barberries, ib.
	To preſerve Raſpberries, 219
To preſerve Pippins red, ib.	Another way, ib.
To preſerve Pears, ib.	To preſerve your Pomcitrons, ib.
Another way for white Pippins, 212	To preſerve Oranges and Lemmons, 220
To preſerve Medlars, ib.	To preſerve Saterion roots, ibid.
To preſerve Peaches, ib.	
Another way, 213	To preſerve red Roſe-leaves, 221
Another way, ib.	
To preſerve Quinces, ib.	To preſerve Enula Campana roots, ib.
Another way to preſerve them white or red, 214	To preſerve Currans, ib.
To preſerve Gooſ-berries, ib.	To preſerve Mulberries, 222
Another way, ib.	To preſerve Eringo-roots, ibid.
Another way, 215	
To preſerve Mellacatons, ib.	To preſerve green Walnuts, ibid.
To preſerve Damaſins, ib.	To

THE TABLE.

To preserve Angelica roots, 223
The time to preserve green fruits, according to other Authors, ibid.

Conserves.

Conserve of Barberries, pag. 224.
Another way, ib.
To make Conserve of Violets, ib.
To make a Marmalade of Quinces, 225
To make conserve of Borage flowers, ib.
To make conserve of Rosemary flowers, ib.
To make conserve of Buglos flowers, ib.
To make Pectoral rolls for the Cough, 226
To make conserve of Strawberries, ib.
To make conserve of Prunes or Damsins, ib.
To make conserve of Red and Damask Roses, ib.
To conserve Cowslips, Marigolds, Violets, Scabions, Sage, and Roses, &c. 227.
To make a Pomander, ib.
Another way to conserve Strawberries, ib.
To make conserve of Cichory flowers, ib.

Sirrups.

To make sirrup of Pomcitrons, pag. 228.
To make sirrup of Liquorish, ibid.
To make sirrup of Hoarehound, 229
To make sirrup of Hyssop, ib.
To make sirrup of Violets, ib.
Another rare way, ib.
To make sirrup of Mulberries, 230
To make sirrup of Clove-Gillyflowers, ibid.
To make sirrup of Roses solutive, ib.
Another way to make sirrup of Damask Roses, 231
To keep your liquor of Roses all the year, ib.
To make sirrup of Cowslips, ib.
To make sirrup of Lemmons, ibid.
To make sirrup of Maidenhair,

THE TABLE.

hair, 232
To make sirrup of dry Roses, ibid.

To keep Cherries all the year, and to have them at Christmas, ibid.

Candying.

To candy Violet flowers, pag. 233.
To candy Pears, Plumbs, Apricocks, to look clear, &c. ibid.
To candy Borage flowers, 234
To candy Rosemary flowers, ib.
To candy all sorts of flowers after the Spanish way, ib.
To make Manus Christi, ib.
To candy Goos-berries, 235
To dry Apricocks, ib.
To candy Enula Campana, ibid.

To candy Eringo-roots, 236
Another way, ib.
To dry Pippins, ib.
To candy Rose-leaves as natural, as if they grew on trees, 237
To candy all sorts of Flowers, Fruits and Spices, the clear Rock-candy, ib.
To candy Marigolds in Wedges, the Spanish fashion, ib.
To candy all manner of flowers in their natural colours, 238
To candy Ginger, ib.

Pastes.

To make Paste of Pippins the Genoa fashion, some with leaves, some like Plumbs with stalks, and stones in them, p. 239

To make Paste of Oranges and Lemmons, ib.
To make Paste of Goos-berries, 240

Certain

THE TABLE.
Certain Old useful Traditions of Carving and Sewing, &c.

Erms of a Carver, p.241
The *Office of the Butler, Pantler, Yeoman of the Seller, and Eury,* 242
Of the Sewing of Fish Service, 245
Of Carving of Flesh Service, ib.
Sauce for many sorts of Fowls and Flesh. 246
Of the Feasts and Service from Easter *unto* Whitsuntide, 248

General directions for the Carving up of Fowl.

Lift that Swan, 249
Rear that Goose, ib.
To cup up a Turkey or Bustard, 250
Dismember that Heron, ib.
Unbrace that Mallard, 251
Unlace that Coney, ib.
Sauce that Capon, ib.
Allay that Pheasant, ib.
Wing that Partridge, 252
Wing that Quail, ib.
Display that Crane, ib.
Dismember that Heron, ib.
Unjoynt that Bittern, ib.
Break that Egript, ib.
Untach that Curlew, 253
Untach that Brew, ib.

Break that Sarcel, ib.
Mince that Plover, ib.
A Snite, ib.
Thigh that Woodcock, ib.
From the Feast of Whitsuntide *unto* Midsummer, ib.
From the Feast of Saint John *the Baptist, unto* Micahelmas, 254
From the Feast of Michaelmas, *unto the Feast of* Christmas, 255

Sewing of Fish.

First Course, 256
Second Course, ib.
Third Course, ib.
Of carving of Fish, ib.
Sauces of all Fish, 257
An excellent way for making Ipocrus, 258
An approved Receipt for a Consumption that hath long remained, ib.
To coller Flounders, 259
To roast a shoulder of Mutton in Blood, ib.
To make a Portugal Pie, ib.
To stew a Carp, 260
To make a Bacon Tart, ib.
To make Vever Olly, or Cheese pottage, ib.

The

The whole Body of
COOKERY
DISSECTED.

BOOK I.

How to pickle Cowcumbers.

TAke your smallest Cowcumbers, or Gerkins, after *Bartholomew-tide*, dip a cloth in Beer, and rub them clean from the dirt, then put a laying of Bay and Dill leafs in the bottom of your Firkin or Pot, and a quantity of whole Pepper, two or three blades of Mace, and as many Cloves; then place a laying of Cowcumbers thereon ; so continue with your said ingredients till your Pot or Firkin be full; then make a Liquor with fair Water, and good store of Dill to make it strong, with so much Salt as will bear an egg ; you may infuse the Dill, or you may boyl it, but let it be cold, then put it into your Cowcumbers; let this pickle continue to them almost a fortnight then pour part away, and fill it up with white wine Vinegar, so shall your Cowcumbers be green and crisp, and not too sour.

How to pickle Mushroms.

TAke a bushel of Mushroms, blanch them over the crown, barb them beneath; if they are new, they look as red as a Cherry; if old, black; this being done, throw them into a Pan of boyling water, then take them forth and let them drain; when they are cold, put them up into your Pot or Glass, put thereto Cloves, Mace, Ginger, Nutmegs, whole Pepper; then take white-wine, a little Vinegar, with a little quantity of salt, so pour the Liquor into your Mushroms, and stop them close for your use all the Year.

To pickle the tops of Elder.

BReak the tops of your young sprouts of Elder, in *March* or *April*, having a quantity thereof broke in pieces six inches long, boyl them in water half a dozen walms, then pour them out into your Sieve or Collinder, and let them drain; then prepare a pickle of Wine or Beer; put thereto a little Salt, and a little bruised Pepper; so put them into the said Pickle, and stop them. A good sallet.

To pickle Elder buds in March, *before the Tree leaves.*

HAving gathered what quantity you please before they are full blown, and put them into Wine-vinegar, they are a good Sallet. If in case they are full blown, as in *June*, they serve to make strong Elder-Vinegar; and themselves no Sallet: This Vinegar is good to make sauce for divers sorts of meat.

To pickle Clove-gilly-flowers.

WHen you have picked a good quantity of Gilly-flowers, mingle half White-wine and half Vinegar together, with so much white Sugar as will make them sweet and sharp, and so put your Gilly-flowers

flowers in, with a few Cloves, which is a good Sallet, and the liquor thereof will serve for Lears for sweet and sharp boyled Meats, or baked Meats.

To pickle Purſland ſtalks.

WHen they are waſhed, and cut in pieces ſix inches long, boyl them with water and Salt, a dozen walms; when they are taken up, drained, and cold, let your Pickle be ſtale Beer, and Wine-vinegar; add a handful of Salt thereunto, and put them up into your veſſel, and ſtop them up cloſe, and they will keep to the Spring following.

To pickle Artichokes.

TAke your Artichokes before they are over-grown, or too full of ſtrings, and when they are pared round, that nothing is left but the bottom, boyl them till they be indifferent tender, but not full boyled, take them up, let them be cold, then take good ſtale Beer, and White-wine, with a great quantity of whole Pepper, ſo put them up into a barrel, with a ſmall quantity of Salt, keep them cloſe, and they will not be ſour; it will ſerve for baked Meats, and boyled Meats, all the Winter.

To pickle the tops of Turnips.

TAke the tops of young Turnips, cut off the ſuperfluous branches, or leaves, when your water boyls put them in, and let them boyl till they are indifferent tender; then take them out, and let them drain, and put them into a pickle of White-wine Vinegar and Salt.

The ſame manner may you pickle the ſprouts of Cabbage-ſtocks, but take a care you do not over-boyl them.

To pickle green Figgs.

TAke your green Figgs about *August*, cut them in halves, an'd boyl them up in Vinegar, a little quantity of Sugar, large Mace and Cloves, fo put them up into your Pot or Glafs in the fame liquor; they will ferve to Garnifh your boyled meats, or Friggefes, in the Winter.

To pickle Barbaries red.

WHen yourBarbaries are picked from the leaves in clufters, about *Michaelmas*, or when they are ripe, let you water boyl, and give them half a dozen walms; let your pickle be of White-wine and Vinegar, not too fharp, fo put them up for your ufe.

To pickle Sampier green.

TAke your Sampier frefh from the Rock, and pickle it in Water and falt; when you have occafion to ufe thereof, take what quantity you pleafe, and throw it into boyling Water; although before it had loft its colour, fix or feven walms will make it green; drain it, cool it, and put it into a pickle of Vinegar for your prefent ufe; otherwife you may firft boyl it in good ftore of VVater and Salt, and keep it in the fame Liquor; but the firft way is the beft.

To pickle ftalks of Theffel or Sherdowns.

IN *March* or *April*, there is Theffel runs up like an Artichoke; the root thereof is like to the bottom of an Artichoke; both root and ftalk being peeled, and boyled in VVater and Salt, you may pickle them in VVhite-wine; it will ferve either for baked, or boyled Meats, or elfe to be ordered and fent to the Table as Artichokes.

To

To pickle Reddish tops.

YOu must do with this, as you do your Turnips or sprouts of Cabbage; it will serve for a hot Sallet.

To pickle Taragon.

YOur Taragon being stripped from the stalk, put it into your Glass or Vessel, and let your Pickle be half VVhite-wine, half Vinegar, so keep it for your use.

To pickle Cowslips.

THey are only to be pickled with Vinegar and Sugar.

To Pickle Fennel or Dill.

LEt your water boyl, then having your young Fennel tyed up in bunches, half a dozen walms will be enough, drain it, and let your pickle be Vinegar.

To pickle Red Cabbage.

TAke your close-leav'd Red-Cabbage, and cut it in quarters, and when your Liquor boyls, give it a dozen walms, and pickle it in Claret-wine Vinegar; you may put into it your Beet-roots boyled, and your Turnips half-boyled; it will all serve both for garnishing and Sallet; for your Turnips thereby shall be dyed into a crimson colour, a handsom garnishing to the Eye.

To pickle Burdock Roots.

YOur Burdock-Roots being scraped and half-boyled, pickle them with half VVhite-wine, half Vinegar, with a little Pepper and Salt, and when you will make use of them, slice them thin.

To pickle Lemmon and Orange Pill.

THey being boyled with Vinegar and Sugar, put them up into the fame pickle; you muſt obſerve to cut them in ſmall long thongs, the length of half the Pill of your Lemmon being pared; it is an handſome ſavoury Winter-ſallet; theſe ought to be firſt boyled in Water, before you boyl them in Sugar.

To pickle Aſhen Keys.

BOyl your Aſhen Keys in water, and let the pickle be Vinegar.

To pickle curled Endive.

YOu muſt give your Endive a ſcald in a walm of boyling water, and pickle it with half White-wine and half Vinegar.

To pickle Charnel.

YOu muſt give your Charnel two or three walms in boyling water; the pickle muſt be only with Vinegar.

To pickle Quinces.

TAke your fair Quinces, and core them with your boring irons or ſcoop; take the worſt of your Quinces, and cut them to pieces, and boyl your core or pieces in your pan of liquor, ſo that you make the liquor ſtrong, then boyl your Quinces prepared to pickle, till they may be ſuppoſed a quarter boyled, then ſtrain out your liquor with your hair-ſieve, or ſtrainer, and put a ſmall quantity of Salt, add thereto ſome ſtrong Beer, and put up your Quinces whole in your Veſſel or Pot, and pour in ſome of the ſame liquor, and ſtop them cloſe up

To pickle Bramble-Fruit.

IT is a long berry, but full of stones, some call them Services, or Hips: Your pickle is Beer-vinegar, and a little Sugar; you must give them three or four walms; but if they are full ripe, you are to pickle them raw as they are.

To pickle Broom-buds.

PUt your Broom-buds into little Linnen Baggs, tye them up close, make a pickle of Bay-salt and water, being boyled together, so that it will bear an Egg; when it is cold, put it into your Vessel or Pot, to your baggs of Broom-buds, keep it close stopt, and let it lye until it looks black, shift it again once or twice, until it change to a bright or green colour, afterwards take it out, and boyl it, as your occasion calls for, and pickle it in Vinegar. It will keep a Month or two.

To pickle Bog-berries.

BOyl up some Vinegar and Sugar together, and pour it in, being hot, into your Pot or Vessel where your Bog-berries are: and they will serve to garnish your dishes all the Winter; you may do the like to pickle Hog-haws; only boyl them up if they are not ripe.

To pickle Grapes.

LEt not your Grapes be fully ripe; their pickle is White-wine and a little Sugar.

To pickle Red and White Currans.

TAke Vinegar and White-wine, with so much Sugar as will make it pretty sweet, then take your Red or White Currans, being not fully ripe, and give them one walm, so cover them over with the said pickle, keeping them always under liquor.

The whole Body of Cookery Dissected.

To pickle Elder, or many other buds of trees in the Spring, that useth to serve for Spring-sallets.

GIve them one or two walms with Vinegar, Salt, whole Pepper, long Mace, and a Lemmon-Pill cut in pieces, then drain them, and let the Buds and the Liquor cool severally; afterwards put them in a Pot, and cover them with your pickle.

To pickle Cabbage-stalks.

ABout *Michaelmas* you may take your Cabbage-stalks, an handful or more from the Cabbage, or so far as the pith is good; shave off the out-side, and cut them in quarters, half boyl them in water and salt, then cut the pith from the outward pill, and pickle it in white-wine, a little stale Beer, bruised Pepper, large Mace, a few Fennel-seeds and Salt; you may slice out this with your pickled Sallets.

To pickle Shampinnions.

YOu must give them two or three walms; and pickle them in white-wine Vinegar, bruised Pepper, Salt, with a little large Mace.

To pickle Sleep-at-noon.

LEt your water boyl with a little Salt, throw it in, and let it have three or four walms, put it forth into a Cullender; when it is cold, pickle it in white-wine and Vinegar, with a little Pepper and large Mace.

To pickle the stalks of March-Mallows.

IN the latter end of *March*, and in *Appril*, your stalks will be as big as a Childs finger, you may gather of them the quantity of a bushel more or less, break them in lengths, about five or six inches, and pill off the
outward

outward peel, and when your Pan boyls with water and an handful of Salt, put them in, and let them have five or ſix walms, then take them up with your Scummer, and lay them a draining until they are cold, and make your Pickle with ſtale Beer, ſome Vinegar, groſs Pepper, and an handful of Salt; when they are pilled as aforeſaid, you may take an handful of them, and even them at the ends, and cut them as round as you can, about the bigneſs of a Peaſe; thus do until you have cut a good diſh of them, then lay on a skillet of water, and let it boyl with ſome beaten Pepper tyed in a ragg; put them in, and let them boyl quick, (as you do Peaſe) when they are enough, put them into a Cullender, let the water drain from them, put them in a diſh with ſweet Butter, and toſs them up together; diſh them after the manner of Peaſe, with Pepper and Salt on the diſh brims: And they differ very little in their taſte from Peaſe, therefore ſome call them *March* Peaſe.

To pickle Alexander-Buds.

TAke Alexander-Buds before they begin to run to feed, take off their looſe leaves and top, ſo that the Bud may be firm, cut part of the Root to it; let them be half-boyled in Water and Salt, then put them from the liquor, and when they are cold, pickle them with Vinegar, Salt, and a little ſtale Beer; when you diſh them up, you muſt ſlit them in the middle.

To pickle Mallagatoons.

YOu muſt take them before they are ripe, ſo that with a Knife you may ſplit them through the ſtone, then take half ſo much Sugar as they weigh, and put it in as much water as will boyl them up, and when your Sugar and Water boyls well, ſcum it, and put in your Mallagatoons with their skin-ſide downward, and let them ſimper, but not boyl up; after this manner you

may

may do Peaches and Apricocks, being not full ripe, or Apples in halves; pickle them in the said pickle as you boyl them; this will serve for the garnishing of Sallets.

In these varieties of pickles, you have matter sufficient to make Grand-sallets for the Winter, as also for the Summer, being many times desired, for many of them are very wholsom and Cordial for the Stomach.

BOOK II.

How to Sowce, Pickle and Coller all manner of Flesh.

To Coller and Sowce Brawn.

Your Brawn being scalded and boned, of each side you may make three handsom Collers, the neck Coller, the sheald Coller, and so the side or flank Coller; if your Brawn be very fat, you may make also the gammon Coller behind, otherwise boyl it and sowce it; this being watered two Days, shifted three or four times a Day, and still kept scraped, then wash it out, and squeeze out the blood, and dry it with cloaths; when it is very dry, sprinkle on Salt; so begin at the belly, and wind it up into Collers; but in case you can stoe more flesh in the flanck, or in the Coller; you may cut it out of other places where there is too much, or from the Gammon; this being bound up, as you will bind up a Trunk, with all the strength that can be obtained, put it in your Furnace or Copper; when it boyls, scum it; you must be careful it be kept full of liquor, and continually scummed for the space of six hours, then try it with a Wheatstraw if it be very tender, cool your Boyler by taking away your Fire, and filling of it constantly with cold water; so shall your Brawn be white; but if it

stands,

stands, or settles in its liquor, it will be black; then take up your Brawn, and set it up on the end, on a Board, your Sowce drink ought to be beer brewed on purpose; but if it be of the House Beer, then boyl a Pan of Water, throw therein a Peck of Wheaten Bran and let it boyl, strain it thorough a hair Sieve, and throw in two handfuls of Salt, so mix it with your Beer aforesaid, and sowce your Brawn therein; you may take half a Peck of white flower of Oatmeal, and mix it with some liquor, and run it through your hair Sieve, and it will cause your sowce to be White: Milk and Whey is used in this case; but your Milk will not keep so long; you may put both, in the boyling thereof; it will cause it to boyl white; keep your sowce Brawn close covered, and when it begins to be sour, you may renew it at your pleasure, with adding of fresh liquor.

To Coller Venison.

TAke your Venison and cut it fit to be Collered, or to put into your Pot, it being something deep, and slender, so that you may make about three Collers of a large side, or hanch; season your Venison (being larded before) with Pepper, a little Cloves, Mace, Nutmeg, and as much Salt as will turn your Spices grayish; then roul up your Collers, put them into your Pot, put Butter thereunto, so cover over your Pot with some course paste made a purpose; this will ask four or five hours baking; draw them out of the Oven, and let them stand until they are cold, then may you take off your lid, and take out your Venison whole, pour away your gravie, and make clean your Pot, put a little clarified butter in the bottom thereof, then put your Coller in again, and fill it up with clarified Butter, so put on your lid, with a sheet of brown Paper tyed over it; this way shall you keep Venison a Twelvemonth. In a great feast you may break three of your

your Pots to pieces, then take out your Venison whole, being congealed, rowed with Butter, set your three Collers upon a great dish, and plate; then stick all your Butter round about with Bay-leaves and a branch of Bayes on the top of each Coller; in your common dyet one is enough for a Dish, but you must break your Pot, otherwise your Butter will not come forth whole with it; you must also dip your Pot in hot Water to loosen your Butter from the sides. This is as rich and honourable a Second-course Dish, as your Brawn is for the first: you may also if you please, slice it out of your Pots at your pleasure: The same way may you do with Venison baked in Rye-dough; that is, Take out all your Venison when it is baked, scrape out all your gravie and jelly out of your bottom and sides of your Pie, pour in clarified Butter, place in your Venison again, and cover it over with clarified Butter, then put on your lid in its place; it will congeal to the clarified Butter, that none can tell that ever it was cut; but you must remember to lard all this Venison, before you Coller it, or put it into your baked meat.

To Coller Beef Red.

TAke a good flank of Beef, and cut out a Coller three quarters of a Yard long, and almost half a Yard broad; then take a small quantity of Cutchenele prepared, and a little Allum: put this into the value of a pint of red Wine, then season your Beef with Salt-peter Salt, and put it into a Boul or Tray, with your aforesaid Wine, mix it all well together, and let it lye four and twenty hours; then season your Beef with a handful of sweet Herbs minced, two Nutmegs, with a little Cloves and Mace beaten, and a quantity of small Pepper not to be discerned; so Coller up your Beef, and bind it with your Tape; if you have a Pot high enough, you may bake it, put a little Liquor therein; otherwaies you

may

The whole Body of Cookery Diſſected. 13

may boyl it in Pump VVater with a ſoft fire ; when it is cold put it into your pickle, being of white wine, ſtrong Broth, and Vinegar, with a little Salt, if the Coller be too freſh, otherwiſe you need put none ; when you go to diſh this at a Feaſt, you may cut it into four Collers ; it will be of a lovely red, ſtick it with Bay-leaves, and garniſh your Diſh with flowers and green : You may alſo cut many Diſhes of your Coller in ſlices, it will be an handſome Service for your Second Courſe.

To Coller Veal.

TAke a Breaſt of Veal and bone him, and beat him ſquare, fitting to be Collered, ſoak him well in ſeveral Waters, till all the blood is ſoaked out, then take him and dry him, and ſeaſon him with beaten Cloves, Mace, Nutmeg and Ginger, put a handful of ſweet Herbs, about a Spoonful of Salt, ſtrow this all over it, then have your ſlices of fine thin fat Bacon, ſeaſoned with a little Sage and Pepper ; dip each piece in the yolks of Eggs, and arder all over your Veal, ſo begin at the Neck end, and roul it up into a faſt Coller, bind it up faſt with Tape, ſo boyl it with your bones, with a faggot of ſweet herbs, keep it conſtantly ſcummed, till it is boyled, then put it into your ſowſing-Pan with the ſame Broth, adding ſome Vinegar and Salt thereto, with ſome large Mace ; when you ſerve it up, you may cut it in thin ſlices, and fill a great diſh, and garniſh it with flowers, and ſerve it for the firſt courſe.

To Coller Pig.

YOur Pig being ſplit and boned, and ſoaked well in ſeveral Waters, dry it, ſeaſon it with Cloves, Mace, Nutmeg, Ginger, a little quantity of Pepper, with a handful of ſweet Herbs, and ſage, about a ſpoonful of Salt ; all this being mixed, caſt them on both ſides of your Pig ; then Coller it cloſe, beginning at the rail, and

and bind it up : wafh it clean from the Herbs, and put it a boyling in fair Water, keep it conftantly fcummed; when it is more than half boyled, put in a faggot of fweet Herbs, fome large Mace, a race or two of Ginger fliced, with half a pint of Vinegar, and a piece of Izenglafs, or at leaft boyl your Izenglafs and your Spice in fo much of it that you intend to jelly; The Pigg being boyled, put it forth into your Veffel or Pan, take away the top and the bottom of your broth or jelly, melt it, and pour it to your Pigg again, difh up your Pig, when you are ready, cut your Coller into three or four, and difh the head in the middle, on the top of them, with an Apple in his mouth, beat your jelly, and garnifh your Pigg, and difh with flices and gobbets (with fome flices on the back) as alfo with flowers and Bay-leaves.

To Coller Pork.

YOu may take a piece of Pork out of the fide, as you did before of Brawn, being watered all Night, and well fqueezed from the blood, feafoned with a good handful of Sage, fweet Margerom, Time and Parflee minced together very fmall; then having cut out of a fillet of Veal fo many thin Collops, hackt with the back of a Knife, and wafhed over with yolks of Eggs, cover your faid Coller, with your Eggy fide of your Veal downards, then wafh over your Veal on the upper fide with Eggs, and throw on your feafoning, with fo much Salt as you may imagine may feafon it, and it will congeal together by reafon of the Eggs: fo Coller it, and bind it up, and when it is boyled, Sowce it with fome of the faid liquor, and a little Vinegar, beaten Pepper and Ginger : You may flice a Coller thereof when you difh it; it will fill three or four great difhes or chargers, or you may fend it up in a Coller; garnifh about your difh with fage and flowers, and ftick your Pork with Bay-leaves, or Rofemary and Flowers.

To

The whole Body of Cookery Diſſected. 15

To Coller Mutton.

TAke a breaſt of Mutton and bone it, cut off the Neck part of it, ſlice it about the Brisket, ſoak it very well in Water from all the Blood, it being dryed and ſpread abroad, ſeaſon it with an Onion, a little Sampier, a few Capers, a pickle Cowcumber, add to it a little Time; all this being ſmall minced together, throw it on your meat, with Pepper, Cloves, Mace, a little Ginger and Salt, with ſome pieces of Anchovies all over; ſprinkle a top thereof with your feather, the yolk of an egg, then wind up your Coller exceeding cloſe, and boyl it with Water and Salt, with a faggot or two of ſweet Herbs; you may cut a Neck in five or ſix pieces, and lard it with Lemmon-pill and boyl with it; thus you may do with your Chines alſo; but if you Sowce your Chines, you muſt lard them with Bacon, being boyled, put Vinegar into the liquor; This will alſo ſerve for a hot boyled meat, the lear being made as you ſhall ſee in the hot boyled Meats; if you ſend it up cold, you may cut it into ſo many ſlices, as you have larded pieces; put the higheſt Coller in the middle, then garniſh your diſh with Sampier or Capers, your meat with Lemmon.

To Coller Goats-fleſh.

TAke your Goats-fleſh, breaſt or neck, bone it, cut it, and beat it out as thin at one place as another, ſeaſon it with Pepper, Salt, ſome Cloves, Mace, a little Time, ſweet Margerom, Winter-Savory, and Ginger beaten; Coller it, bind it, and bake it in a Pot, put a Pint of White-wine and ſtrong broth thereto, when it is baked, add more Wine to the Liquor, cut it in the middle, and let it lye in the pickle, ſo you may ſend it up in ſlices, or how you pleaſe.

To

To Coller Geese.

BOne your Geese, and cut them square, fit to be Collered, let them soak one Night in their seasoning, it being Cloves and Mace, Pepper and Salt, so in the Morning take it forth, and put small pieces of Anchoves all over, and Westphalie Bacon minced, then roul it up, as aforesaid, and boyl it in strong Broth, with a little whole Pepper and large Mace, pickle them in the same Liquor; when you dish them, cut them in halves, then the two sides will stand upwards, dish them up, garnish the brims of your dish with Westphaly Bacon minced.

To Coller Swan.

BOne your Swan, and part the two sides, season it as the Geese aforesaid, only instead of the Westphaly Bacon and Anchoves, take thin slices of fat Bacon, almost the breadth of the sides, season them with small Pepper and Sage minced, and dip them into yolks of Eggs, and so lay them on upon the sides of your Swan, and roul them up into Collers; let your Pickle as aforesaid, be as to the Geese; boyl the head to set upon your Collers in the middle of your Dish.

To Coller Brand Geese or Wiggens.

DO as you did by your Geese before, only add thereto an Onion or two, before you have Collered it; this will all serve for second Course, in case you want number of Dishes, or else you may use them for the first Course.

By the same rule you may do any other Fowl according to their Nature in the time of Season.

BOOK

BOOK III.

To Sowce, Pickle, or Marble Fish.

To Coller Eels.

TAke your greatest Eel, and cover it well with falt, fplit it down the back clofe to the Bone, then cut out the Bone, as bare as you can, wafh them and dry them well, and lay them upon a Dreffer-board ftrowed with Salt, that he may not flip when you go to Coller him, then take a handful of minced Oyfters, with a little Time, fweet-Margerom, Winter-favory, one Onion minced fmall, then fome Nutmegs, Cloves and Mace beaten fmall; all this being mingled, ftrow it on the infide of your Eels; the Salt that lyes on the flippery fide of the Eel, will be enough to feafon it; if not, add fome more thereunto, fo roul them up clofe, and bind them with Tape, boyl them in fair Water and Salt, with a little Vinegar, a faggot or two of fweet Herbs, and two or three whole Onions, and fliced Ginger, let that be your Pickle; then at your pleafure, you may ferve them up to the Table, garnifh them with Fennel and Flowers, as you fee good.

To Sowce a Tench, to be ferved in Jelly.

TAke a Tench, and fplit him down the Back, only cut off the Head whole, when you have wafhed them clean from the Blood, boyl them up with White-wine, Water, Vinegar and Salt, with large Mace, fliced Ginger, Nutmegs, flices of Lemmon, fo let them boyl in no more Liquor than will cover them, and keep them down under Liquor with a Difh or Plate; when he is boyled, take him up with your Scummer, and lay him in the Dish that you intend to send him up in; then take all the chine bones from the back, and stick them on the Fish, and take a quantity of the said Liquor, and put it on the Fire again; and in case it will not jelly by the strength of the Fish, then boyl a piece of Izenglass, till you find it comes to a jelly; so let it stand till it is almost cold, that it will but run, then pour it over your Fish into the dish, you may keep some to beat; for the garnishing of your Dish, you may mince Sives and Taragon together, and strow the brims of your Dish with your Fish, if you please, when you send it up; after the same manner you may use for Turbert, Breme, or Perch, or any other Fish that you have a desire to serve up in Jelly.

To pickle Smelts white or red.

TAke your large Smelts, and being geld, lay them in a Pan, on them a row of Lemmons, slice Ginger, Nutmeg, large Mace and whole Pepper, then a row of Smelts, so continue till they are placed, then put to them white-wine Vinegar, and Salt, and Bay-leaves a top; but if you would pickle them Red, your Pickle must be red Wine, well mingled with Cutchenele, they will be ready in a Week after they are pickled; part them in halves, as you do Anchovies, and dish them up; strow upon them Lemmon cut square like Dice, with Broom-buds and Barberries, so pour it upon them; garnish them with sliced Lemmon, and serve them up.

To Marble Sowls, Plaice, Flounders, Smelts, or any other Fish that is fitting to Marble.

FIll your Frying-pan with sweet Sallet-oyl, and when it is very hot, your Fish being dryed and flowered, put them into the said Pan; when they are fryed brown and stiff, put them into a large earthen pan, put thereto sliced Nutmeg, large Mace, and whole Pepper, and two

two or three sliced Lemmons; when you have done frying of all your Fish, fry a quantity of Bay-leaves, and put them in a top of your Fish, then put to it so much White-wine, and a little Vinegar, as will cover the Fish, strow a little Salt in it, so dish them up for second Course, when you have occasion.

To pickle Lobsters, and to preserve them.

IN case you are afraid your Lobsters will miscarry after they are boyled, and that they will keep no longer, then take Fennel and bruise it in Vinegar, add salt thereto, and with a branch or two of Fennel, wash them between the Carkase and the Tail, leave your branched Fennel under the Tail, and set them down in a cold place, or a moister with Salt; but if you will be at so much charge, you may preserve them in the said Pickle; however you may preserve the Meat for your use, the tail and claws being broke, in the Pickle aforesaid, and use them as a Sallet. Thus must you preserve your Pranes, or Shrimps, or Crafish.

To pickle a Conger Eel.

YOu must scald your Eel, and scrape it till the outward Skin is scraped off, then boyl your Eel, being cut in pieces, and bound with Tape, in Water, Salt, and Vinegar, and an handful of green Fennel, and when it is boyled, put it into your Sowsing pan, with some of the same Liquor and Beer-Vinegar, with an handful of Fennel on the top of the Fish, so serve it up cold to the Table.

To Pickle and Sowce Sturgeon.

OPen your Sturgeon and take out the entrails; if it be a Female, take out the spawn thereof, and preserve it to make Caveer, then cut out your Sturgeon in lengths, being split equally through the back, first cut off

off your Joul to the bodyward, then your firſt and ſecond Ronde very fair, ſo that the Tail may be the leaſt, ſo that you will have Eight pieces in your Sturgeon; bind it up very cloſe with braces or tape, ſtrow good ſtore of Salt thereon; your Liquor boyling very hard, put it in, then let it boyl for an hour and an half ſoftly, take it up carefully without breaking, and let it cool, then put it into your Caggs or Barrel; let your pickle be half White-wine, half ſtale-Beer, with two or three handfuls of Salt, ſo put it to your Sturgeon aforeſaid, then hoop up your Barrel, and keep it cloſe, ſo that you may take off the Head at your eaſe, which you muſt do ever now and then, and ſupply with Liquor, always ſcumming away the Oyl; otherwiſe your Sturgeon will be ruſty.

To pickle Caveer.

WAſh it with Vinegar, ſeaſon it with Salt, then preſs it two or three Dayes, ſo that all the Liquor or excrements may run away from it, then take it again forth, and mix it together with a quantity of Pepper beaten ſmall to duſt, and Salt as before, then put it into your Preſs again; let it ſtand two or three Dayes, then taſte if it be ſeaſoned high enough; if not, you muſt do ſo the third time; then take it and put it into an Earthen Pot, and ſtrow on Salt on the top of it; when you make any uſe to ſerve up any of it, take out a quantity thereof, and waſh it with Vinegar, and with your Knife ſeparate your Caveer from the ſtrings, and bring it into certain ſmall parcels, as big as a Sprat; diſh it up in your Diſh round about, and in the middle put ſlices of Lemmon between, pour on Oyl and Vinegar, and garniſh it with Lemmons and Barberries.

To Coller Sowls.

TAke out the Bone of the Sowl from the Head to the Tail, in the White fide of him; you muſt only ſcale the Sowl, and not ſtrip him, then take a little piece of Salmon, a handful of ſet Oyſters, the tail of a Lobſter, Pranes or Shrimps; mince all this together with the yolks of half a dozen Eggs, boyled hard, with half a dozen of Anchovies, then take a handful of ſweet Herbs, minced very ſmall, put them all together, make them up into a Body with your yolks of Eggs, and grated Bread, ſeaſon them with Nutmegs, Cloves, Mace, Ginger, and a little Salt : This ſame forced Meat will ſerve for moſt Fiſh : your Sowl, as aforeſaid, being waſhed and dryed, and waſhed over with a few yolks of Eggs, ſpread part of the forced Meat all over the Sowls, then waſh it over with Eggs again, and dip your Oyſters in the yolks of Eggs, with Pranes, Shrimps, or ſliced Lobſter, and ſtick upon the forced Meat, ſprinkling ſome Salt, and more ſpices, if occaſion ſhall require, then roul up your Sowl in Coller, and bind him hard with Tape; you may force as many as you pleaſe, and boyl them in Water, Wine, Vinegar and Salt, and ſeaſoned with whole ſpice, with a faggot or two of ſweet Herbs; let your Liquor boyl before you put in your Coller, pickle them in the ſame; when they are boyled, if you ſerve them up, you may cut them in the middle, and then the middle of your Sowl ſtands upwards in the Diſh.

To Coller Salmon.

TAke a ſide of Salmon, you may cut off a handful of the Tail, it being dry and waſhed; waſh it over with the yolks of Eggs, ſtrow on a good handful of ſweet Herbs, with a little Fennel, ſeaſon it with a pretty ſtore of Salt, and a good quantity of your aforeſaid

said spice, adding a little Pepper thereto, bind it up in Collers with your broad Tape; let your water, vinegar and salt boyl together, then put in your said Coller with a faggot of sweet Herbs, with sliced Ginger and Nutmeg; it will ask an hour and halfs boyling, if it be a great Coller; so put it into your Sowse-pan with your Liquor, until you go to dishing of your cold-meats.

To Sowce Lumps.

SOme flea your Lumps before they boyl them, but that is not proper for any Sowced Fish, to be served in cold; you must only scald and scrape him with your Knife, then boyl him up as the aforesaid Fish, and serve him to the Table; you may serve him with Jelly, as you were shewn before.

After the same manner of boyling Fish, or Pickling, you may do Mullets, Dace, Gurnets, Pikes, Carps, Perches, Tenches, Roches, and many other sorts of Fish, in the Nature of this.

BOOK X.

Cold baked Meats of Flesh.

AFore you go about your baked Meats, I shall give some directions how to make your Paste, because some that may have occasion, may be ignorant therein.

To make Paste of Rye-Flower.

IT is only done with boyling Water, made very stiff, and molded so together that it may not crack; your Paste for your lesser cold baked-Meats, as for Fowl, and the like, is to be made with fine Flower, to every

Peck

Peck a Pound and half of Butter, and about the quantity of eight Eggs, casting away the Whites of Four, put your Butter into your Liquor, and when it is melted, pour it into a hole made in your Flower, but not to your Eggs, and put to it as much Liquor as will work it up, so mingle it together with your Eggs lying round about your Flower ; for if you should put your scalding Liquor to your Eggs at first, you would caudle them, and take away their use and Operation, in making your Paste any whit the better to stand; you are not to strive to make this Paste altogether so stiff as the other, yet it must be somewhat stiffer than your Paste for hot baked-meats, because you raise these higher than them ; And the matter that you bake in these, will ask much more baking than your hot baked-meat ; this must be well molded, that it may work as clear as wax ; and to that end, let not your Liquor be too vehement hot ; the more Butter you put in, the more colder let your Liquor be ; you may well upon that account, put in two Pound of Butter.

To Bake Venison in Crust, or in Pots.

YOur Venison being boned and parboyled, you must lard it very thick with your best larding Bacon, cut in square pieces about the bigness of the top of your Finger, and as long; then season it with Pepper and Salt, only put Salt in your Pepper till it look grayish ; if it be an Hanch, you must cut it with your Knife, till you make it fit for your Coffin ; if it be a side, you must take out the sinews, and the skin that is thereon, and cut off the neck part, to put under your best Venison ; but your sides are more fitting to be baked to eat hot, and your Hanches cold : now your Coffin being made round, or four-square with your Rye Paste, about a Foot high, your best fashion is round ; lay in sheets of lard in the bottom of your Coffin, and strow in season ing, and then place in your Venison; if you please, you may sheet it with lard also on the top, then put on two pound of Butter very smooth; so your lid being ready, indifferent thick, wet it, and lay it on, and close your Pie; so make a funnel upon your lid, with your garnish; so beat two or three Eggs, with a Spoonful of water, and a little flower, indore your baked Meat with the same, with your wetting Brush made of Feathers. This baked Meat will ask six hours baking; take heed your Oven be not too hot at the top, to scorch the brims; when it comes forth of the Oven, if you will keep it any thing long, you must pour out all the Liquor, for the gravie will presently putrifie it; otherwise you must do as you were taught before; then take off your Butter clear from your gravie, and put it to your clarified Butter, and fill up your Pie when it is cold; being thus done it shall keep half a Year; but being done as aforesaid, it shall keep a Twelve-month: keep your funnel stopped with a piece of Butter.

To bake a Fillet of Veal to be eaten cold.

TAke a great Leg of Veal, and cut off a large Fillet; then cut it into three pieces like Fillets, and parboil them: when they are cold, season them with a little Pepper beaten small, and Salt, Nutmeg, Cloves and Mace; your Coffin being ready, put in the first Fillet, and strow on Time, and having slices of Bacon seasoned with Sage and Pepper, lay it on the top of the said Veal: then lay on the second Fillet, and do the like with another laying of Bacon; then lay on the third Fillet, and do the like: So strow on a little minced Time, and a little seasoning, with some large Mace, put on the Butter, and close up the Pye. You must observe to beat all your Fillets of Veal with a Rolling-pin, or with the back of a Clever, put on your Funnel, garnish and indore your baked-meat with Yolks of

The whole Body of Cookery Diſſected.

of Eggs: Let this Baked-meats be made with hot Butter, paſte, and fine flower: when it is baked and cold, fill it up with clarified Butter.

To bake a Calves-head to be eaten cold.

YOu muſt firſt half boyl a fair Calves-head, then take out all the Bones on both ſides, and ſeaſon it with the aforeſaid ſeaſoning, and lard it with Bacon and a little Lemmon-pill; then having a Coffin large enough, not very high, nor very thick, but made four-ſquare, lay on ſome ſheets of Lard on the top, and Butter it; when it is baked and cold, fill it with clarified Butter.

To bake a Fawn or Kid to be eaten cold.

FIrſt, bone either Fawn or Kid, parboil, and lard them very thick with Bacon, then ſeaſon them with a little fine Pepper, Nutmeg, Cloves, Mace, and as much Salt as you think fitting (cold baked Meats ought to have more than hot) then take ſome ſavoury forc'd Meat, and put into the Belly, and ſo make it into the proportion as before it was boned: make your Coffin according to that proportion, with hot Butter, paſte, and put it in fairly, ſo that it bear not down the ſides: So put on your Butter, and cloſe it up, and when it is baked and cold, fill it up at the Funnel with clarified Butter.

To bake a Hare.

TAke a Hare and parboil him, and cut all the Fleſh clean from the Bones, then take a good piece of *Weſtphalie* Bacon, or other lean Bacon well boiled, mince them all together, then beat them in a great Morter, ſeaſon it with Pepper, Salt, Cloves, Mace, and Nutmeg, with a handful of minced ſweet Herbs put to it, a little Vinegar, and three Eggs; beat them again in the

the Morter, till they come into a reafonable Body, not too ſtiff: having your Coffin made in the form of a Hare, lay in part of this Meat over the bottom, then lay a laying of Bacon, of ſquare pieces as big as a Tobacco Pipe, ſo long as your Meat, then lay in another laying of your Meat: This do three or four times, till all the Meat is gone, lay alſo a laying of Bacon on the top of it. Note, that you muſt waſh every laying with the yolks of Eggs, and ſqueeze it down with your hand, then put on Butter, and cloſe your Pye: you ſhouldad, firſt alſo lay ſheets of Lard at the bottom; ſet up the Head and Ears of your Hare in the fore-part of the Pye, in a funnel of paſte, with a Garniſh; and a funnel in the middle thereof, indored with yolks of Eggs beaten, and ſo bake it: when it is cold, fill it with clarified Butter; this muſt be done with hot Butter-paſte: To carve when it is Eating, you muſt begin at the Tail, and cut through to the Head, it will be all madder'd in a Body in your ſlices.

Another way to bake a Hare.

TAke a Hare, being parboiled, and break his bones with a chopping Knife, that they ſtart not up, and break your Pye; and alſo cut the ſinews of the back and other parts, then lard them very well with bacon lard; ſeaſon them with Pepper and Salt, a little Cloves, Mace, and Nutmeg: your Coffin being ready, in the proportion of a Hare, lay ſome leaves of lard underneath, ſeaſoned with Pepper, minced Sage, and ſweet Herbs, ſo put in your Hare, only the head to be on the lid, as aforeſaid; put in your Butter, and cloſe your Pye, indore it, bake it, and fill it with clarified Butter when it is cold.

To

To bake Pork to be eaten cold.

TAke a Loin of Pork and bone it, and cut part thereof into thin collops beaten with the Clever, also take as manny collops of Veal thin beaten; season your Pork with Pepper, Salt, and minced Sage; season your Veal with Cloves, Mace, Nutmeg, and minced Time; put yolks of Eggs to each of your Meats, and mingle them together, with their several seasonings, then lay a laying of the Pork, in a form as you intend to make your Pye, either round or otherwise; and then a laying of your Veal thereon, so continue till you have laid all your Meat, then take a Rolling-pin and beat it well together into a Body, put it into your Coffin made for that purpose, close it, indore it, bake it; when it is cold, fill it with clarified Butter; let your Pork be the fat end of the Loyn, and both undermost and uppermost in your Pye.

To bake Brawn to be eaten cold.

TAke your raw lean Brawn that is not useful to coller, and as much fat Bacon, and mince them small together, then beat them in a Morter, beat a good handful of minced Sage with them; season them with a good handful of Pepper and Salt, and a good quantity of beaten Ginger, pour in a little Vinegar, and break in a couple of Eggs; you may make a cold Butter-paste, and drive out a sheet thereof, and lay in your Meat in the form of a Brawn, and put in Butter and Bay-leaves a top, and so close up your Pasty: Let them be sent up to the Table with an Apple in his Mouth: If you please, you may bake it in a round Pye or any other form.

To bake Rabbets to be Eaten cold.

WHen they are parboiled, take out all the Bones you can well take out, and lard your Rabbets, then season them as you did your Hare, put a good quantity of Savoury, Forc'd-meat, so put them into your Coffin prepared; put on Butter and close your Pye, bake it; and fill it with clarified Butter when it is cold.

To bake Pigeons to be Eaten cold.

PIgeons being parboiled, stuff them full of forc'd-Meat, and Bacon in slices; being seasoned with Pepper and Salt, lay them into your Coffin prepared, and put betwixt each, one slice of Bacon seasoned with Pepper and Sage; so close your Pye, put on a Funnel, and when 'tis baked and cold, fill it with melted Butter.

To bake Bran-Geese, or Wild-Geese.

WHen they are parboiled, take out the breast bones, and as many other as you can, not disfiguring the Fowl: then season the Fowl, and lard them, bake them, so fill them with Butter.

To bake a Turkey.

BOne and lard your Turkey when it is parboiled, being seasoned with Pepper, Salt, with a little Cloves and Mace, put him into your Coffin prepared for it, lay on Butter, and close it; put the Head on the top with your garnish: Indore it, bake it, and fill it with clarified Butter when it is cold.

To bake Herns.

OF your Herns, you must take out what bones you can, not disfiguring the Fowl; so lard it, it, and feafon it with Pepper, Salt, and Cloves and Mace beaten; clofe it, and bake it, and fill it when it is cold with Butter.

To bake a Swan.

PUll all the grofs Feathers from the Swan clean, and all the down; then cafe your Swan, and bone it, leave all the Flefh, lard it extream well, and feafon it very high with Pepper, Salt, Cloves and Mace; fo having your Coffin prepared in the proportion of a Swan, made of Rye dough, put in your Swan, and lay fome fheets of lard and bay-leaves on the top, fo put on Butter and clofe it: put on the Head and Legs on the top, garnifh and indore it, and bake it; when it is cold fill it up with clarified Butter. Your skin being fpread forth and dried, is good to make a Stomacher for them that are apt to take cold in their Breaft. You may bake your Swan, if you pleafe, being ordered as aforefaid and not cafe it.

How to bake a Goofe.

BReak the bones of your Goofe and parboil him, then feafon him with Pepper and Salt, a little Cloves and Mace; if you pleafe, you may bake a Rabbet or two with it, becaufe your Stubble-Geefe are very fat, and your Rabbets dry, you need not lard either: Bake it in good hot Butter pafte. This is the Goodwifes Pye upon the feafon, or againft a good time; by the fame Rules as aforefaid, you may bake any other grofs Flefh or Fowl, according to its nature or quality.

Cold Baked Meats of Fifh.

To bake a Lamprey Eel Pye.

CUt open your Lamprey in the belly, and take the bone out of the back, then fcald it, and fcrape it
well

well of the skin side; season it in the inside with Pepper, Salt, Cloves, Mace, and a little minced Onyon, then close it together again as it were whole; you must also season the outside : make a round Coffin, being ready, of Rye dough, according to the wideness of your Eel, when turned round therein; if your Coffin be very high, you may lay one upon another : put in two great Onyons in the middle, season them on the top with some of your seasoning, with half a dozen Bay-leaves and Butter; close your Pye very high : so with your funnel and garnishing, indore it, and bake it, and fill it up with clarified butter when it is cold.

To bake a Turbert.

YOur Turbert being fin'd and prepared, slash it on the white side with your Knife, season it with small Pepper and Salt, Nutmegs, Cloves, and Mace; your Coffin being ready, according to the proportion of the Turbert, put it in, lay on Butter, and close it : This may only be sent to a Friend; in case there be plenty of Turberts, it is a more honourable dish to be baked hot, with other Compounds, as you shall see hereafter

To bake a Salmon.

SCrape your Salmon, wash and dry him, then run your Pen-knife from the head to the Tail on both sides : otherwise take out the chine, then season him with beaten Cloves, Mace, Ginger, with Pepper and good store of Salt, both in the inside and the outside in the scortches : you may put him in a raised Coffin proportioned for him, otherwise lay him upon a sheet of Pasty paste, and set a border close round him, that he may be formed like a Salmon; then put in Butter, sliced Ginger, large Mace on the top thereof, then turn up the other half sheet of your Paste over the Back, as you do a Pasty, and close them all along by the Belly-side, from Head to Tail,

so

The whole Body of Cookery Diffected. 31

so bring him in proportion with his Fins and Tail, Head and Gills, so set a Funnel and Garnish thereon; being scaled all over, then indore him and bake him, and fill him with Butter when he is cold.

To bake an Eel to be Eaten cold.

COller your Eel, and season as before, when you sowst him; lay him upon the side into the Coffin, so put on Butter, and close him; indore him, bake him, and when he is cold, fill him with clarified Butter.

To bake a Pike.

TAke a fair Pike and lard it with Pickle-herring, being beforehand scaled and made fitting, force his Belly with forst Meat of Fish, then season him with some Pepper, Salt, Cloves, Mace, Nutmeg and Ginger beaten: then bake him as you did your Salmon before, according to his form or proportion. Your cold baked Meat of Fish ought to be according to their proportions or forms, so may you bake any that you have a mind to.

BOOK V.

How to make several sorts of Jellies, Leaches, and Creams.

To make Jellies.

TO prepare and make your stock for Jellies, you must have two pair of Calves Feet, being boyled so that they may be blanched, then take two Knuckles of Veal, cut off the Fillet, break not the Bones; let your Veal and Calves Feet lie in fair Water for the space of four and twenty hours, and for the time shift them in five or six Waters, scruseing forth all the Blood; then put them a boiling in fair Spring Water, so much as will well cover and boil them; keep them

them fcumming for the fpace of an Hour, and put a little Salt therein, with fome long Mace, Cinamon flit, Nutmeg and Ginger, in a Tiffinee cloth : when they have boiled foberly for the fpace of two Hours, try your Broth in a Spoon whether it will Jelly; boyl it not down too low, left it change brown: but if it jellies not to your mind, put into it about an ounce of an Ifing-glafs, and when it hath fimbred about half an Hour, ftrain out your Broth into a Pipkin, and let it ftand till it is cold, or till you go to make your feveral Jellies.

How to feafon and run Chryftal Jellies.

YOur ftock being cold as aforefaid, take away the fat from the top, and dregs from the bottom, and put the reft into a Pipkin; put to it fome Cloves, Mace, Cinamon, and flit Ginger and Nutmeg, alfo of Musk and Ambergreefe, of each a Grain in a Tiffinee Ragg; put in fome Rofe-water, and about a quart of Rhenifh Wine if your ftock be ftiff, or as much as you may imagine will make it a ftrength fit for Jelly : add to it of Oyl of Nutmeg and Mace, two or three drops of each, and as much double refined Sugar as will make it to your tafte, according to the quantity of your Jelly; let all thefe on the Fire in the Pipkin, and let it fimber a quarter of an Hour, then take it off, and put in the Juice of a dozen Lemmons, and having eight Whites of Eggs well beaten with a Spoon, put them into the Jelly, and fet it on the Fire again till it boyls up; then having your Jelly-bag ready hanged up on a Spit between the two racks near the Fire, with a Bafon underneath, put your Jelly into the Bag, and let it run into the Bafon, then fet another Bafon under it, and put up the firft running into the Bag again, fo do till it runs clear, this is the Chryftal Jelly.

How to run Colours.

PUt a quantity of Saffron into a piece of Tiffinee, and some beaten Cutchenele into the like, tyed close with a Thred, you may put Spinage or green Wheat also into another; and when you have run out as much Chryftal Jelly, as you intend, put under your Bason with your Cutchenele in it, bruising it tenderly with a Spoon, that it may colour your Jelly; take heed you bruise it not too hard, for fear of breaking the Tiffinee, and mudding your Jelly with the Dregs thereof: so observe with your other Colours.

To make Jellies of Oranges.

TAke the Juice of two dozen of Oranges, and one Quart of the aforesaid stock; boil or let them simper together for the space of a quarter of an hour, seasoned as the aforementioned Chryftal Jelly: if it be too weak, you may add thereto a quarter of an ounce of Ising-glass; if too strong, add some clear Rhenish Wine: so clarifying of it with four or five whites of Eggs, as aforesaid, run it through your Bags. Thus might you make Jelly of Red Currans, the juice thereof being bruised with a little Rhenish Wine; in the Winter season you may use the Syrrup of Mulberries or Barberries, or clear Syrrup of Orangado: so will you have your several coloured Jellies, with their several tastes.

To make Harts-horn Jelly.

TAke the Brawn of six Cocks, being steept in Water, and shifted for 24 hours, then take a quarter of a Pound of Harts-horn, and boil these together two hours, then strain the Broath out into a Pipkin, and let it be cold, then take off the top and bottom. Return your clear Jelly into a clean Pipkin, and season it as your Chryftal Jelly before; only adding thereto a little quantity of Chainny;

Chainny; if it be too strong, add some Rhenish Wine; if too weak, a small quantity of Ising-glass: You may put herein Majesty of Pearl, or if you please, Corral; after which set it on the Fire again for a quarter of an hour, more or less, according to the strength or weakness of your Jelly; then clarifie it with whites of Eggs, and run it through your Bags as aforesaid, and preserve it in a Glass or Pipkin for your use: This Jelly is a great Cordial, very Restringent and strengthning to the back. It may be taken cold, or else dissolved, being heat again, and so drank.

How to make Leach.

TAke a Pottle of new Milk, half a Pound of Jordan Almonds, being first blancht, then steept in Water for half a Day or better, then let them be beaten very small in a Morter, after which put them into your Milk, set them both upon a heap of coals in a Skillet until they boyl, keeping it always stirring for fear of burning to; and so let it boyl for the space of half an hour, then strain out your Milk through a hair strainer into another Skillet; add thereto one Ounce of Ising-glass being pull'd to pieces, and steept in Milk for an hour before; put thereto likewise a good quantity of whole Cinamon, with some large Mace, & a Nutmeg quartered, together with half a Pound or more of your fine white Sugar; Musk and Ambergreece, of both one grain: then set it on the fire again, keeping it stirring while it continues there: If you feel it to begin to grow at the bottom, shift it into a clean Skillet, it being very apt to burn; when it hath boyled half an hour, take a spoonful, and put it into a cold Sawcer; if when it is cold you find it strong, then add more Milk thereto; if weak then boyl it longer: When it is enough, add to it a little Rose water, then strain it into your Bason.

How

How to run your Leach into colours.

TAke Saffron, Cutchenele and Spinnage; let them be all beaten apart, and tied up in three Tiffinee raggs, by which you may make three colours; wring forth a small quantity of Spinnage, it makes the one green; the other two steept in a little Rose water, bruised tenderly with a Spoon, makes you Red and Yellow; if you would have any other colours, you must use sweet sirrups which are clear; you may cast these to make Ribbon, Leach; dissolve one of the said colours, and pour it into a deep Bason: when it is congealed and strong, dissolve another, and being so cold that it will but just run, run it on the top of your former; thus do with as many as you have.

The use of your Jelly and Leach.

YOur Jelly and Leach is a great Second and Third Course Dish: Your Jelly being sliced forth thin, and placed in your Dish; so is your Leach also cut forth in Ribbons, and placed between the Jelly, with your colours opposite one to another; beat some of your Jelly to pieces, and put a Spoonful in goblets (or more) in the middle; and also garnish it with goblets, or Diamonds of Jelly in every vacant place; you may also run your Jelly into the pill of Lemmon, being cut into half, and the Meat taken out; or into the sets of sweetmeat-Tarts, or little Coffins made for that purpose, or any other way that is proper, according to your pleasure.

To make divers sorts of Creams.

To make Cheese and Cream.

WHen you have run your Morning Milk with about one Pottle of fresh Cream to a Gallon and half, your Curds being cleansed from the Whey, season it with fine beaten Cinamon, Sugar and Rose-water; fill five or six Dishes, about half a Pint a piece, with the said Curd; then lay Trenchers on the top of them, and a Board thereon, and press them until they come into a body like Cheeses; then turn them out whole into your Dish (which you may do the better by buttering the bottom of your Dish) and having a Pottle of Cream boyled up, with whole Cinamon, large Mace, and a Nutmeg quartered; with the yolks of six Eggs beaten with Rose-water, stirred in a little before it comes off the Fire, seasoned with fine Sugar; you may add one grain of Musk in the boyling, which will serve for the same purpose another time; when it is almost cold, put it in with your Ladle between the said Cheeses; scrape thereon Sugar, and serve it up.

Another way.

SEason your pure fresh Cream with beaten Cinamon, Nutmeg, Rose-water and Sugar, with as much Naple-Bisket grated as will make it somewhat thick; so pour it over your Cheeses, as was done with the other; strow on Cinamon and Sugar, and so send it up.

To make Apple Cream.

TAke a quantity of Pippins, and boyl them in a Pint of White-wine, and a Pint of Sack, with a Pill of minced Orangado, some whole Cinamon and Ginger

Ginger sliced, half a Pound of fine Sugar, keep them close covered, until they are boyled unto a Jelly; then lay them by spoonfuls as high as you can into yonr Dish; when they are cold, pour in your boyled Cream as aforesaid; stick your Rocks of Jelly with sliced Cittern.

This may be done without Sack or White-wine, only adding a Pound of Sugar more to fourteen Pippins: you must use no more Water in the boyling than will cover them: you shall know when they are rightly boyled down, they will be as red as Rubie, and clear.

To make Quince-Cream.

BOyl your Quinces unpared; and when they are boyled very tender, pare them, and take the pulp from the Core, season it with beaten Cinamon, and Ginger, Orangado, and dryed Cittern minced small, Carraway-Comfits, and Rose-water, and Sugar; so your Cream being boyled and seasoned (as in the first) and half cold, put it into your Quinces, being dished in Spoonfuls; or if you please, you may mix it altogether, the Cream will not curdle; but if you do this with raw Cream, your Quinces must be quite cold, else your Cream will curdle.

To make a Cream called Sack and Pottage.

TAke about a Pottle of Cream, or new Milk, whilest it boyls, beat the yolks of a dozen Eggs with half a Pint of Sack; and when the Milk boyls put it in, keeping it stirring until it comes to a tender curd, then run it through a Strainer; save your curd, being cleansed from the Whey; season it with beaten Cinamon, Ginger, Nutmeg, Sugar, Rose-water; so put it into your Dish, as a Tansey, strowing thereon beaten Cinamon and Sugar.

To make a Sack-Posset the best way.

SEt a Gallon of Milk on the Fire, put therein a grain of Musk, whole Cinamon and large Mace; when it boyls, stir in half a Pound of Naple-Bisket grated, keeping of it stirring while it boyls; then beat eight Eggs together, casting four of the Whites away; beat them well with a Ladleful of Milk or two amongst them; take off the Fire the aforesaid Milk, and stir in your Eggs; put it on the Fire again (but keep it stirring for fear it curdles) having almost a Pint of Sack in your Bason (upon the Coals, with a spoonful of Rose-water) your Milk being seasoned with Sugar, and taken off the Fire, pour it into your said Sack, stirring of it apace; while it is so pouring forth, take out your grain of Musk, so throw thereon beaten Cinamon, and send it up.

To coddle Codlings green, to serve up with Cream.

TAke Apples from the Tree fit to coddle, put them into a broad Pan (or Skillet) of Water, set them over an heap of charcoal Fire; so that they may be alwayes scalding hot, and never boyl, kept close covered; only to have an Eye on them, that now and then they may be turned in the Pan: This constant sober heat without boyling (and being kept close) causeth their greeness; when they are tender, take off the outward Skin; your cream being boyled up, and seasoned, you may put them in whole or in halves, all over your Cream; being very well sprinkled with Rose water: so scrape on sugar, and send them up.

To make Barly Cream.

LEt your Pearled Barley be well boyled, then set over your Cream, and put therein as much of the said Barley, as may bring it to a reasonable thickness; being boyled up for the space of a quarter of an hour,

boyl

boyl in it whole Cinamon, and large Mace, with a little Lemmon-pill; then having two yolks of Eggs, for each Quart of Cream, well beaten with Rose-water and some of the said Cream, put them in, keeping your Cream stirring, adding a little Salt, when you take it off the Fire; seasoned with Sugar, you may serve it hot to the Table.

To make Rasberry Cream.

WHen you have boyled up your Cream (as other Creams aforesaid) take two Ladlefuls of the said Cream, (being almost cold) bruise them together, season it with Sugar and Rose-water, and put it into your aforesaid Cream, stirring it altogether; so dish it up.

After the same manner may you do your Strawberry Cream.

To make Red Currans Cream.

YOu must first bruise your Currans with some of the said Cream, (being boyled as aforesaid) then strain them through your Strainer (or Sieve) and put the Liquid substance thereof to the said Cream (being almost cold) and it will be a pure Red; so serve it up.

To make Cabbage Cream.

TAke three Gallons of Milk, when it boyleth, put therein a Pottle of Cream, and (after it's in) let it boyl a dozen walms, then take it off the Fire, and put it in four or five broad Milk-pans; let it get a head, until the next Day, that you intend to use it; when you dish it, put half a Cabbage in the bottom of your Dish, (with the cut side downwards) then take off the head, or clouts of Cream, with a Slice or Scummer, and lay them over the Cabbage, sprinkle on Cinamon, Sugar and Rose-water, between each sheet, so lay one on the top

top of the other, until all the heads of your pans is on the Cabbage, and it will appear on the Table like a Cabbage ; you may ſtick it with ſprigs of Roſemary, laying Artificial Snow thereon.

But if you diſh the ſaid Clouts, in the bottom of a ſmall diſh (within a greater) you may then call it Clouted Cream.

To make Snow Cream.

BReak the Whites of ſix Eggs, put thereto a little Roſe-water, beat them well together with a bunch of Feathers until they come perfectly to reſemble Snow; ſo lay on the ſaid Snow in heaps upon ſome other Cream (that is cold) which is made fit for the Table ; you may put under your Cream, in the bottom of the diſh, part of a Penny Loaf, and ſtick therein a Branch of Roſemary or Bayes, and fill your Tree with the ſaid Snow ; ſo ſerve it up.

To make Almond Leach Cream.

BEat a quarter of a Pound of Jordan Almonds in a Morter, until it comes to a Paſte ; (but note in the beating, you muſt mingle by degrees ſome Roſewater and Sugar) after it is well compoſed or beaten thin, with a little Milk, adding thereto a little Riceflower ; ſo make it like a Batter, pouring it into your Cream or Milk over the Fire, and let them boyl altogether (putting thereunto whole Cinamon, a little large Mace, Iſing-glaſs, and a quartered Nutmeg) for the ſpace of half an hour ; but you muſt keep it ſtirring the whole time, for fear of burning ; when you take it off, put into it the yolks of four Eggs, beaten in a little Cream and Roſe-water, with half a Pound of White Sugar ; ſtir all together, and diſh it up ; a Pottle of Milk is enough for all the aforeſaid compounds.

The

The whole Body of Cookery Diſſected.

The aforeſaid compounds being boyled in a Quart of Milk, you may pour it into two Baſons; you may colour one of them green with the Juice of Spinnage, and ſlice it into your Diſh when it is cold; ſtick your green with ſliced Almonds, and your white with green Cittern.

To make Gooſberry Cream.

First preſerve your Gooſberries (as you are taught in the Book of Preſerves) then having a clear Cream, boyled up, and ſeaſoned with old Cinamon, Nutmeg, Mace, Sugar, Roſe-water and Eggs, (as you have read before) diſh it up; and when it is cold, take up your Gooſberries with a Pin, and ſtick them on in rows, as thick as they can lie upon the ſaid Cream; Garniſh your diſh with them, ſtrow them over with Sugar, and ſend them up.

To make Rice Milk or Cream to be eaten hot.

Boyl your Rice in Water about half a quarter of an Hour, put it out into a Cullender, and pick out the unhuskt Rice from it, then put on three Pints of Milk or Cream, or both together, and ſet it on a heap of Coals in a Skillet; put to it large Mace, whole Cinamon, a Nutmeg in halves; then put almoſt a quarter of a Pound of your aforeſaid Rice, being thinned and beaten with Cream or Milk; let it boyl until the Rice be very tender, and it begins to thicken; then take the yolks of four Eggs, and beat them with ſome Roſewater, and a Ladleful of your Cream, off the Fire, ſo ſtir it all into your Cream over the Fire, then take it off, and ſeaſon it with Sugar and a little Salt, diſh it up, and take forth your whole Spice, ſcrape Sugar round the brims of your Diſh. After the ſame manner may you make Barley Milk or Cream; only note, you muſt give Barley far more boyling than your Rice, both in the Water and Milk

To

To boyl Milk or Cream with French *Bread, to be eaten hot.*

TAke a *French* Role, being chipt, and slice it exceeding thin in little pieces, dry it upon the Fire; then having three Pints of Milk or Cream, ready to boyl with Cinamon, large Mace and Nutmeg, put in your Bread, and let it boyl together with your Milk; beat the yolks of four or five Eggs with a little Rose-water, and a Ladleful of your Milk over the Fire: and stir it together with your Cream; season it with Sugar and Salt, and send it up. These two above-mentioned, do use to be sent hot to the Table on Fish-dayes.

To make Spring Pottage.

PUt on about a Gallon of fair Water, with a handful of great Oatmeal beaten small, and a piece of Rib Bacon; then take a handful of Brook-lime, as many Water-Cresses, Nettle-tops, Elder-buds, Violets and Primrose-leaves, with young Alexander-leaves; mince all these very small, put them to your Broth, with a little large Mace; so season it with Salt, and put in Butter when you take it off; and so serve it to the Table on Fasting-days, or eat it in the Morning Fasting. It is good to cleanse the Blood.

To make Water-Grewel.

TAke a Pottle of Water, a handful of great Oatmeal, pickt and beat in a Morter, put it a boyling: when it is half enough, put to it two handfuls of Currans washed, a faggot or two of sweet Herbs, four or five blades of large Mace, a little sliced Nutmeg; let a grain of Musk be infused a little while in it; season it with Sugar and Rose-water when it is enough, and put to it a little drawn Butter.

The whole Body of Cookery Diſſected. 43

To make Punnado.

TAke about one Quart of Running-water, put it on the Fire in a Skillet, then cut a light Roul of Bread in ſlices, about the bigneſs of a Groat, and as thin as Wafers, dry it in a Diſh on a few Coals, then put it into your Water, with two handfuls of Currans, pickt and waſhed, a little large Mace, ſeaſon it with Sugar and Roſewater, when it is enough ; and infuſe or rub the bottom of your diſh with Musk : You muſt add Salt to this, and the abovementioned.

To make Barley-Grewel.

TAke half a Pound of Barley, and give it one or two walms, in two or three Waters, then put it in a ſtone Morter and beat it ; ſo ſet it a boyling in a Pottle of Water, or more, with two Ounces of Harts-horn ; when it hath boyled about two Hours, ſtrain it through a Strainer ; then add a little more Water to your Barley, to get out the Heart and Strength of it ; then ſet your Liquor a boyling again, with half a Pound of Currans, a faggot of cold Herbs, as Sorrel, Strawberry, and Violet leaves, &c. alſo a little Time, three or four blades of Mace ; and when the Currans are boyled enough, your Broth will be ready ; then add about a quarter of a Pint of the Juice of Sorrel, let it boyl one walm ; take it off the Fire, and ſcruiſe in the Juice of four Lemmons ; ſeaſon it with Roſe-water, with Musk infuſed therein, with a little Salt : there is nothing better than this, to give any one in a Feaver, all the time of their ſickneſs : if you ſerve it to the Table, leave out cold Herbs, and add ſweet Herbs, you may alſo ſend up the Barley with it, but for weak Stomachs ſtrain it.

To make a Pearmane Cawdle.

MAke a Poffet with a quart of Milk and White-wine very clear, then flice half a dozen great Pearmanes and boyl them in your Poffet; when they are boyled enough, ftrain the Liquor forth, with as much of the Apple as will run; lay it on the Fire again, with two or three blades of Mace; when it boyls, beat the yolks of three Eggs into, to thicken it, feafon it with fome Muskified Rofe-water, and Sugar: this is very good to give fick People which are fubject to Melancholly.

To make a Lemmon Cawdle.

TAke a Pint of White-wine, and a Pint of Water, and let it boyl, put to it half a Manchet, cut as thin and fmall as you can, put it in with fome large Mace; then beat the yolks of two Eggs to thicken it, and fcruife in the Juice of half a dozen Lemmons, feafon it with Sugar and Rofe-water.

To make a Florendine, or Made-difh of Rice.

THe Pafte for your Florendines ought to be a rich cold buttered pafte, or Puff pafte: take a Pound of Rice, boyl it a quarter of an hour in water, then put it out into a Cullender, afterwards boyl it half an hour in Milk, or as long as you can, provided your Milk burns not too; put four or five fticks of Cinamon in the boyling thereof, and let it ftand in a deep Difh or Bafon, until it is cold, and congealed together; then take the one half of it, or as much as you need, break to it the yolks of fix Eggs, and the Whites of two, put to it half a Pound of Beef-fuet minced fmall, and almoft as many Currans, a dozen of Dates minced; feafon it with Cinamon, Nutmeg, a little Cloves, Mace, Ginger, Salt, and a handful of Sugar, with a little Rofe-water: fo mingle it all up together in a thick Batter, with a little Cream: cover

The whole Body of Cookery Diſſected. 45

ver over your diſh you intend to bake it in with a ſheet of Paſte : put in your Rice, fill it not too full, that it riſe not over the brims of your diſh, then jagg a ſheet of Puff-paſte, the breadth of your diſh, about half an inch broad, twiſt them and lay over your Florendine, from the one ſide of your diſh to the other, faſtening them to the ſheet of Paſte in the bottom, ſo croſs them again, that they may be Chequer-work, then cut your Paſte upon the brim of your diſh, double, over all the ends of your croſs-bars : bake it, and ſtick it in the chequers with Lozenges : ſcrape on Sugar, and ſend it up.

To Butter Rice.

TAke Rice that is after the ſame manner boyled in water, then in milk, bruiſe it with your ladle, with ſome ſweet Cream amongſt it : put butter to it, and ſet it on a heap of coals in a diſh : let it boyl, and keep it ſtirring : ſeaſon it with Cinamon, grated Nutmeg, Salt, Roſe-water and Sugar : when it is enough, diſh it on ſippets of toaſts ; and ſtick them with the ſame, or Lozenges of Paſte fryed and baked : ſcrape on Sugar, and ſend it up.

To make a Florendine or made-diſh of Apples.

PUt on a skillet of water, with ſome Currans a boyling : then pare about a dozen Pippins, and cut them from the Core, into the ſaid water : when they are boyled tender, pour them into a Cullender : when the water is drained from them, put them into a diſh, and ſeaſon them (but if you have time, ſtay until they are cold, leſt it melt your Sugar, beſides it will ſpoyl your Paſte) with Sugar, Roſe-water, Cinamon, and Carraway-ſeeds : then role out two ſheets of Paſte : put one in your diſh bottom, and all over the brims : then lay in your Apples in the bottom round and high ; wet it round, and cover it with your other ſheet, cloſe it, and

carve

carve it about the brims of your dish, as you please prick and bake it: scrape on Sugar, and send it up for a second course.

To make a Florendine or Made-dish of Spinage.

TAke almost a peck of Spinage: when your kettle boyls very fast, throw it in, and let it have half a dozen walms; then put it out into a Cullender and let it drain, and scruise out all the water; mince it very small with a pill or two of Orangado, add to it half a pound of boyled Currans; season it with Cinamon, Ginger, beaten Nutmeg and Salt; then put it in your dish upon a sheet of Paste; put to it Butter and Sugar, cover and close it; prick it over, and bake it: When it is almost baked, put to it a glass of Sack, a little drawn Butter and Vinegar; so shake or mingle it together with your knife, or spoon: and when you have occasion for it, scrape on Sugar, and send it up.

To make Pasties to fry.

TAke of the same compounds, of Apples, and other ingredients, as is in your Florendine of Apples, and make very small Pasties, as you did of the Rice, only add to them a little sliced Orangado.

To make a Florendine or Made-dish of Kidney of Veal.

TAke the Kidney of Veal, fat and all, as much as you have, and mince it small; then mince a few sweet herbs, and about a quarter of a pound of Currans, or more, according to the quantity of your meat; season it with Cloves, Mace, Cinamon, Nutmeg, Sugar, Rose-water, Salt, the yolks of three or four eggs, and a little Sack; if you think it will be too fat, you must add a handful or two of grated bread, a Pippin or two minced, with a little Orangado: so put it on a sheet of Paste in the bottom of your dish, and cover it with

with another, clofe it up, prick it and bake it, fcrape on Sugar, and fend it up for the firft Courfe.

To make toafts of a Kidney of Veal, called Marrow toafts.

Mince it, and feafon it as aforefaid, and put it in a Difh on the coals: as it melts, add grated Bread and the yolks of Eggs, a little Cream; fo ftir it up and down, until it comes into a body like Pap: then take two or three rouls of ftale light Bread, and cut off the two corners of every one of them: then cut them forth in toafts throughout the roul; wafh the one fide with the yolks of Eggs, and fpread on your compofition; being hot, it will fpread like Butter: thus do with all of them, until all be one: wafh them over on the top with the yolks of Eggs; and fo fry them foftly; difh them upon a Plate, ftrow on Sugar and fend them up for fecond Courfe, in a common dyet.

To make a Florendine or a Made-difh of a Calves-Chaldron.

Take one that is very fat, and boyl it, mince it very fmall, with Time, Parflee, a handful of Spinnage, and a few other fweet Herbs; mince all thefe very fmall, with a couple of Pippins; then put to them fome grated Bread, more or lefs, according to the fatnefs or leannefs of your Chaldron: Seafon it with Cinamon, Cloves, Mace, Salt, Nutmeg and Ginger: then break in half a dozen yolks of Eggs, and two Whites: mingle all together, with a good quantity of Currans, according as you put to Mince pyes: all thefe ingredients being well mixed, and your fheet of pafte in the bottom of your Difh, lay your Meat on it, but do not overcharge the Difh, leave room that the Fat boyls not over the brims thereof: then lay over it Dates, Marrow, and Raifons of the Sun; fo clofe it up, and bake it, fcrape on Sugar, and fend it up for the firft Courfe difh. If you

you have a mind to make a Pye, or Mince-pies with the said Meat, you need leave out nothing but the Eggs: Again you ought to put into your Mince Pies a lear of Verjuice: After this manner may you bake Calfs-feet.

To make a Made-dish of Apples and Red Currans.

BOyl up your sliced Apples in a little water and Sugar; let them boyl until the Apples have soaked up all the Liquor, and begins to be dryish: then beat in a Morter a Pint of red Currans, or more, put the Apples and them together, with the yolks of four Eggs, and whites of two: boyl up a quart of Cream, and thicken it up with your Eggs: put your Apples and Currans into your dish on a sheet of Paste, and lay on more Sugar, close it, carve your Paste on the brims: cover your Florendine with another dish, and bake your Paste in a soft Oven: when your Paste is dry, take off your dish, and let it bake a while gently; then when your Cream is cold, put in part of it, and mingle it together: let it stand a little in the Oven: then scrape on Sugar, and send it up for a second Course dish: You may only make it with Currans and Apples, with Sugar, Cinamon, and Rose-water: so let it stand in the Oven for about half an hour while the Paste is dry, and serve it up with a cut: It hath a very good taste, and an excellent colour; and it is the better way.

To make a Made-dish of Artichokes.

BOyl up about a Pint and half of Cream, with two Eggs as before, with a little whole Cinamon, Rose-water and Sugar: then slice five or six Artichokes very thin, season them with Cinamon and Sugar: and season the Marrow of three or four Marrow-bones, in pieces as big as your Thumb, your dish having a garnish opposite on the brims: Butter it in the bottom, then lay a laying of Artichokes all over: strow on the parboyled

Currans,

The whole Body of Cookery Dissected. 49

Currans, and spread over it a laying of Marrow: then pour on that a ladleful or two of Cream, aud let it congeal together a little in the Oven: take it out, and lay over another laying of Artichokes, with Marrow, Currans and Cream, as you did before; so bake it, stick it over with Almonds, and send it up with a cut over it: You may make Florendines with Potatoes, Wardens, Quinces, or Pears: but by what you have already read, you may be able to perform according to their several Natures.

To make forced Meats.

TAke a piece of a Fillet of Veal, and a little piece of Westphaly Bacon boyled, & a piece of Bacon larded, a little Beef suet: (the lean more in quantity than the fat) mince them all together, with one handful of sweet herbs, with some Onions (minced) added to them, seasoned with Cloves, Mace and Nutmegs beaten: put as many raw yolks of Eggs into it, as will make it up into a stiff body: you may mingle amongst it, Pine-Apples, Pistatious. Add Salt to your seasoning: this being rouled in the yolks of eggs, is your savoury forced meat: And you may use it with any savoury baked or boyled meats, as you shall hereafter hear.

To make part of the said forced meats green for your use.

TAke Spinnage, scalded in boyling water, turn it out into a Cullender, and scruise out the water, then mince it small, and mingle it with so much of the forced meat, as you intend to use: you may also mince a handful of Spinnage and Parslee very small: and when you have made your small Balls of forced meat, as big, or little as you please; dip them in the yolks of eggs, and roul them in your green herbs, so that a quick boyling will make them as green as the herbs.

E *Another*

Another forced Meat.

TAke a piece of a leg of Veal, or any other flesh cut out of the skin, that you intend to force: mince it with a quantity of Beef-suet and sweet-herbs, seasoned with Cloves, Mace, Nutmeg and Cinamon beaten: add to it a little Sugar, Rose-water, and one handful of Barberries, a little Salt: make it into a body with the yolks of eggs, and you may put in the Whites of half of them, in this forced meat: It is necessary you put in dryed Citron and Orangado, minced very small: you may green what part of it you please, as you did the other: this serves for your sweet boyled meats, or baked meats of flesh: or to force any thing that you would dress sweet, to please some palates, if desired.

BOOK VI.

Containing strong Broths, and Pottages, with other preparations of Cookery.

To make Strong Broth for your use in dressing of Meat.

TAke a leg of Veal, or other knuckles of Mutton and Veal, being well soaked in divers waters, and the blood dryed clean out: put it a boyling in fair Running-water: keep it scumming during the boyling: when it is almost boyled, you may add a faggot of sweet herbs, large Mace, and a little Salt: your meat may be used for service, but preserve your Broth in a Pipkin.

An excellent Cordial Broth.

TAke a Cock or two, cut off their wings and legs: cleanſe all the blood out of the inſide, parboyl them very well, that when they are boyled, there may ariſe no more ſcum: then waſh them again in fair water, put them in a pitcher with a pint of Rheniſh wine, and as much of your aforeſaid ſtrong Broth as will cover them: add thereto a few Cloves, large Mace, ſliced Ginger and Nutmeg, a little whole white Pepper, if deſired, with a ſmall quantity of Chainie, and an ounce or two of Harts-horn; put in a little Salt, and ſtop up your pitcher cloſe, that no ſteam may come forth: then having a Pot over the fire, let your Pitcher boyl therein about ſix hours, then pour out your Broth through a ſtrainer, into a baſon, and ſcruiſe in the juice of two or three Lemmons: this may be heated as you have occaſion. It is not only Cordial, but good againſt a Conſumption alſo.

To make a Pottage of broth, to ſerve up with a Biſk, or grand boyled Meat.

WHen you boyl up your Fowl, or other Meat for that purpoſe, you may uſe the ſtrong Broth (before cited) and boyl as much meat therein as you have when it is at the full ſtrength; take a quart thereof, add a pint of gravie drawn with Wine, half a dozen of Anchovies, two or three whole Onions, a quarter of a pint of Oyſter liquor, one handful of Raſpine of your French Bread, the juice of two or three Lemmons, the yolks of a couple of eggs beaten into it, when you are ready to uſe it, with a ſliced Nutmeg; ſo draw it up all together; this is a Pottage or Broth fitting for ſavoury boyled meats; if you pleaſe, you may uſe ſome herbs in the ſaid Broth, for ſome of your boyled meats; as Spinnage, Sorrel, Endiff, Lettice, Purſlin, or the like; however forget not some faggots of sweet herbs in the boyling of it up: This is a rich Broth, with a very high hogo.

Another way.

TAke a quart of strong Broth, put to it four whole Onions, a faggot or two of sweet herbs, some large Mace, a handful of Goosberries, with Lettice and Endiff hackt, the yolks of two eggs beaten in half a pint of White-wine, two Lemmons cut dice-wayes; when your Broth is boyled with your herbs, put in your Eggs and Wine, adding to it a sliced Nutmeg; so draw it up till it boyls; then cast in a ladlefull of drawn butter; if it should be too thick, you may add, any quantity of Broth you please to it; this is a savoury sharp Broth, and may be served up with Veal or Mutton, or what Fowl you please. But let not your Goosberries be boyled too much, for fear they turn to mash.

To make a Broth or Pottage, called Skinck.

TAke a leg, or legs of Beef, according to the quantity of broth you would have; cut off the meat in pieces bigger than an Egg; break the bone in pieces, let them lye a soaking in water, washing and cleansing it clean from the blood; put it in your Pot, and a little more than cover it with water; set it over the fire, watch the boyling and scumming thereof; then put a quantity of Pepper tyed up in a rag or cloth, and when it is above half boyled, add four whole Onions, a little Cloves and Mace whole, a Race or two of Ginger sliced; take forth a ladleful thereof, and steep a rag full of Saffron in it, bruise it with the handle of your knife, until you have coloured it, or the vertue of the Saffron gone; then put in the ladleful of Broth again, and let it boyl until your meat be exceeding tender, or to the consuming

The whole Body of Cookery Diſſected

ing of half your Broth; feaſon it with Salt to your pallate, and diſh it up on ſippets of French bread, with ſome of the meat in the middle of the diſh; this is the Skinck; but you may alter it; ſometimes by putting a handful or two of chopt clove-Cabbage; otherwiſe by bruiſed Spinnage and Endiff cut; your herbs in this caſe muſt not be ſhred ſmall; you may add ſliced Manchet to it which way you pleaſe. If you put in any of theſe, they muſt boyl but their time, which is about half an hour, otherwiſe they will loſe their colour.

To make white Broth.

TAke a pint or a quart of White-wine, put it on the fire in a Pipkin, with three or four quartered Pippins, being pared, eight Dates cut in halves, a faggot of ſweet herbs, large Mace, whole Cinamon, a quartered Nutmeg; let them all boyl together; (if you want liquor, add a pint of ſtrong Broth) take the marrow of three Marrow-bones, put it alſo in (when your aforeſaid Broth boyls) but if you pleaſe, wrap it up in the yolks of eggs, and a little grated Bread, left it melt away; then take the yolks of four eggs well beaten with wine, or ſtrong Broth; (your Broth and ingredients being boyled) ſtir it therein; ſo ſeaſon it to your pallate with white Sugar, and take it off the fire; ſome add a pint of Cream to the eggs, but there is great danger therein, that it turns when the Wine and Cream comes together; let both of them be boyled firſt, and almoſt cold before you compound them together; then you may ſet them on, and heat it again, by a continual ſtirring of them together; this Broth you may ſerve up with boyled Capons or Chickens; garniſh the Marrow and Dates upon the breaſt; you may if you pleaſe uſe Spaniſh Potatoes boyled and ſliced, or skirrets in this Broth; but for diſhing and ſending away your meat, you may ſee further in the Book of boyled meats.

To make Stewed Broth.

TAke your shins of Beef or Mutton, otherwise what meat is allowed, being washed and set on, scum it clean; then slice your brown bread, and soak it in the said Broth; when it is so soaked, rub it through a strainer with your hands, put in as much as you judge will make your Broth thick in the boyling; when it is half boyled, add thereto your Raisins, Currans and Pruins according to the quantity of your Broth, with beaten Cloves, Mace, Cinamon and Ginger; taking a good quantity of your Pruins up when they are boyled, mash them together, and strain them as you did the bread with Clarret; so let it continue till it's boyled, then season it further with Sugar and Rose-water, and serve it up with some of the best of your meat.

Another, a Consumption Broth.

TAke the Broth that certain pieces of Marrow-bones have been boyled in, which you may have for nothing at any Feast; boyl therein a great quantity of great Turnips: when they are boyled, press out all the liquor out of them, and put it again into the pot: then take two red old Cocks, scalded, beaten to pieces with the back of a Cleaver: then put them into the said Broth with a pair of Calves-feet; let them boyl together, being well scummed: when they are half-boyled, put in some Raisons of the Sun stoned, sliced Lickerish, a few Anniseeds, with a handful of Pine-apples and Pistatious beaten in a Morter: then put in Cloves, Mace, and Nutmeg, adding to it a pint of red wine: when this meat is boyled all to pieces, strain it forth into your Bason or Pipkin: then put to it white Sugar candy: and you may clarifie it too with the whites of eggs when you boyl it again (if your mind be to have it clear) and so run it through your Jelly-bags: you may take this

Morning,

Morning, Evening or Noon (the Dose being a quarter of a pint.)

To make Red Pottage.

TAke a hanch of Venison, cut him in five or six pieces, and place them in the bottom of a Pot or Pan: then do more than cover it with fair water; after it boyls, and is scummed, add to it a good quantity of whole Pepper, and when it is half enough, put in four whole Onions, Cloves and large Mace, of each a little, sliced Ginger and Nutmeg, three or four faggots of sweet herbs, (with good store of time in the faggots) let it boyl together untill the Venison be very tender, and a good part of the Broth consumed: so done, pour out the Broth from the meat into another Pipkin; keep your Venison hot in the same Pot, either by being covered, or adding other hot Broth: then take a couple of great red Beet-roots, being above half boyled before, cut them in square pieces, three times so big as Dice, and put them into your Broth taken from the Venison; then set it over the fire again, and let it remain there untill the roots are boyled tender, but not masht to pieces; only add more in the boyling four Anchovies minced, then dish up your Venison on sippets of light bread, in order as it was in the hanch: then pour in your Broth, so much as will almost fill the dish: then take your roots by themselves, and toss them in a little drawn Butter, and lay them all over the Venison: you may make use of boyled Colly-flowers, to garnish it out further if you please. Let your red Broth be seen round about the dish sides: if the Beet be good it will be red enough: if not, you ought to colour it with Sanders: this is savoury red Pottage, and to be esteemed above the Venison.

I have explained this here for the Broths sake, rather than for the boyled-meats: in that Book I shall also speak of more variety of Broths.

Another Broth.

TAke a pottle of strong Broth, infuse twelve sliced Onions therein, this Broth may you use to make any of your sauces for wild-fowl, and to draw gravie out of your meat: you may add to it a piece of Lemmon-pill, and a faggot of sweet herbs.

How to draw Gravie.

WHen your meat is above half roasted, put underneath thereof a dish with a good quantity of the Onion Broth (before cited) then you may stab and cut your meat, when you think the gravie will run best: so lade on your Broth on the meat, to draw down the gravie: and likewise White-wine or Clarret, if you have it: when your gravie meat is roasted enough, cut it off, and press it, that you may lose none of the gravie thereof: so preserve this gravie in your Pipkin, adding half a dozen of Anchovies, with a little Nutmeg to each quart or three pints of gravie; you may also put some Oyster liquor therein: this will be called for in your Feasts, to use for sauce for much of your meat, especially your Range.

How to draw Butter.

TAke a quarter of a pint of strong Broth, and put it into a Pan or Pipkin: break in two pound of butter, set it upon a heap of coals, keeping of it drawing or stirring with a Ladle; then break in two pound more, or as many as you have occasion for, so you add liquor proportionable to it; still keep it drawing up to the end, till it be dissolved: when it looks white, thick and smooth, it is in a good condition, and you need not fear the oyling of it: but if it looks yellow and curdled, you will hardly recover it, but it will oyl.

How

The whole Body of Cookery Diſſected. 57

How to Recover it.

TAke a ladleful of ſtrong Broth, put it on the fire in another Pipkin, then put to it half a pound of Butter in pieces, and when it is drawn white, you muſt pour in your oylie Butter; and as you pour it, be ſure to keep it alwaies ſtirring together; ſee that the oylie Butter overcomes not the drawn Butter, by putting it in too faſt: but in caſe you have no Butter in the houſe, yet there is a way to fetch the oylie Butter again; let it ſettle in a cold thing for a pretty while, then pour forth the moſt oylie of it, leaving the dregs and whey behind, add a little ſtrong Broth to the ſaid dreggs, and put it on a hot heap of coals, and ladle it up until it become like to drawn Butter in a body; then take it off the fire, ſtill keeping it drawing and ſtirring; in the mean time, pour in the oylie Butter very ſoftly; ſo let it on the fire and draw it, and when it becomes ſtrong take it off and pour in your oyl again, ſo that the leſſer may comprehend the greater, and draw it all into a body again.

How to make Barley Broth.

TAke a knuckle of Veal, and a neck of Mutton, cut your Mutton in pieces, put them in a Pot with as much water as will contain to boyl them; then take a quarter of a pound of French Barley, having had two or three walms before, in two or three ſeveral waters; ſo put it out of your Cullender; and put it into your meat, ſcum your Broth well when it boyls; put in two or three great Onyons, two or three faggots of ſweet herbs and Parſlee, almoſt one pound of Raiſons of the Sun, ſome whole Cloves, large Mace, two races of Ginger, a piece of Lemmon-pill; ſeaſon it with ſalt and let it boyl ſoberly until it be enough; ſo ſerve up your meat with Raiſons and Barley on the top of it, and
garniſh

garnish your dish with Raisons; But if you please to have it with herbs, you may add Endiff and Spinnage hacked with a knife, and put it in a quarter of an hour before it be enough: or in the Summer, you may use Lettice, Purslin, or any other good herbs.

BOOK VII.

Which teacheth to make all manner of hot boyled meats of Flesh.

How to make a Bisk.

THere is a grand boyled meat, called a Bisk, and it is much mended by the English, of what was practised by the French, according to their Original, because an English man never thinks a thing well, nor rich enough, but usually doth augment according to reason, and disalloweth of unnatural compositions. The best way for dressing the said dish, now in use, and allowed, is, That you take all the choicest wild-fowl, and tame-fowl, of the smaller sort; the biggest that is to be made use of, is a Capon or Pullet, to be forced; Put the said fowl (that you make choice of) a boyling, with a piece of good Bacon, belonging to the rib; then having your forced meat in balls, about the bigness of an egg, but longer, rouled up in the yolks of eggs (as is shewn in the Book of Forced meats) put twenty of the said Balls in the aforesaid Fowl; you may wrap up some of the same Balls in the Caul of Veal, after the same bigness and length; then charge a second Pipkin with Lamb-stones, sweet-breads, Lambs tongues larded on both sides; these must first be all fryed brown, only scorcht, not thorow, before they are put into the
Pipkin;

Pipkin; put to them blanched Cocks-combs and sliced pallets: let them simber up in strong Broth, and a little white-wine: add two or three whole Onions, a little large Mace and Nutmeg: then charge your third Pipkin, with bottoms of Artichokes cut in quarters, and the Marrow of four or five bones: let them boil with strong Broth; then having all your Fowl drawn, and trussed, whether peeping Chickens, squab Pigeons, or in season, Plovers, Partridge, Ruffs, Knots, Godweaths, Quails, Larks, or any other; your proportion in these being trussed, parboyled, and made ready, boyl them up according to their time of boyling, either in water and salt, or strong Broth; let all these ingredients be ready together: then having your great Charger, with a soop and light bread in sippets, then dish up your Capon (or great Fowl) in the middle of your dish, and place your worser Fowl round about, and your next sort towards the brim of the dish, and your best and smallest sort on the top of all; your forced meat between the Fowl and round the dish; and your Lamb-stones and sweet-breads in every vacant place; then slit your Lambs-tongues in halves, and put them in the most necessary place, with the larded side upwards; so put your Pallets and Cocks-combs between and about the whole, as also your Artichokes and Marrow about the top of the boyled meats; then take your Bisk Broth, being boyling hot, adding half a pint of Clarret gravy thereto, pour it all over your boyled meat; you may garnish your boyled meat with fryed Bacon, fryed Potatoes, fryed Oysters, and all over with sliced Lemmon; then strow it over with one handful of Pistatious Kernels; you may make this Bisk lesser, or bigger, as you please.

To

To make a brown Bisk.

TAke all your aforesaid Fowl, or what Fowl you have, and half roast them; (yet let their breast be a yellowish brown) put them into your Pipkin, with strong Broth; and likewise all your other ingredients mentioned in the other Bisk (except your Marrow and Artichokes) season this your great Pipkin with Mace, Nutmeg, half a dozen of Onyons, some faggots of sweet herbs, with a dozen Anchovies; let these stew all up together; put a ladleful or two of drawn butter to them; then having your soop in your Charger upon a heap of coals, dish up your grossest Fowl in the middle, and all your other round, as flat as you can; and your most gross ingredients between, and your best over all: In these boyled meats, you may use both Mushroms and Oysters stewed up in gravy, cast this over your boyled meat: so lear your boyled meat as before; and garnish it about the brims with Petteets, and Bacon fryed brown in eggs, with sliced Lemmon on the top; strow over it all yolks of eggs minced small. In this way of boyling, Reason must guide you, to know what Fowl or Ingredient will ask most boyling, and what least; and so boyl up the whole accordingly.

To make an Olue.

IN this Olue, you must take all manner of Fowl that is allowed you, both of great and small; some whereof you may force, others you may lard; these being all roasted, take a gammon of Bacon, that is well boyled, skinned and larded with Lemmon-pill and Sage, wash it over with the yolks of eggs, and strow thereon minced Sage, Pepper, and hard yolks of eggs: then having another Pipkin charged with balls of forced meat, Sassages, Lamb-stones, and sweet-breads, Artichokes in quarters, and what other Ingredients, or
vari-

The whole Body of Cookery Diſſected. 61

varieties you have; Let them all boyl up together in ſtrong broth, with a faggot of ſweet herbs, Large Mace, and two or three Onions: your Gammon of Bacon being Roaſted for the ſpace of an hour: Elſe baked in an Oven: Diſh it up in the middle of your diſh, and your fowl in order round about your forced meat, and Saſſages place likewiſe round about, and between the fowl: your other Ingredients all over your Olue in vacant places: Let your Leare be half a pint of gravy, and ſome of your ſtrong broth, boyled up with ſome Anchovies, and three or four whole Onions, with ſome grated Nutmeg; ſo pour it all over your Olue, and garniſh it with ſliced Lemmon.

How to force all manner of Meats.

SUppoſe you have a deſire to force a leg of Mutton, or Lamb, or any ſuch like meat, you muſt let your knife run round betwixt the skin and fleſh of your leg of Mutton, (or other meat) take heed you cut not the outward skin: Cut out all the meat from the bone within the leg: then waſh your leg in the In-ſide with the yolks of eggs, being ſeaſoned after your forced meat is made, as before was taught: you may force it ſavoury or ſweet, at your pleaſure: And when its full in the room of your fleſh, waſh it at the butt end with the yolks of eggs; And cloſe your skin to the forced meat, in the form as it was at firſt; ſo ſet it on a piece of a Caul of Veal, in the diſh or pan you intend to bake it in, waſh it over the top with the yolks of eggs: and let it bake ſoberly: then you may make both of your white and green forced meat, as many proportions of birds, in the manner of Pigeons, Quails, or Plovers, as you pleaſe, waſhing them over with the yolks of eggs: So if you have the heads of any of the fowl before mentioned, joyn them on with your Proportions, with the yolks of eggs: your leg of Mutton

being

being half baked, put them in the same pan, or into some other, in the Oven; when it is baked, you may dish up your leg of Mutton, with the greatest proportions next round about it, and the lesser to garnish your dish about the brims; In the baking thereof you should put some Wine or strong broth, being thickned up with a yolk or two of an egg, will serve for a leare to put over it, so garnish it.

Your Leare for your sweet forced meats.

TAke a little strong broth, White-wine, or Verjuice, Sugar, Cinamon, and Nutmeg; one handful of stript Barberries, a Lemmon cut in dice or slices; thicken it up with the yolks of two or three eggs; when it boyleth, put therein a Ladle full of drawn butter, and pour it over your forced meat. If you force Fowl, you must cut the flesh from the breast of both sides your Fowl, up to the breast-bone, so let your knife run betwixt the flesh and the skin, meeting at the breast-bone, rounding of the flesh, take it out: Let the breast-bone continue, and the skin that groweth on the top of it, and take heed you cut no holes in the skin: Wash it in the inside with the yolks of eggs where the meat is taken out; And force it again, with a sweet, or savoury, which you please. After this manner, must you force all Fowl.

How to make a forced boyled meat.

YOu may force one Capon, three Chickens, and three Pigeons, and some thin Collops of Veal; first let your Capon be half boyled, and more; then put in your forced fowl, and as many of the same kind unforced; your Collops of Veal being seasoned, and washt over with yolks of eggs, and rouled up with forced meat, put them in also, bound up with a thred; boyl a quantity of forced meat-balls, both green and white,

The whole Body of Cookery Diſſected. 63

white, by themſelves, (about the bigneſs of a little egg) in a pipkin; your diſh being laid with Sippits; put your Capon in the middle thereof, with the ſix forced fowl round about; and the unforced fowl between, your forced Collops (which ought all to be larded) cut in the middle, and varniſhed in all the vacant places among the fowl, as alſo your green, and white forced balls, round about the diſh, between, and upon the fowl, your proportion of Birds (as before taught) round about the brims of your diſh; if your fowl was forced ſavoury, you muſt have a ſavoury Leare made with Gravy and ſome of your ſtrong broth, Oyſter Liquor, and Anchovies diſſolved, beaten up with the yolk of an egg: when you Boyl it, pour this over your Boyled meat: Then ſtrow it all over with Weſtphalie Bacon cut very ſmall; Garniſh it over likewiſe with Lemmon and Barberries at your pleaſure.

Your Leare and garniſh for ſweet forced boyled meat of the ſame kind of Fowl.

TAke half a pint of ſtrong Broth, and as much Verjuice; put them over the fire, add thereto a quantity of Barberries, one handful of Grapes, or Gooſberries (if in ſeaſon) the yolks of three Eggs beaten up in a little white-wine, ſeaſon it with Sugar, Nutmeg, and Cinamon, (beaten) draw it up, and pour it over your boyled Meat: ſtick your boyled meat with ſprigs of Paſte, garniſh it over with Barberries, red Currans, Lemmon, or what you pleaſe.

To boyl Capons or Chickens in white Broth.

BOyl up your Fowl white in ſtrong Broth, if you have it, otherwiſe in fair water and Salt, with a faggot of ſweet herbs, and large Mace: your diſh being ſippeted, and garniſhed with Barberries boyled up (and Lemmon) lay your Fowl therein, and pour
on

on your Broth and ingredients: as it is shewn in another place.

To boyl a Hanch of Venison.

YOu may force your Venison, with a handful of sweet herbs and Parslee minced, with a little Beef-suet, and yolks of eggs boyled hard: season your farceing with Pepper, Nutmeg, Ginger, and Salt: put your Hanch of Venison a boyling (being powdered before) then boyl up three or four Colly-flowers in strong Broth, and a little Milk: when they are boyled, put them forth into a Pipkin: add to them drawn butter, and keep them warm by the fire: then boyl up two or three handfuls of Spinnage in strong Broth: when it is boyled, pour out part of your broth, and put in a little Vinegar, a ladleful of drawn butter, and a grated Nutmeg: your dish being ready with sippets in the bottom, put in your Spinnage thereon round towards your dishes side: then take up your Venison being boyled, and put it in the middle of your dish, and put on your Colly flowers all over it: pour on your drawn butter over your Colly-flowers: garnish it with Barberries, and the brims of your dish with some green Parslee minced. In the same manner may it be done with Cabbage.

To boyl Legs, Necks, or Chines of Mutton, four wayes.

YOu may lard your Mutton with a little Lemmon-pill, boyl it in water and salt, with a faggot or two of sweet herbs: then take a pint of Oysters, being washed and set: put to them some of their own liquor in a clean Pipkin, a little strong broth, and half a pint of gravy, as much white-wine, put to them two or three whole Onions, and a little quantity of Time, grated Nutmeg, and three Anchovies, let them boyl together, beat up two or three yolks of eggs in a little

The whole Body of Cookery Diſſected. 65

of the ſaid Broth, and draw it up thick, with a ladleful of drawn butter amongſt it: diſh up any of the ſaid meat upon ſippets, and pour on your Lear, with your Oyſters on the top: garniſh it with Lemmon and Barberries, and ſend it up.

Another way.

TAke half a handful of Sampier, a handful of Capers, a few ſliced pickled Cucumbers, put them in a little ſtrong Broth, White-wine and Verjuice, let them boyl together, (put to them a Lemmon cut in Dice) when you bring them off, and a grated Nutmeg; beat them up thick with two yolks of eggs, and a ladleful of drawn butter; put therein a ſmall quantity of Sugar, that it may be a ſharp ſweet; diſh it upon ſippets, pour on the Lear, garniſh it with Barberries, Sampier and Capers, and ſerve it up.

Another way.

CUt Turnips in ſquare pieces, boyl up a pottle of them in a little ſtrong Broth and Milk; when they are tenderly boyled, pour them forth into a Cullender, then having a great handful of Parſlee boyled green, and chopt very ſmall, with a handful of boyled Barberries, ungrated Nutmeg, and a little ſmall Pepper, put theſe together with the Turnips in a great Tinn diſh: add to it two or three ladlefuls of drawn butter, a little Vinegar and ſtrong Broth: ſet them upon the coals, and toſs them up together: then diſh up your meat, as before, and lay them all over by ſpoonfuls, Broth and all.

Another way to make a Lear for the ſaid meat.

TAke a little white-wine and ſtrong Broth, with ſix Onyons minced exceeding ſmall, boyl them well together; then put in ſome ſmall bunches of grapes, and

F　　　　　　　　ſome

some loose, with a handful of minced Oysters, a handful of parboyled Parslee minced very small likewise, and a Nutmeg sliced; thicken it with the yolks of two eggs, so pour it all over your Meat; garnish it with Grapes on the top of it; pour over all your Oysters a ladle-ful of drawn butter, and strow on the yolks of hard eggs minced small.

To boyl a Leg of Veal and Beacon.

LArd your leg of Veal with Bacon all over, and a little Lemmon-pill amongst it, then boyl it with a piece of middle Bacon; when your Bacon is boyled, cut it in slices, season it with Pepper and dryed Sage mixed together; dish up your Veal with the Bacon round about it; send up with it, saucers of Green-sauce, strow over it Parslee and Barberies.

To make your green sauce two ways

1. TAke a handful or two of Sorrel, beat in a Morter, with two Pippins pared and quartered; add thereto a little Vinegar and Sugar; this is your Green-sauce to send in Saucers.

2. Take two handfuls of Sorrel, beat it well in a Morter; scruce out the juice of it, put thereto a little Vinegar, Sugar, drawn Butter, and a grated Nutmeg; set it on the Coals until it is hot, and pour it into your dish on your sippets; so dish up your Veal and Bacon.

To boyl a Breast of Veal.

BOne your Breast of Veal, and beat it well, then wash and dry it, having one handful of sweet Herbs, Parslee and a little Sage, minced small, with a small quantity of Cloves, Mace, and Nutmeg beaten, adding to it a little salt; wash over the inside of your Veal with the yolks of eggs, and strow your herbs all

over

over it, and lay over it some slices of Bacon dipt in the yolks of eggs, so roul it up into a Coller, and bind it with Tape; boyl it with a piece of middle Bacon; when it is enough, cut out your Coller in eight slices, and dish it on sippets; slice out your Bacon in the same number, dished between your Veal; let your Lear be made with gravie and strong Broth, with a sliced Nutmeg, drawn up thick with drawn Butter, and the yolk or two of an egg, pour it over your meat; garnish it with slices of Bacon, fryed up in yolks of eggs.

To boyl a Knuckle of Veal with the Neck cut in five pieces to be skrved in Broth.

LArd the pieces of the Neck with Lemmon; put it a boyling in fair water, or strong Broth (if you have it) let it be clean scummed; put therein a faggot of sweet herbs, a little large Mace; when it is almost boyled, put in some small forced meat-balls, both green and white, two handfuls of Spinage, with one Manchet in slices; when it is enough, dish up your Knuckle upon sippets in the middle of your dish, and the pieces round about, with the forced meat between, and the herbs and broth over your meat; you may lay on slices of Bacon, if you please.

To boyl a Leg of Pork.

LEt your leg of Pork be well-powdered for a week, then boyl it and having a handful of boyled Sage minced very small, put it into a little strong Broth with butter and Pepper; then let your Turnips be boyled as before for your leg of Mutton toss your Sage and them together, with more drawn butter; dish up your Pork, and lay on your Turnips over it; you may stuff your leg of Pork first with Parslee and Sage, and boyl it up with Cabbage; after the same manner, bring chopt a little, and toſt up in drawn butter.

To boyl Capons or Hens for the Winter-ſeaſon.

AFter your Capons or Hens are boyled, with a piece of Bacon; take a pint of ſtrong Broth and white-wine: put in a pound of Saſſages, two or three whole Onyons, a little Nutmeg and large Mace, a faggot of ſweet herbs, a quart of Oyſters, a little minced Time; let them boyl up together; thicken them with the yolk of an egg, and a little drawn butter: diſh up your Capons or Pullets on your ſippets: then pour on your Lear and Oyſters upon the breaſts and the Saſſages round about, with ſlices of bacon betwixt: garniſh them with Lemmon: ſtrow them over with the yolks of hard eggs minced.

Another way with Muſhrooms.

IF you gather your Muſhroms, peel off the outward skin and barb them underneath, throw them into water: then take them up, and part them in a Tin diſh, put to them ſome whole Pepper, Mace, and three or four whole Onyons: ſet them on the fire for a while, and there will run from them much liquor: ſtir them about in the ſaid liquor; when they are well ſhrunk, pour the liquor from them, and put to them a little white-wine and ſtrong Broth, Oyſter-liquor, with three or four Anchovies, a little minced Time and ſliced Nutmeg; add to them half a pint of the beſt gravie, thicken the liquor with the yolks of two eggs beaten and little drawn butter: your Capons or Pullets being diſhed upon ſippets, toſs up your Muſhroms, and pour them on your Capons garniſhed with Lemmon.

To

To Boyl Chickens.

BOyl your Chickens in water and falt, with a faggot of fweet herbs, and large Mace; put in a piece of butter, keep them white; then take a little ftrong Broth and white-wine, fome bunches of Grapes; when they are boyled together, put in a fliced Nutmeg, the yolk of an egg to make it thick, with a handful of Parflee fcalded and minced, with a ladeful of drawn butter; fo difh up your Chickens, and pour on your Lear; garnifh them with Lemmon, and put your bunches of Grapes on the breafts of the Chickens.

Another way.

TAke half a pint of the juice of Sorrel, fet it on the fire, then take three or four bunches of Sparragrafs, (being already boyled, but not too much) cut off the buds fo long as your finger, then cut off another cut from your Sparragrafs, if they be not ftalky, put them into your Sorrel that is heating on the fire, and with them a ladleful of drawn butter, and grated Nutmeg, a little fet Parflee minced; if you add a little Vinegar, you muft do the like with Sugar, that it be not too fharp, neither muft it be too fweet: fet your difh with fippets on a heap of coals (which you ought to do with all your meat) put ftrong Broth to your fippets that the fire may make them fwell, difh up your Chickens, fhake your Lear together, put the Sparragrafs on the breafts, with a little drawn butter thereon.

Another way.

TAke your bottoms of Artichokes (being already almoft boyled) cut them in flices (not too thin) then take the marrow of two or three Marrow-bones, and boyl it in a little white-wine and ftrong Broth; put in in your Artichokes, and let them boyl together until they be enough, thicken it with a litle drawn butter, and the yolk of an egg, cut your Chickens in halves, and diſh them on your ſippets; ſo take out your Marrow and Artichokes, with your little ladle, and lay it all over the Chickens; then pour in your Lear, and a little drawn butter thereon, ſet them on the coals, and grate on a Nutmeg all over your boyled meat; this you may do in Winter as well as Summer, having pickled Artichokes by you.

Another way

TAke Shirdowns, and boyl them as you do Artichokes; take likewiſe the ſtalks of them, being cut a handful and half long; ſplit them in the middle, and peel off the out-ſide, and boyl them pretty tender; then take them out, and put them into a Pipkin, with the Shirdowns being quartered; put to them a glaſs of Sack, as much white-wine, and the like of ſtrong Broth (from your Chickens, if you have no ſtronger let them boyl until they are very tender, with a blade or two of Mace, ſome ſet Parſlee minced, and a ladleful of drawn butter; when they come off the fire, add ſome Vinegar and a very little Sugar, that may hardly be taſted: ſet your diſh on the coals, with ſippets in the bottom, diſh up your Chickens cut in halves: lay on your Shirdowns and ſtalks all over them: pour on your Lear, with a little drawn butter on the top.

Another way to Boyl Pullets and Chickens for the Winter.

BOyl your Spaniſh Potatoes, but not too much, then cut them to pieces about the bigneſs and length of your thumb: then take a handful or two of Skirrets boyled and blanched, with two or three pills of Orangado, ſliced in pieces long ways, put them altogether into a Pipkin, with a little ſtrong Broth,

White-

The whole Body of Cookery Diffected. 71

white-wine, and Vinegar, a blade of Mace, let them boyl together; then beat them up with the yolks of two eggs, and a ladle-ful of drawn butter, and a little Sugar; when you take them off the fire, put in a grated Nutmeg, diſh up your Pullets or Chickens on ſippets, lay all over them your Potatoes, Skirrets and Orangado mixed together; pour on your Lear, and garniſh it as you do your ſweet boyled meats, with Orangado and Barberries.

Another way.

TAke your Cabbage Lettice, cut out the hard Cabbage thereof; force your outward leaves (dipt in the yolks of eggs) with your ſavoury forced meats; then make your forced meat-balls green and white; when your ſtrong Broth boyls, put in your forced Lettice, and afterwards your ſmall Balls; then take the hard of your Cabbage Lettice, and ſome curled Endiff, and give it a quick boyling in ſtrong Broth; when it is almoſt boyled quarter your Lettice, and cut your Endiff as long as your finger; put it into a Pipkin with half a pint of gravie ſeaſoned, a ſpoonful or two of Vinegar, and a little ſtrong Broth; you may add an Anchovie, with a grated Nutmeg, and a ladle-full of drawn butter; if it be not thick to your mind, you muſt help it with the yolk of an egg; then diſh up your Pullets or Capons; take up your Cabbage-Lettice, cut them in the middle, and place them round about your diſh, as alſo your green and white forced meat, then pour on your Lear with your Endiff and Lettice upon the breaſt of your Foul; you may garniſh your diſh with a Cucumber boyled and forced; after the meat is taken forth, cut it in pieces, and lay it round the diſh.

F 4 *To*

To Boyl Wild-Ducks, Wigeons or Teal.

First half roast them, then take them off, and put them in a shallow broad pan that will contain them, with a pint of Clarret-wine, and a pint of strong Broth, a dozen of Onyons cut in halves, a faggot or two of sweet herbs, with a little whole Pepper, and some slices of Bacon; cover your pan, and let them stove up: add gravie to part of the liquor at last, so much as will serve to dish them: garnish them with the Bacon and Onyons if yon please.

Another way.

Take Clarret-wine, and strong broth, as before, slice in half a dozen Onyons, and let it boyl together: then put in the quarters of half a dozen Pippins, (pared) two or three blades of large Mace: and when your Ducks or Wigeons be half roasted, cut them in halves, and put them in, and then stove them up together until they are enough: put a ladleful of drawn butter to them, and a grated Nutmeg: dish up your Ducks, &c. on sippets, pour on your Lear, and let your quartered Apples lye all over your Fowl, garnish it over with Bacon fryed yellow with eggs, and strow it over with hard yolks of eggs minced: You may also use savoury forced meat, and Sassages in the boyling of these: however neglect not the larding of them, before you roast them: this way of boyling will serve both for Duck, Teal, or Wigeon, being much of a nature.

To Boyl Rabbets.

You must truss them for boyling, by pricking down the head to the shoulders, and their hind legs toward the belly: you may lard them with bacon, and boyl them up white: take the Livers, being boyled, mince

mince it small with a little boyled fat bacon, cut like Dice; put this in a little Wine, strong broth and Vinegar, to the quantity of half a pint: let it boyl with a little large Mace: then put into it a little set Parslee minced, a few Barberries: you may use Grapes if you have them: add thereto a ladleful or two of drawn butter; if it be to thick, or lack Lear, you may add a little more Vinegar and strong Broth: dish up your Rabbets on your sippets, and pour your Lear all over them, and garnish them with Lemmons and Barberries.

How to boyl Pigeons.

Take Spear-mints, one handful of Parslee, a few sweet herbs, with a small quantity of Time, two or three Onions, mince all this together very small: put to it some thin slices of bacon, about an inch in length and bredth, add to it one handful of grated bread, the yolk of an egg, and a little piece of hard butter; make up this into a body, and fill your Pigeons bellies therewith: then put them into a deep dish, with their bellies downwards; put to them a little white-wine, strong broth, and vinegar, with two or three whole Onions; let them boyl together; when the are boyled, take out the first matter in their bellies, put it in a pipkin, with some of your Pigeon broth; (you must not forget to have savory forced meat, both white and green, boyled up with the Pigeons) And as many slices of bacon (as you have Pigeons) being before boyled; put in a grated Nutmeg and a ladleful of drawn butter, with a handful of scalded Goosberries, if you have them, dish up your Pigeons round your dish, and a piece of bacon cut square, in the middle larded with Lemmon, and your force meat round your dish and your other bacon between your Pigeons, then pour your Lear all over your boyled meat, with a ladie of drawn butter on the top of that, and ftrow it over with Weftphalie bacon minced; the common way of boyling Pigeons or an old Coney may be ufed, which is to ftuff their bellies with parflee, and a little Onion; And when they are boyled, to be taken out and minced, and put into butter and vinegar, fo poured over your Pigeons and Bacon.

To boyl Plovers.

YOu muft almoft roaft them, then ftew them up in ftrong broth and gravy, with three or four whole Onions, good ftore of fmall force meat balls, and Saffages, two or three Anchovies; when they are enough, add to them a grated Nutmeg, and a ladle of drawn butter; to this kind of boyled meat you may ufe Lamb, ftones Sweet-breads, and Pallets: fo difh up your Plovers and order your Ingredients round about, as you have feen, In other boyled meats.

To boyl Caponets or Pullets.

TAke two or three, according to the greatnefs of your feaft, or difhes : take a Gammon of Weftphalie bacon, boyled very tender, and about half a dozen of Marrow-bones, trimed with a Cleaver; that is to fay, cut of both ends of the bones that they may not be cumberfome, then cut them round in the middle as you ought (and ufe to cut a Marrow-bone) All thefe ingredients being boyled, (only the Gammon of bacon by its felf, (you muft have in readinefs a Pipkin full of parboyled Spinnage, with a good quantity of parflee; (afterward ftewed up in a little Wine, ftrong broth, adding to it a little Mace, Salt, and Nutmeg) then difh up one half of your fpinnage, in the bottom of your difh on fippits; remember you put in it drawn butter, and a little Vinegar, when you take it off the fire: your Gammon of Bacon being blanched, lay it

in

in the middle of your dish, then cleave your Caponets, or Pullets in the middle from the breast to the back, and place them round about your bacon; then place your Marrow-bones between every side, and Sparagrass upon your Pullets, with toasts about your dish brims and Marrow-bones: so put the rest of your spinnage, &c. by spoonfuls on the top of your bacon, and pour on drawn butter with a little very strong broth over your meat, and garnish it with Lemmons, you may make this boyling meat in the winter season with Oysters, Lamb-stones, sweet-breads, pallets, fryed, and stewed up with Gravie, Claret-wine, Anchovies, Nutmeg, Mace Salt, a faggot or two of sweet-herbs, and a couple of Onions, adding Pigeons, or what other foul you please place all this upon, and about your boyled meat, in the room of your soop or Spinnage.

To make a forced boyled Meat.

Take six Chicken Peepers, as many squob Pigeons, and so many Quails, with what small foul is in season, boyl them in water, salt, and sweet herbs: then take two dozen of Larks; Truss and farse them with a piece of Whestphalie Gammon of Bacon minced with the yolks of hard eggs, Parsle, Spinnage and Time, some grated bread and Nutmeg, made into a body with the yolks of raw eggs, then mince some parboyled Spinnage, and Parslee, and dip your Larks in the yolks of eggs, and roul them up and down in your green herbs; Let your Pipkin boyl with strong broth, and put them in, with about forty forced meat balls as big as a Walnut, green, and yellow, put to them about six Sweet-breads, as many Lamb-stones, two or three pallets sliced and fryed, some Artichokes cut in quarters, a handful of Chestnuts, with Pistaches and Pineapples; then having about a dozen of Marrow-bones cut in halfs, cleared from the flesh, and the ends of the

bones

bones Trimmed, clofe them on force meat balls with the yolks of raw eggs, that they may ftand together upright, then ftop your other bones with a little paft and eggs, and lay about them: bake them in an Oven, then force your half Orange, Lemmon, and Pomgranate Peels, and put them unto your bones before they are baked; your difh being ready with Sippets. put in the middle thereof your three Marrowbones upon forced meat balls; then lay your other bones round about by the fides, and your Chickens, Pigeons, Quails, or what ever foul you have, between all: then pour out part of your Liquor, from your Larks and other Ingredients, and put it in a pint of gravy with four Anchovies, a handful of Mufhrooms, a ladle of drawn butter, and a grated Nutmeg: Difh your green Larks all over your boyled meat, with all the reft of your Ingredients; fo lear it, and ftrow on Weftphalia bacon minced fmall: garnifh round, and upon your pills of Orange and Lemmon; and ftick fome branches of Rofemary on your Marrowbones ftanding upright, elfe fome fprigs of Artificial Birds made with Almond pafte; you may garnifh the brims of your difh with toafts, and your boyled meat with fliced Lemmon.

To Boyl Udders and Tongues.

WHen they are boyled enough in the Beef pot, and blancht, you muft have your Turnips ready boyled, cut in pieces and toft in Butter, as alfo your Colly-flowers and Carrets: put your Turnips all over the bottom of a large difh, then flice on your Tongue or Tongues, and lay them one againft another; flice your Udders, and lay them between, oppofite: garnifh your Collyflowers all over them, and the Carrets up and down between your Colly-flowers: you may add of the fat of your Pot, if it be pure, unto your drawn butter and Vinegar, and pour over it.

A

A boyled meat after the French fashion.

Take bottoms of boyled Artichokes, the yolks of hard eggs, young Chicken Peepers, and squab Pigeons, truss with Veal sweet breads, Lamb stones, Cocks stones and Combs, and knots of eggs, put all these into a Pipkin with strong broth, White-wine, Salt, Pepper, Nutmeg, Mace, Butter, stew all these together softly, then boyl up your Marrow, in a little pipkin, with a handful of Barberries, Grapes, or Goosberries, pour your liquor from your Marrow, and put in half a pint of gravie, and a ladle of drawn Butter, grated Nutmeg, and some Pistaches, when your pipkin is ready with the Ingredients; dish your fowl on Sippets, and place all your other on and between them, and your other Leare with Marrow, over your boyled meat, and lay Sparragrass round that, garnish it with Lemmon, and set in on coals till you send it up.

Another way according to the French fashion.

Take part of a Capon minced and stampt with Almond paste, Muskified bisket bread, some yolks of hard eggs, and sweet herbs minced very small, some yolks of raw eggs, Safforn, Cinamon, Nutmeg, Currans, Salt, Marrow, and Pistaches, mingle all these together, then take six Manchets of French bread of a day old chipt, cut a round hole in the tops of them, and save the pieces, then rake forth all the crum, and fill the said loves with composition prepared, and stop them at the top with your pieces you saved, then bind it up in a clean cloth, and boyl them in a skillet, or bake them in an Oven: then take three Chickens and three Pigeons, and cut them down their back, take off their skins without holes, with the legs, wings and neck on: then force them with the flesh made into a savory force meat, as elsewhere. When they are forced,

forced, sow up their backs, then put them into a deep dish with strong broth: you may boyl with them Quails, Martins, Sparrow, pieces of Artichokes, Sparragrass, Marrow, Pistaches, Pine apples: when all is ready, dish your forced loaves, in the middle of your dish, the Chickens and Pigeons round about the Quails with other small birds, with your Marrow, Artichokes, or what other Ingredients you have in the Summer: to these and the like boyled meat, you may use Artichokes, Sparragrass, Collyflowers, Grapes or Goosberries, &c. but in Autumn and Winter, you may use Skirrits, Potates, Dates, Cheftnuts; to this Lear you may add gravie and drawn butter, unto your strong broth.

BOOK VIII.

Containing how to make several sorts of Puddings.

How to make a Quaking Pudding.

Take a pint of Cream, and a manchet grated: take three or four spoonfuls of the Cream, and mingle it with two spoonfuls of Rice flower, beat it into a batter, so it doth not clod, put it into the aforesaid Cream, then beat six eggs, mix them all together, and beat them very well with a little Rose water, Nutmeg, Cloves, Mace, and Cinamon beaten, with a little salt; if it be too thick, you may add a little more Cream; then take a thick, cloth washt over with butter; spread it over a narrow Bason, your Pudding being well beaten together; put it in, gather up your Cloth close together, tying it hard with a packthred, giving it some liberty to rise: your liquor

boylig

The whole body of Cookery Diffected

boyling very hard, take up your pudding in your hands, and turning it up and down, so that your bread and cream be mingled very well, then put it into your boyling Liquor, let it boyl for three quarters of an hour covered close, keep constantly turning for the first quarter, but it must boyl fiercely left it soak water when its enough take it up, open it and turn it forth into a dish; stick it all over with blancht Dates and dried Cittern-all over; perfume a little Rose water with musk, with som vinegar, drawn butter, and a good quantity of sugar; when its very hot, pour it on your puding, scrape hard sugar on the brims of your dish, and send it up.

Another way.

Take a little Manchet, slice it exceeding thin, put it into a Quart of Cream, then put it over the fire, and let it boyl with a stick or two of Cinamon; you may pour into it before it boyles, two spoonfuls of flower beat into a batter, and keep it stirred, then pour it forth into a bason, put to it a grated Nutmeg, a little Cinamon and Ginger, some Orangado and dryed Cittern, cut very thin; when this is cold, put to it half a douzen eggs beaten, with some Rosewater, and mix them all together; if it be too thick you may add cream, so that it may become a quaking pudding when it is boyled (as the aforesaid.)

To make a dish of Puddings of several Coulours.

To this end you must have five or six dishes bespoke on purpose of the Turner with Covers to fit them you must butter over all your dishes in the Incide; fill one of them with the Ingredients aforesaid, put on the Cover, and bind it down with a Cloth prepared for the same purpose, and packthred: take a quantity more of the said stuff, that will fill a dish, Colour it with Spinnage:

Spinnage: if you think it will thin it too much, add part of an egg to it, and beat it together: Put on the Cover, and bind it up so that no water may run in; then take a handful of Cowslips, a handful of Violets, a handful of Clove Gillyflowers: mince each of these by themselves, and beat them severally in a Morter: so add as much of the aforesaid stuff to each as will fill three several dishes, you may thin them as you please, by mixing more Cream to either of them, so bind them up as aforesaid, and when your pot boyls very fiercely, shake your dishes, that the matter may mingle together, and put them in: When they are boyled, uncover your dishes, turn out your puddings into a large dish: Stick them as before: Else with any Rich Suckets: Your Lear, is Butter, Vinegar, Rose water and good store of Sugar; scrape on Sugar, and send them up: they are an exceeding handsome, and Rich service. fitting for any feast: you may make but one or more of the above four sorts of puddings, as you please.

To make Marrow Puddings to boyl in Skins.

Take a pottle of Cream, two rowls of French bread, sliced very thin, being cut over again the contrary way, you may put it over the fire a soaking with a little whole Cinamon, till it begins to boyl, then beat a dozen of eggs together: and when your Cream is almost cold, beat them in, put to them the Marrow of five Marrowbones minced, with some minced Orangado, and Cittern, beaten Cinamon, Ginger, Cloves and Mace, Rosewater and Sugar, with some salt: You may thin it with cream, if your Manchet sweels to much: (for it must be but a little thicker than Pan cake batter) then having your hogs guts, the smallest of the great ones, being well scoured and cleansed, fill up your guts, and tye them up like beads, being

about

The whole Body of Cookery Diffected. 81

about the bigneſs and length of an egg (or ſomething longer) you muſt give two Inches ſcope to every one of theſe in the tying, elſe they will break, not having room to riſe: boyl them very ſoftly in a Kettle, for the ſpace of above half an hour, then take them up, and keep them for your uſe, and heat them for ſervice or pleaſure.

To make black-Puddings to be kept.

TAke a gallon of great Oatmeal, and put to it two gallons of very good ſtrong broth, let it boyl ſoftly over the fire about half an hour, keeping it continually ſtirred, then put it out into a great earthen pan; let it be cold, and put to it about a gallon of hogs bloud ſtrained; mix it together with the congealed Oatmeal; if it makes it not thin enough, add to it a quart of milk or more, let it ſteep together all night; then take a good handful of Winterſavory, as much Pednyroyal, a little Hyſſop, and Roſemary, half a handful of Time, a handful of Sives: if not, take Onions or Leeks, and a handful of Sage, mince all theſe exceeding ſmall, and put them into your puddings: ſeaſon it with Pepper beaten ſmall, Cloves, Mace, Ginger, Cinamon, and Nutmegs, with a quantity of Salt; then having about two flecks of Lard cut with your Knife twice as big as a dye, put all in together, with about ſixteen *Eggs*, mingle it all well with your hands: if it be thick and not high coloured with blood, add more to it, your ſmall guts of a hogg being cleanſed and watered for a day before; cut your guts an ell and half long, and blow them up all, to ſee whether they are ſound, then fill a taſte of theſe puddings, and obſerve what ſcope you give to your taſte, that you may know how they ſwell, as alſo to know what they want in their ſeaſoning, ſoftneſs or hardneſs; for they ought not to have ſo much bloud in them to congeal them hard; and according to this

G Tryal,

Tryal, you may order the rest; so fill up your lengths, and tye them up in six links, or but four if you please; you must allow at least three inches scope in each link; let your water boyl very sober, and when they have boyled half an hour, take them forth, and put others in; then afterwards put them in for half an hour again: as you fill your Puddings, you must supply your Pan still with Hogs suet, and order your hand in the filling, that the ingredients may all carry a due proportion; these Puddings, with some white Puddings made with Beef suet, after the manner of the little ones, (but of a span length) will be a very good service for a common diet, especially at night; you may add to your white Puddings a pretty quantity of flower, with your grated bread, but then you must put in the fewer eggs, but the more Beef suet minced exceeding small.

To make Polony Sassages to keep all the year.

YOU may take a piece of a Gammon of red Bacon, & half boyl it, mince it very small: if your Gammon be not fat, take half as much bacon lard, mince it likewise: season them with time and Sage minced very small, and good store of Pepper beaten to dust, with a little Cloves, Mace and Nutmeg, and a pretty quantity of Salt, for they ought so to be; add to them the yolks of two eggs, and so much red wine as will bring them up into a stiff body; mingle them well with your hands, fill them into middle skins, as big as four of your ordinary Sassages, so hang them in your Chimney for a time, and when you will use them, they must be cut out very thin round ways, and put them in your dish with Oyl and Vinegar, and serve them for a Sallet for the second course, or for a Collation before you drink

Another

Another way for Saſſages.

TAke Pork, not as much fat as lean, mince it exceeding ſmall together, then take part of the fleck of Pork in pieces about the bigneſs of the top of your finger, ſeaſon each apart with minced Sage, good ſtore of Pepper and Salt, ſome Cloves and Mace, mix in your ſeaſoning into each of theſe; take your ſmall ſheeps guts and cleanſe them, ſo fill them with your funel, always putting ſome of the pieces of fleck between the minced; you may ſprinkle a little wine on the top of your Saſſage meat, it will fill the better. I have made rich Saſſages of Capons and Rabits, and could ſhew a receipt for it; but none ſo ſavoury as thoſe of Pork, by reaſon that Sage and Pepper is not ſuitable to the nature of the other; ſo tye up your Saſſages in links, and keep them for your uſe.

To make a Pudding of Hogs-Liver.

BOyl your Hogs-Liver and grate it; put to it more grated bread than Liver, with as much fine flower as of either; put twelve eggs to the value of a gallon of this mixture, with about two pound of Beef-ſuet minced ſmall, with a pound and half of Currans, half a quarter of a pint of Roſe-water, a good quantity of Cloves and Mace, Nutmeg, Cinamon and Ginger, all beaten, and as much Salt as it requires, with ſome Wintertſavoury, Penniroyal, Sweet Margerum and Time, all minced very ſmall: mix all theſe with ſweet Milk or Cream; let it be no thicker than Fritter Batter, ſo fill your Hogs guts; you may make one for the Table in the maw, to be eaten hot: in your knitting up the guts, you muſt remember to give them three or four inches ſcope: in your putting them into your boyling water, you muſt handle them round, to bring the meat equal to all parts of the gut: they will ask above an
hours

hours boyling: the boyling muſt be ſober; if the wind riſe in them, you muſt obſerve to prick them.

To make a baked Marrow Pudding.

SEt a quart of Cream a boyling, with Cinamon, and large Mace: take eight eggs, caſting away the whites of four, beat them well together, with a little more Cream or milk: when your Cream boyls, take it off the fire, and ſtir in your eggs, let it not be too hot leſt it curdle, ſeaſon it with Roſe-water, Sugar, and grated Nutmeg: your diſh being ready, with a garniſh of Paſte about the brims, cover the bottom of your diſh with thin ſippets of light bread, lay raw Marrow thereon all over, alſo Dates and Raiſons, with Orangado and other ſuckets: then put in a ladleful or two of your Cream boyled up, and lay on the top of that a laying of ſippets, put alſo a laying of Marrow and ſuckets (as before) on the top of that; then pour in your Cream again; if your diſh be deep enough, you may go three ſtories high; fill it not to full till it comes in the Oven, leſt it ſpill over, it will not ask half an hours baking; you may garniſh it if you pleaſe with Lozenges, or otherwiſe.

To make an Oatmeal Pudding.

TAke two handfuls of great Oatmeal, and beat it exceeding ſmall in a Morter, ſet on three pints of Milk in a skillet, put into it two or three ſticks of Cinamon, and large Mace, ſtir in this Oatmeal into your Milk before it is hot, ſo much as will make it reaſonable thick, fit to be eaten; boyl it for the ſpace of half an hour, but keep it ſtirring; put therein a good handful of Beef ſued ſhred ſmall; then take it off the fire, and put it in an earthen Pan, and let it ſtand until it is almoſt cold; if it grows thick, thin it with a little more Milk; beat in four eggs, with almoſt a handful of Sugar, a grated

grated Nutmeg, and some Rose-water; butter the bottom of your dish, and pour in your Pudding, for it ought to be as thin as batter; bake it softly; it will ask but half an hours time; so scrape on Sugar, and send it up.

To make a Pudding of Rice flower.

THicken three pints of Milk, with about a handful of Rice flower beaten into a batter, put in Cinamon and large Mace in the boyling; keep it continually stirred till it be thick, put into it a piece of butter, let it boyl a quarter of an hour, then put it in an earthen Pan, and let it be cold; add to it two handfuls of Curans, a little Sugar, beaten Cinamon, and a handful of Dates minced, beat half a dozen eggs (casting forth three whites) beat them together, put butter in the bottom of your dish, and pour in your Pudding; you must add Salt, and all things else in this nature, according to your discretion; you ought to have a garnish of Paste on the brims of your dish; when it is baked, scrape on Sugar, and serve it up, adding a little Rosewater.

To make a hasty Pudding.

SEt on three pints of Cream, two grated Manchets or French rolles sliced thin and minced, put to this a grated nutmeg, a little Cloves, Mace, Cinamon and Ginger beaten; add thereto half a handful of flower, mingle it together, and stir it into your milk; when it boyls, throw in a piece of Butter; then having four or five eggs beaten, with the whites of half cast away, put them also into your Pudding, with a handful of Sugar, and a little Rose-water, stir them together again, till they begin to boyl and thicken, then put it out into your dish you serve it up in, set it on a heap of coals, put a fire-shovel to be red hot in the fire, then hold it close to your Pudding until it is brown on the top, so scrape on Sugar and send it up.

To make Andolians.

TAke the great guts of a Hog, let them be clean scoured and shifted in several waters, for four and twenty hours together, then take a handful of very good sweet herbs and Parslee, with a piece of Beef-suet, mince it together very small, and put to it a good quantity of Cloves, Mace, Ginger, a little Pepper, Salt and beaten Nutmeg; add to it a handful of grated bread, mingle it all together; then cleanse and stroke your guts from the water and slime, through a cloth very clean, and season the fat side of them with your aforesaid ingredients; so pull one length over another, your least underneath, and your greatest on the outside; you may put five or six lengths over one another; but for the more sure way; for after-service, you ought to wash every length over with eggs, and then season it, before you pull over the other length; when you have done all, bind them up at both ends, and boyl them softly until they are enough, then sowce them: When you use them, you may cut them in slices, and fry them, so serve them up with Mustard. but if you think they will be better, you may dip them in the yolks of eggs, and so fry them.

BOOK IX.

Contains Hash, Stewed, Broyled and Carbonadoed meats.

To farce a Fillet of Beef.

CUt your Fillet of Beef into three great Collops, throughout from side to side, beat them very well with a Rouler, or back side of a Cleaver, so that you have made them flat and thin, then mince a great handful of Parsley, with Time and other sweet herbs; having your meat seasoned as it lyeth, with Pepper, Salt, Cloves, Mace and Nutmeg, and being washed over with the yolks of eggs as you joyn them together again, throw on a handful of sweet herbs, and a handful or two of Beef suet purely minced; then joyn on the other Fillet with the washed side downward to the herbs; so do with the third, having the herbs and Beef-suet between; beat them close together with the flat side of the Cleaver, so put it into a great Pan, and put a pint of Claret and a pint of strong Broth, with half a dozen of Onions and whole Pepper to it, but it is better to wrap it up in two Veal Caules, being washed over with the yolks of eggs, so cover it with a sheet of course Paste, and let it stew up in an hot Oven for about five hours; you must note, that this I call a Fillet, is but three great Collops of one side the Fillet, containing the bigness of a Fillet of Veal; when it is baked, you must dish it up in good store of sippets, and pour in the Broth it was baked with; then having a red Cabbage boyled, hacked and tost up in drawn Butter, garnish it upon, and the sides of the meat, in the inside the dish.

To

To stew a Breast of Mutton.

TAke a Breast of Mutton, and joynt it well, and farce it with some sweet herbs, and minced Parslee; then put it in a deep Stewing-dish with the right side downwards; put to it so much White-wine and strong Broth as will stew it; set it on a great heap of Coals, put in two or three Onyons, a faggot of sweet Herbs, and a little large Mace; when it is almost stewed, take a handful of Spinnage, Parslee and Endive, and put into it; at the last you may put some Goosberries or Grapes: in the Winter time you may stew it with Sampier and Capers; it will not be amiss to add these to them at any time: dish up your Breast of Mutton, and put by that liquor you do not use, and thicken the other with yolks of Eggs and drawn Butter, so pour on the Lear, and the herbs over the meat, and garnish the dish with Lemmon or Barberries.

To farce a Fillet of Veal.

CUt two Fillets out of a large leg, take a handful of sweet herbs and Parslee minced, with a handful of Beef suet minced, and some yolks of hard eggs: season this with two grated Nutmegs, and a little Salt, and so farce your Fillets of Veal: being well larded with Bacon, and drawn with Time, let them be roasted almost enough: then in the mean time take the rest of your farced meat, being about a handful, put half a handful of Currans to it, and a little strong Broth, Vinegar, and a little Claret, with some large Mace, and a little Sugar: your meat being almost roasted, draw it off, and let it stew in this: when it is enough, add a ladleful of drawn butter, so dish up your meat, and pour your sauce all over it.

To stew Venison.

THey which have much Venison, and make many cold baked meats, may stew a dish in haste after this manner; when it is sliced out of your Pye, Pot, or Pasty, put it in a Stewing-dish, and set it on a heap of coals, with a little Claret-wine, a spring or two of Rosemary, half a dozen Cloves, a little grated bread, Sugar, and Vinegar; so let it stew together a while, then grate on a Nutmeg, and dish it up.

How to stew Calves Feet.

YOur Calves-feet being boyled and blanched, split them in the middle, take from them the great bones put them into a stewing-dish with a little strong broth, two or three Onyons, a faggot of sweet Herbs, with a little large Mace and Salt; when they boyl put to them a handful of Parslee, Spinage and sweet herbs minced, with a handful of Currans; when they are enough, beat the yolks of two or three Eggs, with four or five spoonfuls of Vinegar and a little Sugar; so thicken your Lear with that, and a little drawn butter; dish up your Calves feet on sippets, and pour on your Broth.

To hash a Shoulder or Leg of Mutton.

YOur shoulder or leg being almost roasted, you must hash them in as thin slices as you can, into a deep dish; put into it a ladleful of strong Broth, three or four whole Onions, a faggot of sweet herbs, a little large Mace and Salt, put it on a good heap of coals, when it is boyled up to an heighth, put into it two or three Anchovies, half a handful of Capers, a little Sampier minced, two yolks of Eggs beaten with a little White wine, toss up together, so dish it up, and garnish it with Lemmon.

How to make a raw Hash of a more excellent way, new invented.

Take a couple of legs of Lamb, or a leg of young Mutton, hash it exceeding thin with your knife; then having half a handful of sweet herbs minced consisting most of Time, put into your meat, with a little Cloves, Mace, Nutmeg and Salt, with the yolks of five eggs; work up all these together between your hands; your Pan being on with a good quantity of Clarified butter, put it in all over the Pan, so keep it stirring and tossing, until it be almost eatable, then put out your butter out of your Pan you fryed it in; put in a ladleful of strong Broth, a little White-wine, four Anchovies, two or three whole Onions, a faggot of sweet herbs, so let them stew up all together; put in towards the last a pint of Oysters, then take the yolks of two or three eggs, and beat them in strong Broth, or White-wine, and throw them into your Pan, keeping it still tossing and stirring; you may add half a pint of gravie if you have it, your dish being garnished with sippets, pour in your Hash, and put Sassages round about, so garnish it with Lemmon, and strow on the yolks of minced eggs; if it be well done, it will look white with a smeered froth on it.

To Hash a Calves head.

Take your Calves head and cleave it in two, and wash it out in certain waters, that it may boyl white; then put it a boyling and scum it: when it is almost boyled, take it up, and let it cool; Hash it in slices as thin as you can, then put it into your Stew-pan, with a ladleful or two of Strong Broth, and as much White-wine, three or four Onions whole, and a little Time minced, with two or three Anchovies, a little Salt, with a little Oyster liquor, if you have it; put all

all these a stewing together, when they are enough, toss it up with the yolks of two eggs, and a little drawn butter; you may have a Pipkin with about half a pint of Oysters stewed up in a little gravie, with as many Mushroms, being thickened with a little drawn Butter, and seasoned with Nutmeg; take off your Pipkins, lay the bones of your Calves head in the bottom of your dish with sippets, then pour out your Hash with your Lear into the dish, and spread it abroad, and put your Oysters and Mushroms, and that Lear all over your Calves head; then having your thin sliced Bacon, before boyled, and part thereof fryed in eggs, lay it round on the dishes side: the one fryed and the other boyled; you may add Sassages also about it, so garnish it with Lemmon; only grate a Nutmeg, strow it on the top, and let it go up smoaking.

To Hash Hens or Pullets with Eggs.

YOur Hens or Pullets being roasted before, cut them up as you would carve them for the Table; then hash off all the meat very thin and clean from the bones, only leave some upon the thigh bones and pinions; put them into your stewing dish with strong Broth, with two or three Onions; so let them stew up, with a faggot of sweet herbs, and a grated Nutmeg; when they are almost enough, mince half a dozen hard eggs, and put to it; so being seasoned with Salt, add a little drawn Butter and Claret-wine to it, and toss it up together in your dish; let the Lear be thick; if not, add the yolk of a raw egg or two; take out all your bones, and place them on the side of your dish to the brim-wards, upon your sippets; then put your meat all over the dish; scruise a Lemmon with some drawn Butter, and pour on the top of it; strow on yolks of eggs minced, and garnish them with Lemmon.

To

To make a Hash of Capons.

HAsh your Capons in the same manner as your Hens before, put into them a little Claret-wine and strong Broth, two Onions, two Anchovies, a faggot of sweet herbs, let it boyl all together; put to it a little gravie, if you have it, and some Oyster liquor; toss it together with a little drawn butter, so dish it up, and strow over the meat a Lemmon cut in Dice, and send it up: you may stew up Sassages with them, and put them round your dish, if you please.

To Hash Partridges.

YOur Partridges being roasted, take all the flesh off the bones, and hash it very thin; only preserve the legs and wings of two or three Partridges; then put a little Claret-wine into your Pan, with a little strong broth and gravie; put to it an Onion or two, a Nutmeg grated, with an Anchovie, and a few crums of bread; when this boyls in your Pan, put in your wings and legs, with the bones of your Partridges, with all your Hash on the top of them: so cover your Stew-pan, and let it boyl up, and when it is enough, put in a ladleful of drawn butter, and toss it up together; dish up the bones in the bottom of your dish on sippets; lay your legs and wings round about, and your Hash on the bones in the middle, so pour on your Lear, with a little drawn butter, and garnish it with Lemmon.

To Hash Ducks, or other water-fowl.

HAsh your Ducks as you have heard before in the Partridge; put strong Broth, with a little Vinegar, and set them on the coals in the stewing-dish; put to them four Onions minced exceeding small, a little small Pepper, let all this boyl up together with a little Salt;

The whole Body of Cookery Diſſected. 93

Salt; alſo put in a pound of Saſſages into the boyling with your Haſh-Ducks; when they are enough, toſs them up thick with a little draw Butter; ſo diſh them to your beſt Advantage.

To Haſh a Rabbet.

YOu muſt take the fleſh from the bones of your Rabbet, being before roaſted, and mince it ſmall with your mincing knife; ſo put to it a little ſtrong Broth and Vinegar, an Onion or two, with a grated Nutmeg, and let it ſtew up together; then mince a handful of boyled Parſlee green, with a Lemmon cut like Dice, & a few Barberries, put it into your Haſh, and toſs it altogether, and when it is enough, put a ladleful of drawn Butter thereto, and diſh it upon the bones; ſo garniſh it with Lemmon.

Carbonadoes and Broyled meats.
To Carbonado a Gooſe.

YOur Gooſe being roaſted, and carved, ſcorch it with your knife long ways, and croſs it over again (ſo that it may be like Checquer work) both within and without, then waſh it over with butter, ſtrow it with Salt, put it into a diſh, with the skinny ſide downwards, ſo ſet it before your fire, in your dripping Pan, that it may take a gentle heat; when it hath ſtood a while, turn the other ſide; then lay it on your Gridiron, and put it on a moderate fire of Charcoals; when it is done, take it off the fire, and baſt the upper ſide with butter, and dreadg it over with flower and grated bread then turn it and froth it on the fire and diſh it up in order; your ſawce muſt be Butter, and Vinegar, Muſtard and Sugar, being mingled together: put it into your diſh, ſo lay on a little drawn Butter, and garniſh it with Lemmon: you may lay on Saſſages round your diſh if you pleaſe. To

To Carbonedo Turkies.

YOu muſt obſerve the ſame order as you did in the Gooſe, your ſawce muſt be a little gravy and ſtrong broth, boyled up with an Onion, and a little grated bread, with ſliced Nutmeg, an Anchovie, and a ladle of drawn butter; add a little ſalt, diſh up your Turky, and put your ſauce all over it, ſtrow it over with Barberries, and garniſh it with Lemmon.

To Carbonado Henns.

LET your ſawce be a little White-wine and Gravy, half a dozen of the yolks of hard eggs minced, boyled up wtih an Onion, add to it a grated Nutmeg; thicken it with the yolks of an egg or two, with a ladle of drawn butter; diſh up your Henns, and pour over your ſawce, ſtrow on yolks of eggs minced, and garniſh it with Lemmon.

To Carbonado Veal.

TAke a breaſt of Veal, lard it very thick with bacon, and when it is boyled, Cardonado it long, and croſs-ways; waſh it over with a little butter, and the yolk of an egg, ſtrow it over with ſalt; put it on your Gridiron with the right ſide downward, until it be of a yellowiſh brown, diſh it up, garniſh it with a little fryed bacon; let your Lear be a little ſtrong broth, boyled up with ſome minced Time, and ſome Nutmeg grated, a little Vinegar, and a ladle of drawn butter, pour it over your meat; ſo ſcruile in an Orange, or two, and garniſh it with Oranges cut in quatters.

To Carbonado Mutton.

BOyl a ſhoulder or breaſt of Mutton, then ſcorch them over as aforeſaid, and ſtrow on minced Time, Salt,

Salt, and a little Nutmeg; when they are broyled, diſh them up; let your ſawce be Claret wine boyled up, with two Onions, a little Sampier. and Capers minced, with drawn butter and gravy, pour this all over your Meat, and garniſh it with Lemmon.

A diſh of Collops of Mutton, Broyld.

CUt off a piece of your Leg of Mutton cloſe to the bone, cut it into Collops very thin, hack them as broad as you can, with the back of a great knife, and lay them in a broad diſh, then having a little Time ſmall minced, and a Nutmeg grated, mingled with a little ſalt, ſtrow the one half on the upper ſide of your Collops, your Gridiron being clean rubbed with the skins of Bacon, put on your Collops with the ſeaſoned ſide downwards, then caſt the reſt of your ſeaſoning on the other ſide, and let them broyl on a moderate fire; when the one ſide is enough, turn them, they muſt not be brown; ſo let your diſh be on the coals with a little gravy, diſh them up in a heap, pour on a little butter, and gravy hot, cover them with a diſh, and ſend them hot to the table, being garniſh'd with ſliced Lemmon.

Steaks of Pork Broyled.

TAke a Loyn of Pork, cut off the skin, and about an inch or more of the fat: (if the Loyn be ſo fat) then cut of your ſteakes with your Cleaver very thin, and beat them with the flat thereof, as broad and as thin as you can lay them on a diſh, ſtrow them over with a little ſalt, and Sage minced very ſmall; ſo lay them on your Gridiron, and ſeaſon the other ſide; let your ſawce be drawn Butter, Vinegar and Muſtard with a little Sugar, when they are ready, diſh them up, and put the ſawce to them.

To

To Carbonado a Calves head.

WHen it is boyled according to the ufual manner, Carbonado it, and ſtrow on ſalt; ſo waſh it over with the yolk of an egg, and drawn butter, rub the bars of your Gridiron with the skin of fat Bacon, and let it broyl gently, to a yellowiſh brown; diſh it up with your tongue about it; your Lear may be a pint of Oyſters ſtewed up in gravy and wine, with a ladle of drawn butter put to it: ſo pour it all over your Calves head, and put your ſliced Bacon round about; Garniſh it with Lemmon.

To Broyl a Chine of Park.

WHen your Pork is boyled, waſh it over with a little butter, and broyl it: then take your raw Turnips cut to pieces in the length and bigneſs of your thumb, being boyled in a little ſtrong broth and milk, toſt up with ſome drawn butter and vinegar: your Pork being diſh'd, pour this all over it: Garniſh your diſh with Barberries, ſtrowing ſome over the meat and ſend it up.

There are many Gentry who delight in Carbonadoes and broyled meats: for indeed it is a very good ſavory, and wholeſome meat: therefore I do acquaint the Student in Cookery, that he may make uſe of this way for any other meats or Joynts, which I have here omitted, provide the ſawſe be natural to the meat: Butter and Vinegar being the good old ſawce for moſt broyled meats: As for Example,

Boyl a Brisket of Beef, take off the skin, and Carbonado it, then broyl it: diſh it and ſerve it up, with Cabbadge or Turnips: your Lear is butter and Vinegar, In the ſame mannner you may do the gooſe or skin that you took off.

BOOK

BOOK X.

Containing Frigasies and Frying.

How to fry all manner of Garnishing.

YOu must beat the yolks of eggs, put in the beating a little flower, and Sack, make them into a batter, add to the batter some grated Nutmeg; if you make much, you may put in four whites amongst eight eggs: let it be thick.

How to fry Oysters in Batter.

LEt your Pan be hot with your Clarified Butter or tryed Suet, and your Oysters being set and dryed, dip your Oysters in the aforesaid Batter, and put them into your pan; do not over charge your pan; if you do, it will Rise up in a froth, and spoil that which you fry; hold your pan on a hot fire with your Oysters, and when they are come to a lovely brown, take them out with your Scummer; thus you may fry sliced Lobsters, Pranes, or Periwinckles, the tayls of Crafish, to serve for the garnishing of your fish; you may fry Rosemary dipt slightly in Batter: Your Pan must be very hot to fry Bay-leaves, Fennel, or Parslee; your scummer must always be in your hand; for as soon as they become green and crisp, they will turn black if you take them not forth; these things you must not dip in batter: you may fry Skirrets, sliced Potatoes, and bacon in thin slices in the said batter; If you would fry green, then you must scald some Spinnage in boyling water, and mince it with your knife exceeding small; you may strain in a little of the juice of it, but then

H   you

you must add more flower; beat this in with the yolks of eggs, and fry your green away with your pan seasoned) as your other before; to know if your pan be hot, if it leave hissing, and begin to smoak, then it is hot, take it off, else it will burn and spoil all: If you would fry any other thing in batter, you must fry it after the manner afore prescribed: thus much for a garnish

A Frigacy of a Hen or Capon.

THey being either roast or boyled before, almost enough, and carved up, the Pinions being cut off from the wings, and the brawn of the Capon cut off from the joynt, and being so ordered that it may lye handsome in the pan: put to them (as they are in the dish) the yolks of four eggs, with a little minced Time and sliced Nutmeg: then mingle them up together between your hands: your pan being on the fire, with clarified butter (or sweet suet) half hot, put them in, and let them fry until they be yellowish, then turn them: so take a little white-wine, and beat it with three or four yolks of eggs: add to it a little strong broth and gravy, an Onyon or two cut in quarters, two Anchovies minced with a grated Nutmeg, then pour out all your stuff from your Capon or Hen, and put to it a ladleful of drawn butter: so put this Lear into your pan, and keep it continually shaking over a sober fire, until it turns thick, or is ready to boyl, then dish up your Capon or Hen in order: if your Lear in your pan be too thick, you may thin it with Gravy, Wine, or strong broth: so pour over your Lear: strow it with the yolks of eggs minced, and garnish it with Lemmon.

To make a Frigacy of Chicken brown.

Take about four Chickens, scald them, and cut them in qurters: beat them flat with your Cleaver, and break their bones, dry them with cloth very well, ane flower them all over the skinny sides; your pan being hot with clarified butter, put them in with the skinny part downwards, fry them brown, then turn them: let your Lear be a little Clarret-wine and gravy: then put your liquour out of your pan, and put in your lear, with pieces of Saſſages wrung off as long as your thumb, and a pint of Oyſters, two or three onions, with a faggot of ſweet herbs, a grated Nutmeg, and two or three Anchovies, let them boyl up in the pan; then beat the yolks of four eggs with a little ſtrong broth, take the pan off the fire, and put them in: if it turns too thick, you may thin it with Wine, Gravy, or ſtrong Broth: keep it ſhaking whileſt its on the fire, then diſh up your Chickens on Sippets, and pour on your Lear, and Oyſters, with your pieces of Saſſages by the ſides of your diſh, and garniſh it with Lemmon.

Another way for Chicken or Rabbets.

Take your Chickens or Rabbets, and let them be almoſt half boyled, cut them in haves or quarters: put them into your pan with a little freſh butter, (heat not your pan at all for them) then lay your pan on the fire, and let them fry ſoberly: Let your Lear be ready, the yolks of three or four eggs beaten, with about half a pint of Verjuice, a little white-wine, and ſtrong broth, a Nutmeg grated, and a handful of parſlee, boyled up green and minced, with about a ſpoonful of Sugar, adding one handful of ſcalded Goosberries, Grapes, or ſliced Artichoke-bottoms; put all theſe in the pan to your Chickens, being kept ſhaking over the fire, until it be ready to boyl, then dish your Chickens, or Rabbets on Sippets, shake your Lear, and let it be as thick as drawn butter, so pour it all over your Chickens, strow on a Lemmon cut like dice, and garnish it with boyled Parflee and Barberries.

To smear Collops of Veal.

TAke a piece of your Fillet of Veal, and cut it into thin Collops, and hack it with the back of your knife, and lard them with Bacon very thick, then put them into your pan, it being pretty hot, and fry them with clarified butter very brown on both sides; And let them be so hastily done, that they may not be fryed quite through; then having half a pint of Claret wine, and half a pint of Gravy, put it in your pan (with four Anchovies, three or four Onions, a little minced Time, and grated Nutmeg) amongst your burnt Butter; when it is boyled up, thicken it with the yolk of an egg, so dish up your Collops, and pour on your Lear on the top: if your Pan be little, you may fry them at twice, and let them boyl up after the same manner, in your stewing dish, Garnish them with Lemmon.

To fry a dish of Lamb-stones and Sweet breads.

BLanch your Lamb stones, taking off the outward skin, and split them through; also slice your Veal sweat breads, let your Lambs be whole, so let your pan be very hot, and your Lamb stones and Sweet breads flowered exceeding well; you may fry them up into a pure brown, if you do not overcharge your pan; let your sawce be gravy, butter and vinegar, dish them up and strow over them parsle fryed crisp.

How to make a Frigacy of Lamb.

TAke a leg of Lamb, and cut it into Collops, and beat it with the back of the knife; put into a dish with the yolk of four eggs, a handful of Parsle, Time, Sweet Margerum and Spinnage minced very small, put to it a little beaten Cloves, Mace, Nutmeg, and a little Salt, mix them all together, your Frying pan being over the Fire with clarified Butter almost hot; put them in, and fry them softly, let them not be brown, but rather green; when they are almost fryed, put to them a little White wine and strong broth, three Onions in halves, and a ladle of drawn Butter: let it boyl up in the pan, then beat the yolks of two eggs, with a little Vinegar, a little Nutmeg, and a little gravy; dish up your Lamb on Sippets, and pour on the Lear, and garnish it with Lemmon sliced.

A Frigacy of Veal.

YOur Veal being cut from the fillet, very thin, but not very large, do by it as before by your Lamb, add yolks of eggs, and green minced herbs, until your Veal looks green; fry it up as before, and put it into a stewing dish, with a little White wine, and strong broth; then cut some thin slices of Bacon, and throw into the dish amongst the sweet herbs, where the Veal was before; season it with a little Pepper, and minced sage, throw in the yolk or two of an egg: your pan being hot, fry it a little on both sides, so put it into the Lear with the Veal, and also that in the pan it was fryed withal, so let it boyl up together, and beat the yolks of two eggs, with a little Vinegar; put it into your meat, and toss it up together, with a ladle of drawn butter, and two Nutmegs grated; dish up your Veal with your Bacon about it, and pour over your Lear.

A dish of Collops of Mutton with a savoury hogo.

CUt your Collops of your Mutton through your Loyn, and beat them with the flat of your Cleaver; sprinkle them with Salt, and put them in your Pan, with some butter to them, fry them pretty brown on each side, then put them out into your stewing-dish, with some Claret-wine and strong broth; set them on the coals to boyl, then mince two or three Onyons; (as many as your hand will contain when they are minced,) put your pan on the fire with a piece of sweet butter, let it continue until it burn, then throw in your Onyons, when they are crisp, put them to your steaks with the burnt butter, with two or three Anchivoies minced, a handful of Capers, and Sampier minced, with a couple of sliced Nutmers; let it all boyl up together, take the yolks of one or two eggs beaten in, when they are enough; if you have gravie, make use of it also, dish up your steaks, and pour on your Lear.

To fry Coller'd Pork.

YOu may see how to coller it, as before; all that you have to do, is to slice the Coller, and your Pan being very hot, fry it with clarified stuff: you may eat it with Mustard as you do Sowse; this may serve when you have occasion to add a dish to your common dyet.

Another way.

BReak the yolks of eggs, and beat them with a little Nutmeg; then dip in your Collers, and your Pan being hot as for egs, put them in, and fry them away; you may dish them about a forced leg of Lamb, or fillet of Veal, or any other dish of that nature; you may also fry your coller'd Veal up with eggs, as you did your Pork, so dish it up with a slice of one, and a

slice

slice of the other, and put to it a little Gravie, Butter and Vinegar boyled up to a heighth, and garnish it with Lemmon.

A Frigacy of Partridge or Woodcocks.

THey must be first almost roast, and then carved as at The Table, and fryed with sweet Butter, and an Onyon minced exceeding small, put to them half a pint of Gravie, and two or three Anchovies, half a handful of grated bread, a garted Nutmeg, a little drawn butter, and the yolk of one egg, beaten with a little Claret wine ; so tols them all together, when they boyl well, and come to a thickness, so dish them up, and garnish them with Lemmon.

A Frigacy of Ducks or Widgeons.

YOu must cut them out raw in quarters, and beat them with the flat of your Cleaver; then dry them well, and put them into your pan with some Butter, and fry them well ; when they are pretty well fryed, put into them one handful of minced Onyons, and a little while after, put in some Clarret-wine and eight slices of Bacon, having been boyled before, you may add a handful of Spinnage and Parslee boyled up green, and minced small ; when it is stewed up in your Frying-pan, beat in a couple of yolks of eggs, with a grated Nutmeg and a little Pepper; so tols it up with a ladleful of drawn Butter, and dish it up ; pour on your Lear over it, and your Bacon on the top of your Ducks.

A fryed meat of Bacon.

FIll your pan very full of slices of Bacon, very thin, then take of Time, Winter-savoury, sweet Margerum, and Pennyroyal all minced ; strow a little of this over all your Bacon in the pan, with a grated Nutmeg; then

then beat fourteen eggs together, and when your pan is hot with your Bacon in it, and begins to fry, take a ladleful of eggs, and pour it round by the Bacon, all along by the pans side; then pour it crosſways from side to side, both wayes, then fill up all the vacant places, ſo that you hide all the Bacon; let it fry very ſoberly, then butter a plate, and put it into your pan, ſo turn it thereon; put more butter in your pan, and ſhift it into the pan, off your plate, ſo pour on ſome eggs on that ſide of the Bacon, but do it very lightly; and when the underſide is fryed, you may turn it on your plate again, and fry the upper ſide; then take it up, and diſh it on a diſhing-plate, and ſcruiſe on Lemmons; garniſh it with quartered Lemmons.

To make a fryed meat, ealled an Amlett.

BEat in according to your pan, ſixteen eggs, (more or leſs) with a grated Nutmeg, and a Lemmon cut in the likeneſs and quantity of Dice, beat them together well, put butter in your pan, ſet it over the fire, let it be indifferent hot (but not to burn) then put in your eggs, keep them ſtirring that they grow not to the pan, put in butter by the ſides, to make them ſhift up and down, and when they begin to harden and congeal, ſhake them round; by conſtant putting in of butter, they will move round; then turn them on your plate, put butter into your pan, and turn the other ſide downward; fry it of a pure yellow brown, ſo take it out of the pan on your plate, and diſh it up, ſcruiſe on a Lemmon or two, garniſh it about with Oranges, and ſcrape on Sugar.

Another way.

TAke twelve eggs, whites and yolks, and about a pint of Cream, with two handfuls of grated Manchet, beat theſe together, with a little Roſe-water and Sugar,

Sugar, grated Nutmeg, and some Cinamon, put a little melted butter into a skillet, set it on the fire, and pour your eggs and cream into it; keep it stirring until it grows thick into a body, and clears it self from the bottom of the skillet; your pan being hot with butter in it, put it out of the skillet into your pan, and flat it with your slice about your pan, fry it brown, and turn it with a plate, put more butter in your pan, and shift in the other side; when it is enough, take it out upon your plate, and dish it up; scruise on it a Lemmon or two, and garnish it with Oranges.

To fry Primrose-leaves in March *with Eggs.*

TAke a handful or two of Primrose leaves, mince them very small, beat them into a dozen eggs; your pan being very hot, cool it a little, and put in a piece of butter, so put in your eggs, fry them very soberly; when it is enough on that side, turn it, and lay it in again on the other side; when it is enough, scrape on Sugar, scruise on the juice of a Lemmon or two.

To fry Clary.

GAther the youngest Clary and string it, then beat some yolks of eggs, a grated Nutmeg or two; (in the number of eight eggs, you may put in two whites) put on your pan with some butter on the fire, that it may be hot enough for eggs, then dip your Clary into your yolks of eggs, and put it into your pan; fry it of a lovely brown on both sides; dish it up, and strow on Sugar, adding a little Butter, Vinegar and Sugar to it; it is good for break-fast, or second course dish.

To fry Apples.

YOu must first half coddle your Apples, then cut them in slices, and having a dozen eggs beaten toge-

together, and your pan hot with sweet butter, put so many eggs in as will run round your pan, and will make it no thicker than a Pancake; when it begins to harden and turn round, cover it all over with the slices of your Apples, and sprinkle over them good store of Cinnamon, Ginger and Sugar; then pour on eggs all over your Apples, (as much as you put under them before) take them off the fire, and with a red hot fire-shovel harden them on the top; butter your plate and turn them, so fry them on the other side; then dish them up, and scrape on Sugar.

How to make an Orangado Phraise.

MInce your Orangado very small, with some Cittern amongst it, then beat them in a Morter to mash, put to them twelve eggs, casting away the whites of four, add to that a little Rose-water, with two Naple Biskets grated, let your pan be hot with a little sweet butter, this being mixed together, put it into your pan; when it is fryed, so that it turns round, take a red hot fire-shovel, and congeal it on the top, then turn it on a plate, and put it into your pan again with some butter, and when it is fryed tenderly, dish it up; scrape on Sugar, and garnish it with Orangado and Cittern.

A Tanzie of Cowslips or Violets.

BEat your Cowslips or Violets in a Morter, put into them a pint of Cream, a handful of grated bread, a dozen of eggs, casting away four whites, some beaten Cinamon and Nutmeg, half a handful of Sugar, with a little Rose-water, put a piece of butter into a skillet over a fire, and stir them until they come into a body; then put a little butter into your pan, being hot, and proportion it in your pan, and fry it; when it is fryed on that side, turn it on your plate, being washed with
butter,

butter, so turn the other side into your pan, and when it is fryed, dish it up, scruise on the juice of Lemmon, and garnish it with quartered Oranges, and scrape on Sugar.

A Tanzie of Spinage.

TAke a pint of Cream, a handful of grated bread, fourteen eggs, cast away the whites of six, season it with a grated Nutmeg, and Sugar, and green it with the juice of Spinnage ; so bring it into a body, in a skillet, and fry it, as before you did the other; this will be a very tender Tanzie ; but if you intend to cut it according to the vulgar way, you must add the other whites of eggs, else deminish in your Cream ; dish it up, scruise on the juice of a Lemmon, and garnish it with quartered Oranges, then scrape on Sugar. After this way and manner aforesaid, have I made Tanzies of Wallnut-tree-buds in Lent, and of Pine-Apples and Pistaches at other seasons.

To fry Artichokes, or Spanish Potatoes.

WHen they are boyled and sliced, fitting for that purpose you must have your yolks of eggs, beaten with a grated Nutmeg or two ; when your pan is hot, you must dip them into the yolks of Eggs, and charge your pan ; when they are fryed on both sides, your Lear to your Artichokes is drawn Butter, and to your Potatoes, Butter; Vinegar, Sugar and Rose-water; these for a need may serve for second course dishes.

To make Fritters.

TAke a pottle of flower that hath been dryed in an Oven, put to it six Eggs, and the curd of a pottle of Milk, made with Sack and Ale, scruise all the Whey out of it, season it with Cinamon, Cloves, Mace, Nutmeg,

meg, and Ginger beaten, with a little Salt; then make it into a batter with milk, and put therein a dozen of Pippens sliced thin, beat it all well together, let it be so thick with the Apples and the Batter, that it may not run apart if it be put upon a pye-plate; then let your tryed lard be hot in the pan, continuing over the fire; put a ladleful of batter upon a pye-plate, and put it off into your boyling lard upon the point of a knife, to the value of a small Wallnut at a time; you must be very quick to scrape it from your plate into your pan, till it is fully charged; keep them stiring about until they are brown and crisp, then take them forth, and dish them up into a hot dish, and strow them with Cinamon and Sugar; you may also slice the Pippen through the Apple, to the tail-ward, being cored, and dip them into a thick batter, and so put them into your liquor as before.

To make Pancakes.

Put to a pottle of flower eight eggs, casting by four whites, season it with Cinamon, Nutmeg, Ginger, Cloves, Mace, and Salt, then make it into a strong Batter with Milk; beat it well together, and put in half a pint of Sack, make it so thin, that it may run in your pan as you please; put your pan on the fire with a little butter or suet; when it is very hot, take a cloth and wipe it out, so make your pan very clean, then put in more butter, and hold on your pan till it is melted, put in your batter, and run it very thin, supply it with little bits of butter, so toss it often, and bake it crisp and brown.

Another way to dress a dish of Collops of Veal.

Cut a piece of a leg of Veal into thin Collops, with part of the dugg, beat it thin with the back of a knife, and lard it very well, then mince very small a

good

The whole Body of Cookery Diſſected.

good handful of Spinnage, a handful of Parſlee, a little Time, ſweet Margerum, and Winterſavoury, ſeaſon them with a little Pepper, Cloves, Mace, Nutmeg and Salt, then beat about eight yolks of eggs, and dip your Collops therein, ſo roul them in your green herbs, that they may ſtick to them, and put them into your pan with clarified Butter (being hot, as for eggs) when they are fryed on both ſides with a fine green colour, put to them ſome ſtrong Broth, a little whitewine, two or three ſpoonfuls of Vinegar, two or three Onions, a bunch of ſweet herbs, with a grated Nutmeg, and let it ſtew altogether, then add the yolks of two eggs beaten with ſome of their own liquor, and a ladleful of drawn Butter, ſo ſhake it altogether, diſh up your Collops, and pour on your lear; garniſh it over with Bacon fryed in the yolks of eggs.

To fry Calves Feet, or Sheeps Trotters.

WHen they are boyled very tender, and ſpilt in the middle, cutting away the bunchy hair between the toes of your Trotters, ſeaſon them with a little ſmall Pepper, Salt, Cloves, mace, Nutmeg beaten; then take about the yolks of ten eggs, with the whites of three or four put to them, a handful of Parſlee, Spinnage, Time, ſweet Margerum, and Winterſavoury, minced exceeding ſmall, beat them together in batter; your pan being hot with clarified butter, dip your feet into this batter, and put them in, fry them ſoberly on both ſides, then put to them a little ſtrong Broth, Vinegar and Sugar, ſo let them ſtew together, beating them up thick with the yolk of an egg, and drawn Butter, diſh them on ſippets, and ſcruiſe a Lemmon over them-

How

How to Frigacy Neats Tongues and Udders.

WHen they are boyled enough, take your Tongue and Udder, and cut them in slices or Collops, beginning at the butt end, until you come within five inches of the tip, and cut that in sippets length ways, both of your Udder and Tongue, then take a handful of Spinage, Parslee, Time, sweet Margerum & Winter savoury minced exceeding small, and put it into your dish with the Udder and Tongue: put to it Cloves, Mace and Cinamon beaten, with a little Salt, the yolks of six or seven eggs, and mingle it alltogether very well with your hands, then fry it in clarifyed Butter, put it forth into a great stewing-dish on a heap of coals, with Claret-wine, beaten Cinamon and Ginger, Sugar, a little Vinegar, a branch or two of Rosemary, and a handful of grated Bread; when it boyls up together, add a ladleful of drawn Butter, so dish it up with the slices of your tops of Tongues, &c. round about like sippets, and pour on your Lear.

To potch a dish of Eggs for a weak stomach.

TAke a handful of very good Sorrel beaten in a Morter, strain it forth with the juice of Lemmon, and a little Vinegar: put to it a little Sugar and grated Nutmeg, then take some sippets hardned upon a Gridiron, and lay them on the bottom of your dish; put on them a little strong Broth, and a spoonful of drawn butter, then pour in your Sorrel, and set it on a great heap of coals; your eggs being potched in a little water and salt, either in a clean frying pan, or a broad bottomed skillet, with a little more water then will cover them; then take them up, drain them from the water, and lay them on your sippets, so cover them and send them suddenly away; you must observe that your sauce must never be no hotter on the fire, than that you may

eat

The whole Body of Cookery Diſſected. 111

eat it without cooling it again ; for if you do, it will change the colour of your Sorrel, and give your Lemmon and it a bad taſte.

Another way rich and ſtrengthening.

PUt ſippets in your diſh, as aforeſaid, then beat half a handful of Piſtaches, and put them into half a pint of very good Mutton gravy, diſtil them over the fire, adding a grated Nutmeg, and the juice of a Lemmon, with two or three Anchovies diſſolved in ſome of the gravy ; then put it to or on your ſippets, being on a great fire, then diſh up your potched eggs (drained clean from the water) on your ſippets, put all your Piſtaches over your eggs, with a little drawn Butter, to make them look handſom.

Another way.

FIll your diſh with toaſted ſippets, as aforeſaid, put to them a pint or half a pint of Tent, or Muſcadine, grate a Nutmeg on them ; your eggs being very rarely done, and drained clean from the water by a little falſe bottom, or ſpoon made for that purpoſe ; lay them on your ſippets and wine, being moderately warm, ſend them up,

How to Butter Eggs.

BReak about ſixteen eggs, or what you pleaſe ; beat them and put them into a deep diſh, with about half a pound of Butter or more in pieces, and almoſt melted ; ſet them upon a great heap of coals until they begin to come together in the bottom ; then have about a dozen toaſts ready (through the roul) put them all over the bottom of your diſh, and with a great ſpoon rake them round from one ſide to the other, and lay the fleaks as they riſe, upon your toaſts in the diſh ; this muſt be done with much quickneſs and diligence, leſt it

burn

burn to the bottom; when all is laid on the toasts, pour over every one of them drawn Butter, stick them with small toasts, and send them up.

Another way.

BReak them on Butter, as aforesaid, then bring them up into a tender body with your spoon; dish them into a dish with toasts round about; this is your common way.

To fry Collops and Eggs.

CUt your Collops out of middling Bacon, exceeding thin, and about four inches long, so cutting off the rhine at once, part it into a dish of fair water, and let them lye an hour or two to take away the Salt; then take them forth and dry them from the water, and fry them in a pan with Butter or tryed stuff, keep them tossed while they are a frying, put them in a dish before they are through crisp, and set them before the fire, then pour the liquor out of your pan, and make it exceeding clean, by scouring of it with the shells of eggs, then almost fill your pan with pure clarified dripping or butter; when it is hot, but not to blister your white much, break in your eggs one by one, then put them on your Trivett on Charcoals, and part them asunder with your knife, and shake your liquor all over them, so will they fry on the top, you need not turn them, in case your pan be not full enough, you may just turn them, and dish them upon your Bacon, and part of the Bacon on the top of them, this way they will be as white or whiter than potched.

Many more things of this nature, is or may be used in Frigasying or Frying; but by the knowledge of these, all other things according to their nature, may be performed by an ingenious Practitioner.

BOOK

BOOK XI.

Containing all manner of Sallets and Roast-meats, with their several Sauces.

To make Sallets.

To make a Grand Sallet for the Spring.

YOur Gardiner, or those that serve you with herbs, must supply you with all manner of Spring-Sallets, as buds of Cowslips, Violets, Strawberries, Primrose, Brooklime, Water-cresses, young Lettice, Spinnage, Alexander-buds, or what other things may be got, either backward or forward in the Spring; having all these things severally and apart, then take by themselves Sampier, Olives, Capers, Broom-buds, Cowcumbers, Raisons and Currans parboiled, blanched Almonds, Barberries, or what other pickles you can obtain; then prepare your Standard for the middle of your dish; it may be a wax tree, or a standard of Paste (like a Castle) being washed in the yolks of Eggs, and all made green with herbs, as also a tree within that, in the like manner may be made, with Paste made green, and stuck with flowers, so that you may not perceive it but to be a tree, with about twelve supporters round, stooping to and fastened in holes in your Castle, and the other end bending out to the middle of your dish; they may be formed with Paste; then having four rings of Paste, the one bigger than another (like unto hoops) your biggest must come over your Castle, and reach within three inches of the foot of your supporter, the second to be within two inches of that, and so place as many as you please gradually, that they may be like as many steps going up to a Crofs; you may have likewife four Belconies in your Caftle, with four Statues of the four feafon; this done, place your Sallet, a round of one fort on the uppermoft ring, or ftep, fo round all the other, till you come to the difh, with every one a feveral fort; then place all your pickles from that to the brims of your difh feverally, one anfwering another: As for example, if you have two of white, and two of green, let them be oppofite, the white againft the white, and the green againft the green, and fo all the other; fo your difhes bottom being wholly covered below your Mount, garnifh your difh with all kind of things futable, or afforded by the Spring; your Statues onght to have every one a Cruitt placed in their hands, two with Vinegar, and two with Oyl; when this Sallet is made, let it be carried to the Table, and fet in its place; and when the guefts are all placed, unftop the Cruitts, that the Oyl and Vinegar may run on the Sallet; thefe Cruitts muft be glaffes not a quarter of a pint apiece, fized over on the out-fide, and ftrowed with flowers: After the fame manner may you make your Sallet in Summer, Autumn, or Winter; only take thofe Sallets that are then in feafon, and changing of your ftandard; for in the Summer, you ought to refemble a green tree; and in the Autumn, a Caftle carved out of Carrets and Turnips; in the Winter, a tree hanged with Snow: This only is for great Feafts, and may inform the Practitioner in fuch Feafts, for the honour of his Mafter, and benefit of himfelf: the Pafte that you make your Caftle or Standard with, muft be made of Rye.

The Flefh Sallet of a Capon or Turkey.

TAke of either, flice it very thin, as for a Hafh, put that which is white of the breaft and wings by its felf,

The whole Body of Cookery Diſſected. 115

ſelf, and that which is black of the legs, or other part of the Fowl, by it ſelf; put the rump and ſides of the rump in the diſh, and the other bones of the legs and wings about the ſides of the diſh like ſippets; then ſeaſon your meat with a few Sives, a little Tarragon, Speermint and Parſlee, with the Cabbage or two of Lettice; mince theſe exceeding ſmall, add a little ſmall Pepper Salt, and ſliced Nutmeg, with a little Horſe Raddiſh, ſcraped and minced, mingle your ſeaſoning together, and ſtrow it on your Sallet, pour on Oyl and Vinegar, ſo toſs it up together; let your blackeſt fleſh be laid, all over the bottom of your diſh and bones, and your whiteſt on the top of all; ſtrow on a Lemmon cut in Dice, and garniſh it at your pleaſure.

A made diſh of Parmizant.

TAke a Grater, and grate half a pound of Parmyzant, then grate as much Manchet, and mince ſome Tarragon together with Horſe Raddiſh; ſeaſon this with almoſt a handful of Carraway Comfits; put to it a little briſk Claret-wine to moiſten it over, then diſh it in a ſmall diſh, from the middle to the brim, in parcels as broad as your knife; garniſh it with Carraway Comfits, Horſe-Raddiſh and Tarragon; ſend it up the laſt diſh of your meſs or meſſes, with Muſtard and Sugar; becauſe at a Feaſt it is not common to ſend up a whole Cheeſe.

A Sallet of a dryed Neats-Tongue.

LEt your tongue be exceeding red, ſliced as thin as a groat, and about the ſame bigneſs, put to it a little Tarragon minced ſmall; toſs it with Oyl and Vinegar, and diſh it; put Bay-leaves round your meat, and ſtrow on Weſtphalie Bacon on the brims of your diſh.

I 2   *A*

A Sallet of Fennel.

TAke young Fennel, about a span long in the Spring, tye it up in bunches as you do Sparragrass; when your skillet boils, put in enough to make a dish; when it is boiled and drained, dish it up as you do Sparragrass, pour on Butter and Vinegar, and send it up.

A Sallet of green Pease.

WHen your green Pease appear, about a handful and half from the ground, cut off enough to boil for your Sallet, let your liquor boil before you put it in; when it is tender, pour it forth into your Cullender, let all the water be drained clean out of it into a dish, with some drawn butter; season it with salt, and hack it with your knife, and toss it together in the Butter, so dish it up. Thus may you do with Turnip or Raddish-tops, that are young.

A Sallet of boiled Spinnage.

BOil your Spinnage, as before you did your Pease, but in broth if you have it; you must boil it exceeding quick, else it will change colour; put it out into your Cullender, and drain it from the water; hack it with a knife, and put it in a Stewing-dish, with a handful or two of parboiled Currans, a little Vinegar, drawn Butter, Sugar, a grated Nutmeg and Salt, mingle it all together, and let it stand on a heap of coals, until it begins to boil up; have ready a matter of a dozen toasts, cut thin through the penny Mancher, put them into the bottom of your dish, and put your Sallet on them with a spoon in heaps, so scrape on Sugar.

I having before hinted of several Sallets in the Spring season, need not speak to you of the Summer, because there is none almost, but knows so many varieties of that season, and so much made use of by the vulgar, that

that it would take up not only a great deal of my time (which may be better spent) to recite them, but fill my volume, which I have intended for a better use: As for part of the Autumn and Winter, I have before prescribed you the Rules to pickle, I shall leave you to that, and so proceed to what is behind.

Rules how to roast Meats, with their several Sauces.

To roast a Hanch of Venison.

IF your Venison hath been seasoned, you must water it, and stick it with short sprigs of Rosemary; let your sauce be Claret-wine, a handful of grated bread, Cinamon, Ginger, Sugar, a little Vinegar, boil these up so thick as it may only run like batter, it ought to be sharp and sweet; dish up your meat on your sauce.

To roast a Jegget of Mutton.

YOur Jegget of Mutton is the leg and half the loyn cut to it, draw it with Lemmon-pill and Time, roast it soberly, save the gravy in a dish under it, put therein Claret-wine, two or three Onions cut in halves, two Anchovies, a spoonful or two of Elder-Vinegar, let this boil up together; then put in a few minced Capers and Sampier, with a Nutmeg sliced; this is sauce for your Jegget of Mutton, or for any other roast Mutton; you may add what gravy you have to it, and Oyster-liquor.

To roast a Shoulder of Mutton with Oysters.

YOur Oysters being parboiled, put to them some Parslee, Time and Wintersavoury minced small, with the yolks of six hard eggs minced, a handful of grated bread, three or four yolks of eggs, so mingle all together

together with your hands; yonr shoulder, or other joynt of Mutton being spitted, lay it upon the dresser, make holes with your knife, and put in your Oysters, with the herbs and ingredients after them; about twenty Oysters will be enough; take the rest of your quart, or as many as you have, put them into a deep dish, with some Claret-wine, two or three Onions in halves, a couple of minced Anchovies; put all this under your Mutton in the Pan, to save your gravy, and when your meat is ready, put your sauce upon a heap of coals; put to it the yolk of an Egg beaten, a grated Nutmeg, and drawn Butter; dish up your shoulder of Mutton, and pour out this thick Lear of Oysters all over it; strow on the yolks of hard Eggs minced, and garnish it with Lemmon.

To roast a Chine or Neck of Veal.

DRaw them with Time, and put them a roasting; then take some great Oysters, seasoned as afore in the shoulder, having some slices of Bacon cut four square, a little larger than the Oyster: then having two or three square rods, as big as your little finger, put thereon a piece of Bacon, and then an Oyster, so long, until you have spitted all your great Oysters: tye these rods on your Veal, when it is more than half roasted, then put under it a dish with a little Claret-wine, minced Time, and a grated Nutmeg: when your Oysters and Veal is ready, cut off your rods, and slip the Oysters and Bacon into the Wine, let them boil up thick, adding the yolk of an Egg, with a little drawn Butter, put it all over your Veal, whether Chine, Neck, Fillet, or Leg.

To roast a Breast of Veal.

RAise up the skin of your breast of Veal, almost to the end of it, towards the belly, and likewise almost to the place the shoulder was cut off; force it with

The whole Body of Cookery Diffected. 119

with a Saſſage force-meat, good ſtore of Lard in it: but ſeaſon it with Time, Winterſavoury and Parſlee minced, as alſo with Cloves, Mace, Nutmeg, Salt and ſmall Pepper: let it not be ſo hot in your mouth as your Saſſage-meat; mingle this in two Eggs, and farce it between the skin and Veal: and draw your breaſt all over with Time, and let your ſauce be Butter, Vinegar, a little minced Time, and Nutmeg grated: garniſh it with Lemmon, and ſend it up.

A Fillet or Leg of Veal Farced.

TAke a good quantity of Time and ſweet herbs, and make farcing, as is before ſhewn, and farce your Leg of Veal, and ſerve it up in farcing ſauce.

To roaſt Olives of Veal.

CUt out of a Fillet of Veal large Collops, hack them thin with the back of your chopping knife, then having minced your farcing herbs with Beef-ſuet, and ſeaſoned, then ſeaſon your Collops with a little Cloves, Mace, Nutmeg and Salt: mix them with the yolks of four or five Eggs, and ſpread them abroad, ſtrow on your farcing, and roul them up cloſe, ſo put them on a ſpit, and roaſt them; boil up the reſt of your farcing in a little White-wine and ſtrong Broth, with a little Sugar, then draw your Olives, pour on your ſauce, and garniſh it with Lemmons.

To roaſt a whole Lamb or Kid.

TRuſs your Lamb (or Kid) pricking the head backwards over the ſhoulder, tying it down; ſet it, and lard it with Bacon, and draw it with Time, and a little Lemmon-pill; then make a Pudding with a little grated bread, a handful of ſweet herbs, a handful of Beef-ſuet; put in about a handful of flower, and a little Saſſage or forced meat minced; ſeaſon it with Cloves, Mace,

I 4

Mace, Cinamon, Ginger, Nutmeg and Salt; make it up into a tender body, with two or three Eggs, and a little Cream; stuff it into the belly of your Lamb, or Kid; put some Caul of Veal or Lamb over it, so prick up the belly: Roast your Lamb or Kid, and when it is enough, serve it up with Venison sauce.

To make a Kid of a Pig, and a Pig to be roasted.

TAke a large Pig and flea him as carefully as you can, so that you make no holes in his skin; cut off the Ears and Nose to the skin, then truss up your Pig like a Kid, with the head over the shoulders, laid it over with Bacon (being set) and draw it with Time, so put it on your spit to roast; then take a piece of parboiled Veal, and as much Beef-suet, with a good handful of Spinnage, an handful of sweet herbs and Parslee, mince these together exceeding small, season it with beaten Pepper, Cloves, Mace, Cinamon, Ginger, Nutmeg, Sugar and Salt; then put to it two or three handfuls of Currans, and as much grated bread; mingle it with a little Cream, and about four Eggs, so that it may be as stiff as forced meat; then wash over your Pig on the inside with the yolks of Eggs, and sow up the holes in the skin; so force your Pig with this, and let him be in the same form as he was before he was flead; sow up his belly, and put him in a Tyn dish, with a ball of forced meat in his mouth, and a little butter in the bottom of the dish, so put him into the Oven, and bake him up crisp, and roast the other for a Kid; dish them up when they are ready, with a pretty sharp farcing sauce under them, and strow them over with the yolks of Eggs minced.

To roast a Calves-Head.

TAke a handsom white Calves-Head, cut a little hole in it, and take out his brains (after he is par=

The whole Body of Cookery Diſſected. 121

parboiled) then lard it with Bacon, and draw it with Lemmon and Time on both ſides, and put in ſavoury forced-meat inſtead of the brains, being ſtopt in with a leaf of Bacon lard; put it upon your ſpit and roaſt It; otherwiſe, for more ſafeneſs, you may break it (in a diſh) in the Oven; ſo may you well take it out when it is half baked, and prick on Artificial ears, being made with Bacon, waſhed over with the yolks of Eggs, and the whole head likewiſe; put it into the Oven again, and when it is enough, diſh it up, your Lear and ingredients being ready; which is Claret-wine, gravy, a pint or more of Oyſters, a couple of Anchovies, boiled up with two Onions, and a faggot of ſweet herbs, with a grated Nutmeg, ſome ſlices of Bacon, and Saſſages; ſo thicken it up with the yolk or two of an Egg, and a Ladle-full of drawn Butter; put your Oyſters over your Calves head, and your Bacon and Saſſages round about your meat, ſo garniſh it with Lemmon; you muſt take notice that the tongue muſt be taken out before the head is parboiled; and when it is boiled, to be uſed in the Lear.

To roaſt Leverets, and Rabbets.

CAſe your Leverets, but cut not off their hinder legs, nor their ears, but harl one leg through another, ſo likewiſe cut a hole through one ear, and put it through the other, ſo roaſt your Leveret; in the mean time, make your ſauce with a little Parſlee, Time, ſweet Margerum and Winterſavoury minced very ſmall, with the liver of the Hare parboiled, and the yolks of three or four hard Eggs, with a little Bacon and Beef-ſuet; boil this up well with ſtrong Broth and Vinegar; when it is boiled, add a grated Nutmeg, drawn Butter, and a little Sugar; put it into your diſh with your Leverets: The ſame way may you make your counterfeit Leverets of Rabbets; but you muſt

remem-

remember to lard them when they are parboiled, if defired.

To roaſt a Lambs Head.

TAke four or five white Lambs heads waſhed well, ſet and ſoak them in many waters; if you pleaſe you may take out the brains, and force them with a ſavoury forced meat, being drawn with Time Lemmon-Pill; then ſpit your Lambs Head and roaſt them; when they are half roaſted, put on your ſpit as many Lambs tongues larded on both ſides, and let them roaſt with three ſticks of Oyſters, and ſweet-breads amongſt them; then having ſome gravy drawn with Claret-wine, put to it three Onions, a faggot of ſweet Herbs, three Anchovies, and a grated Nutmeg; when your Lambs tongues are roaſted, cut them in the middle, and put them into your wine and gravy; then draw your Oyſters and ſweet-breads off your broaches, with your tongues; then diſh up your Lambs heads upon ſippets, well ſoaked in ſtrong Broth; lay the ſides of your tongues round your diſh by the heads, and put all over them your Oyſters and ſweet-breads, ſo pour on your Lear, with a Ladle-full of drawn Butter; you may boil theſe, and add forced meat balls, and Bacon fryed yellow and green; they will either ways ſerve for good handſom boiled meats, pallatable.

To roaſt Veniſon.

TAke the leg part of your Hanch of Veniſon, and cut it in thin Collops, hack it with your knife, as you do the like of Veal, then lard it very thick, with a ſmall larding pin; then take a handful of Parſlee and Spinnage, good ſtore of Time, a little Roſemary, Winterſavoury, and ſweet Margerum, mince it exceeding ſmall, with a little Beef-ſuet, ſo put it in the diſh with your Veniſon; put to it ſome beaten Cloves,

Cina-

The whole Body of Cookery Diffected. 123

Cinamon, Nutmeg, with a pretty quantity of Salt, the yolks of half a dozen Eggs, or more, mingle it up all together with your hands, then fpit your Collops on a fmall fpit, or long Broaches made with fticks; you muft fpit them fo by doubling of them, or bringing in the ends, that they may not hang too long, but equal; when they are all fpitted, put your herbs amongft them, and tye them together with a packthreed; as they roaft, put a difh under them with Claret-wine; when they are almoft done, take your difh and fet it on the coals, put grated bread, beaten Cinamon, Vinegar and Sugar to your wine, with a Ladle-full of drawn butter; fo difh up your Venifon, and pour on this Lear, being not too thick, all over it.

Several Sauces for your Fowl in general.

For Capons.

A Little fliced Manchet, foaked in fome ftrong Broth with Onions, boil it up in gravy, Nutmeg, Lemmon cut like Dice, and drawn Butter; put it under your Capons.

For Hens.

THe yolks of three or four hard Eggs minced, a little drawn Butter, a fpoonful or two of Claret-wine. gravy, and the juice of a Lemmon.

For Turkie.

TAke the fame prefcribed for your Capons.

For Chickens.

MInce a handful of Parflee very fmall, and wrap it up into a ball with a grated Nutmeg; put this into

into the bellies of your Chickens when you spit them, and take it forth when you draw them, adding some drawn Butter, put it to your Chickens; otherwise, the common way is drawn Butter, and Parslee minced.

A sauce for roast Pigeons.

THese are to be done as your Chickens before, only adding a little minced Bacon (to your Parslee) with a few Mints, so force their bellies when they are roasted, take out their forced meat, put it into a little Claret-wine, and add to them grated bread and drawn Butter; you may use your Vine-leaves roasted, and mince them in.

Sauce for Rabbets.

TAke Butter and minced Parslee, and roast it in their bellies; otherwise you may use the like sauce you have for Leverets.

Sauce for Pheasants, Heath-Poots, or Cocks of the wood.

TAke the same as was used for your Capons.

Sauce for Woodcocks.

YOu must for each Woodcock make a toast made of a Manchet; put to it gravy boiled up with an Onion, a little strong Broth, drawn Butter, and a little Nutmeg; pour this on your toasts, and dish up your Cocks.

Sauce for Quails.

TAke a little Claret-wine, gravy, Nutmeg, Vine-leaves minced, with a little drawn Butter.

Sauce

Sauce for Ducks, Wigeons, Teal, or Plover.

BOil some Onions sliced very thin in a little strong Broth, put thereto gravy and a little drawn Butter, but your general rule for wild-fowl, is gravy boiled up with an Onion, a little Nutmeg and Butter; and for water-fowl, sliced Onions boiled up in strong Broth, with gravy, and a little drawn Butter.

BOOK XII.

Treats how to boil or stew Fish to be eaten hot with Compositions.

How to boil, or stew Fish, to be eaten hot.

TO boil a Turbet, your Pan must be seasoned with good store of Salt, Wine-Vinegar, a faggot or two of sweet herbs, a sliced Lemmon, and Ginger; when it boils put in your Turbet, and let it boil for above half an hour; take for your Lear, or sauce, some Oysters, Pranes, or Shrimps stewed up in a little Whitewine, a little large Mace, thicken it with the yolk of an Egg, and put to it two or three Ladles of drawn Butter, dish up your Turbet on Sippets, lay it on a good heap of coals to dry up the water; pour on your Lear, with the Oysters all over the top; garnish it with fryed bay-leaves and Lemmon; strow on the brims of your dish beaten Ginger.

To boil a Pike.

YOu may split your Pike in the middle almost from the head, within a handful of the tail, so turn him round:

round: Let both sides be brought over the head; the one over one side, and the other over the other side, and let the tail be thrust into his mouth: or if you please, either you may cut off the head beyond the gills to the bodywards, that the head may stand upright in the dish, leaning forwards: Cut the tail likewise off sloping, allowing two handfuls of the fish with it. Then cut the body of the fish into two or three parts, and split it in the middle, your pan being well seasoned (as when you boiled the Turbet) boil it up very quick; then take a little White-wine, and a little Horse-Radish scrapt, a little Oyster liquor, a grated Nutmeg, and two or three Anchovies, beat them up with the yolk or two of an Egg, and put to it two or three Ladles of drawn Butter, or as much as will serve: so dish up your Pike, the head standing up before, and the tail behind, and the rest of the Pike between; otherwise, as it was truss'd round, so put on your Lear, with your Horse-Radish over the top; you may use shell-fish to it if you please, so stick it about with green Bay-leaves fried, or Rosemary fried in batter, and garnish your dish with Lemmon; Remember to season all your Lear with salt.

To stew a Carp.

TAke a living Carp, and knock him on the head; open him in the belly, take heed you break not the gall: pour in a little Vinegar, and wash out all the blood, stir it about with your hand, and preserve it: then have a Pan or Skillet on the fire, with so much White-wine as will almost cover your fish, put to it an Onion cut in the middle, a Clove or two of Garlick, a Race of Ginger sliced, a Nutmeg quartered, a faggot or two of sweet herbs, three or four Anchovies; your Carp being cut out (as the Pike before) and rubbed all over with salt, when your Wine boils put him in, cover him close, and let it stew up for about a quarter of

an

an hour, then put in the blood and Vinegar, with a little Butter, fo difh up your Carp upon your Soope, and pour on your Lear; let your fpawn, Milt and Revet be laid over the Carp; you may thicken this Lear if you will, but it is generally eaten as a broth; fo garnifh it with Lemmon, and ftrow the brims of the difh with beaten Ginger.

Another way to boil Carps.

KNock them on the head, and cut them up, preferve the fpawn and the Liver, fcale your Carps and wafh them, falt them well, and put Vinegar to them, and when your pan boils, and is well feafoned with falt, put in your Carps whole with the Vinegar and Salt they lie in, then diffolve two or three Anchovies in a fpoonfnl or two of Wine; mingle it with your drawn Butter, fo difh up your Carp, and fet them on Coals; lay on the Liver or Spawns, and lear them all over; fo garnifh it with fried Bay-leaves, and Lemmon.

To ftew a difh of Flounders.

TAke your Flounders being drawn and wafhed, and fcorch them on the white fide, and lay them in a deep difh, put to it a little White-wine, a couple of Onions cut in halves, a bunch of fweet herbs, a race of Ginger fliced, a little whole Pepper, a handful of Oyfters minced, and as much falt as will feafon it; cover thefe clofe, and ftew them up with as much fpeed as may be, then difh them up on Sippets, and take fo much of the bottom of your Lear as will ferve you, thicken it with the yolk of an Egg, and put drawn butter to it, and pour it over your Flounders; fo garnifh it with Lemmon, and ftrow on the brims of your difh beaten Ginger.

Another

Another way.

WHen you have fcorcht them, and laid them in your deep difh, put about a pint of fweet Sallet Oyl, half a pint of White-wine, and the like of Vinegar to them, with two Races of Ginger fliced, fome whole Cloves and Mace, a fliced Nutmeg, and a faggot or two of fweet herbs, with a couple of Onions cut; ftew all thefe together, fo difh up your Flounders on Sippets, then take a handful of minced Parflee parboiled green, and throw it into your Lear; let it boil two or three Walms, and pour it over your Flounders, fo garnifh it with Lemmon and green Parflee minced.

To boil Perches.

LEt your Liquor boil, and your Pan be feafoned, as aforefaid, boil them up very quick, then blanch them on both fides, and difh them upon Sippets; then take a little White-wine, gravy, and vinegar, with a grated Nutmeg, and a handful of Oyfters cut in funder; put this all over yonr fifh, and let it be ready to boil in the difh you fend it up in, fo fhake it together, and pour drawn butter all over it; garnifh it with Barberries and Lemmons.

How to make a Bisk of Fifh.

TAke a very good Carp, feal him, take out all the bones, leave nothing but the fifh, mince it or cut it with your knife in pieces, then charge a Pipkin with White-wine, and a little Vinegar, an Onion, a faggot of fweet herbs, fome Ginger, a fliced Nutmeg, three Anchovies: then charge another Pipkin with Pranes, Shrimps, Crafifh, and fliced Lobfter; then charge a third Pipkin with all manner of Shell-fifh that you have, put of the fame Lear, and feafoning to thefe as was in the firft Pipkin: Let your firft Pipkin boil three or

four

The whole Body of Cookery Diffected. 129

four walms, and put in your Carp as it boyls, with a pint of Oyſters cut in ſunder; ſeaſon it with ſalt, beat (when 'tis done) a yolk of an egg to thicken it, and draw butter; let it boyl very haſtily for the time, elſe it will eat flaſhy, and not criſp, thicken up your other Pipkins with drawn butter, and make them ready, then you muſt have in readineſs about five Collerd Sowls, indored over with eggs, and baked in an Oven with a good many balls of forced meat of fiſh, both yellow and green; you may alſo bake up in the ſame thing the Carps head, and four heads of other fiſhes; have likewiſe in readineſs Smelts and Gudgeons fryed Criſp, and Sowls cut in pieces, and Whitings fryeed whole: then have four ſmall Jacks boyled, and four Trouts, or ſuch like fiſh: let your great diſh be on the coals with a ſoop of light ſipets, ſtrow it all over with beaten Nutmeg, and Ginger; then diſh up your great collerd Sowl, as a ſtandard in the middle of your diſh; and your ſtiff ſmelts as ſupporters round about it; then diſh up your four Pikes, oppoſite one to another, their tails to the ſtandard-wards, and their heads to the brims of the diſh: diſh the other four oppoſite to them, ſo that there be eight partitions in the diſh left; fill two of them with your Carp and Oyſters aforeſaid, two of them with fryed Whitings, and the other four with Pranes, Shrimps, Cockles, and Perriwinckles, then you may diſpoſe of your other four Coller'd Sowls croſs wayes, about the ſtandard, in the four partions, between the fiſh; then garniſh on all the fiſh that you fryed, in vacant places, not hiding your ſmall fiſh i But if they are pieces of fryed Sowls or Plaice, you may lay them over your bigger fiſh, then take ſome of your former Lear and Oyſter Liquor, adding more Wine if you want Lear; and the meat in the Shell of a Crab or two: boyl theſe up with a beaten Nutmeg and Anchovie, adding drawn butter, and let

K your

your Lear be as thick, or thicker than it; and when it is ready to boyl, take your Ladle, and pour it all over the fish in your Bisk, (except the Carp;) so take your sliced Lobster, Crafish, and Oysters fryed in Batter, and garnish it every where, according to your own discretion; also take your forced meat out of the Oven, shake it with butter, and do the like as before: garnish round the sides of your dish with the heads of your fish, or how you please; then take the Carps head which was baked with the forced meat, and fasten it on the top of the standard in the middle, and the other four heads upon the other four Sowls: take five hranches of Rosemary, and put through their mouths, and fasten it to the Collers, prick Bay leaves round the Collers, and sides of your forced meat. Although I have prescribed these kind of fishes, yet you may make use of such fish as the season will afford, or you can get.

To dress a Codds head the best way.

Cut off your Coods head beyond the Gills, that you may have part of the body with it, boyl it in water and salt, and having ready about a quart of Cockels, with the meat out of the shell of a Crab or two, put these in a pipkin with about a quarter of a pint of white-wine, a bunch of sweet herbs, an Onion or two, with a little large Mace, and a grated Nutmeg; add to it a little Oyster Liquor, set it on the fire, and when it boyls, and the liquor in it is wasted, put to it two or three Ladles of drawn butter, or as much as will serve; then dish up your Codds head on sippets, and put it on a good heap of coals to dry up the water; then cut the tripe of your Codd, as you cut pallats; also cut the pease, or spawn in thin slices, and the Liver in pieces; take likewise the Gill and pick out the bones, and cut it as you did the other; dish up your spawn or pease round about your

your Codds head, and some on the top, and put all over it your Tripe- Gill, and Liver, then take a ladle, and pour your lear over it, with a little drawn butter on that, and stick all your gill bone with Oysters fryed in batter, and stick them on the pease of the fish, and all over the head where they will enter; so garnish it over with the same Oysters, grate on a Nutmeg and send it smoaking up: take notice that the pease of your fish will ask more boyling than the head, if it be a great one: also remember that you blanch off all the skin of your Codds head, when you dish it, and garnish it with Lemmon and fryed bay leaves.

To make an Olive of Fish

TO this you may have all manner of fish, (that are not flat) as Carps, Pikes, Mullets, Base, Rotchets, Gurnets, Trouts, oa Salmon-peel, &c. being all dress'd and wash'd: take the firmest and biggest for boyling, and the other for frying and forcing; when your Pan is seasoned, and your fish boiled off quick, according to the time that each takes its boyling; as also your other fish being all ready, dish on your sippets, some great fish turned round in the middle of your Charger else a Coller of Salmon baked in an Oven, with the heads of four fishes on the top of it; then dish your boyled fish round about, and your fryed fish between them, your Smelts and Gudgeons round towards the brims of the dish: if you have forced meat of fish made in little balls you may garnish that between the boyled and the fryed; then having your Oysters, Cockles, Perriwinckles; Pranes, Crafish, or sliced Lobster, or any of these ready in your Lear of thick butter, Lear your fish therewithall over; stick your Coller with fryed bay leaves at the heads, and round the dish: so garnish it with Lemmon, grate on a Nutmeg, and send it up smoaking.

ing. I have heard of Cooks heaping up an Olue of fish on the top of one another, but that way is neither Honourable or Profitable; the biggest Fish here that I advise you to lay on the other, are only Smelts, Gudgeons or pieces of Sowls, or Flounders, fryed up very crisp and brown; and all manner of shell-fish, as is shewn.

To boyl Mullet or Base to be eaten hot.

YOu must scal your Mullets or Base, and wash them, saving their Livers or Tripes, Rows, or Spawns; Boyl them up in Water, Salt, Vinegar, Wine, faggots of sweet herbs, sliced Lemmon, and two or three whole Onions, your lear must be drawn butter, large mace, whole Nutmeg cut in quarters, and two or three Anchovies dissolved in the wine you drew your butter withal; so dish up your fish, pour on your lear, (you must always remember to season all your lear with salt to your Pallat.) and garnish it with fryed Oysters and Bay-leaves; season your liquor after this manner for the boyling of most of your fish.

To stew or make broth, with Whitings or Smelts.

PUt on the coals in a deep dish half Wine and half water, put to it a race of Ginger sliced, a little large mace, a Nutmeg quartered, and two or three faggots of sweet herbs with Parslee, adding as much salt as will season it; let this all boyl up together half a dozen Walms; then put in your fish orderly, as they are to lye in your dish, when you send them up, and let them boyl hastily, with a little butter put into them; less than a dozen walms is sufficient for them: when they are enough, pour all the liquor into a pipkin, and set it on the fire again with your spice and sweet herbs that were in it; then mince a handful of parslee small, and a little fennel, and time, and let it boyl with the fish-broth:

broth: then wash out with Vinegar the meat of a shell or two of Crabs, with the Carkass of a Lobster, the yolks of two or three eggs, a ladle of drawn butter, beat all this together with some of the said liquor, and stir it into the pipkin until it thickens, shift out your Smelts, or Whitings, on sippets as you will send them up, and pour on your lear, as it comes from the fire; this is an excellent broth and good for a weak stomach.

How to stew or boyl Eeles.

YOu may Coller np one of the biggest of your Eeles, and boyl him up, and the other being flead, cut in pieces twice as long as your finger, stew them up with half white-wine, and half water, with an Onion or two, and some faggots of sweet herbs, large Mace, and whole Pepper: when they are half stewed put to them a pint of Oysters with a little minced parslee and Time; when they are ready, put to them drawn butter, and vinegar, if your lear be not thick, you must add the yolk or two of an egg; dish up your Collered Eel in the middle, and your pieces round about it to the dish brim, and your Oysters, and lear over the whole; you may garnish it with brown pieces of fryed fish about the breadth of a Plaice.

Another way.

CUt youn Eeles as aforesaid, and stew them up; when they are above half done, take a spoonful or two of Ale yest beaten up with a little vinegar, and put therein, with a greater quantity of parslee and sweet herbs than was in the last, so dish them up, served to the Table in their broth, adding salt.

To dress a dish of smalls Jacks.

CUt off the heads of them, put them into balls of forced meat made of fish, so that the heads may stand ſt and upright, or looking forwards; indore them over with yolks of eggs, and put them into an Oven a baking then cut your Jacks in pieces, ſtew them up in a diſh, with a little whitewine, water, ſalt, vinegar, ſweet herbs, two or three Anchovies, Mace; ſliced Ginger, and Nutmeg; when this boyls up in your deep diſh, put in your Pike and ſome ſmall forced meat balls of fiſh, both green, yellow, and white; let them boyl, then turn the other ſide with a knife, let them boyl again, then take out your forced heads, and ſet them round in the diſh; take out your Jacks with your ſlice, and place them in the beſt manner; between and about them, all over the diſh, put Smelts fryed ſtiff in the mouths of your Jacks, and put your forced meats round about them; you may if you pleaſe add fryed fiſh, Oyſters, or others.

To ſtew a diſh of Breams.

YOur Breams being dreſs'd, waſh'd, dried well, ſcorcht, buttered and ſalted over, put them upon your Gridiron, being very hot, (over charcoals) when they are pretty brown on both ſides, but not burnt, put them into a great diſh boyling on the fire, with a little Claret wine, half a pint of gravy, two or three Onions, as many Anchovies, with a little minced Time, and a pint of Oyſters; put to this ſome drawn butter, and a grated Nutmeg; ſee that your lear be pretty thick, then diſh up your Bream with your Oyſters and lear on it, and ſtrow it over with the yolks of eggs: but if there be any Roman Catholicks, or others, whoſe conſcience ſcruples to eat of fleſh on faſting dayes, you may ſtew it up after another manner; which is, take the Breams broiled as aforeſaid, with a little Claret wine, Vinegar, large Mace, ſweet herbs, and Anchovies, put to this about a pint of ſweet Sallet Oyl, then put in your fiſh, and let it ſtew together with ſome Oyſters, if you pleaſe;

The whole Body of Cookery Diſſected. 135

pleaſe; diſh up your fiſh on ſippets, and pour your lear thereon: you may do the like by divers ſorts of fiſh.

BOOK XIII.

Containing how to Bake, Fry, Broyl, Roſt, and Frigacy certain ſorts of Fiſh.

How to make Sawce or Lear without Butter, or thickning with Eggs.

YOu muſt clarifie your Oyl to take away the taſt and ſtrength of it; then take part thereof, or ſo much as you uſe, for your fiſh, and when its hot in your pan, put in a handful of ſliced Onions, and let them fry, then put in as much Whitewine and Vinegar as your oyl contains, with ſome large mace, a quartered Nutmeg, ſliced Ginger, Oyſter liquor, and minced Oyſters, three or four Anchovies, boyl this together; you may thicken it with the meat, or carkaſs of a Lobſter, and Crab, otherwiſe with the Raſping of ſtale grated bread, diſh up your fiſh when they are broyled, fryed, or boyled, and lear them over with the ſame: to boyl fiſh you may add a handful of parſlee and ſweet herbs minced to be boyled up in your lear.

To fry Fiſh, and all manner of Garniſhing with Oyl.

YOu muſt let your Oyl boyl in your Pan, until it hath done bubling; your fiſh being dryed and flowred, put them in the Pan, and fry them away criſp, as before, in clarified butter: ſo muſt you fry your Oyſters in batter, or other ſhell fiſh, and when you

K 4   have

have done frying your fish, fry up your garnishing, as Bay leaves, Alexander leaves, young Fennel, Parflee, Rosemary, and toasts of stale bread.

Another way, how to thicken your lear for fish without eggs.

TAke the deafe of a Codd, or the spawn of Salmon, and the Livers withal, or else the Livers of Rea, Skeate or Thornback: let them all be well boyled, beat them all in a Morter together, with so much of the peafe as you intend to ufe; beat this into your aforesaid lear of Oyl and Wine; this is a wholesom and good way for dressing fish, and those which are used to it desire it more than without butter.

To stew a dish of Trouts.

FIrst let your pan be very hot with clarified butter, and give them a sudden brown, with what violence you can: have a stewing dish ready on the fire with gravy, Oyster liquor, a little Claret wine, and Vinegar; put your fryed fish therein, (you must note they were to be split in half before frying) fry three or four sliced Onions, and when they are brown, put them to your fish, with a handful of parflee fryed green, a sliced Nutmeg, two or three Anchovies, and let it just boyl up together; then dish up your Trout in your dish upon sippets; whilst your Lear is boyling on the fire, if it be not thick enough, you may add an egg, drawn butter, and some of the butter the Onions and Parflee was fryed in. But your better way for crispness and sight of yuor fish is to fry your split fish, as Trout, Salmon Peal, and Salmon, very crisp and brown: dish it up with the inside uppermost: so pour on your aforesaid Lear, and strow all over it parflee fryed green.

To

To boyl and serve a whole Salmon.

WHen you have drawn and washt out your Salmon, you must run your penknife on both sides towards the back, in and out, in Scollops, from the head to the tail, then take a string and truss up the head to the tail; and put him upon your falfe bottom: your liquor boyling in a deep pan, being highly seasoned, especially with falt and vinegar, put in your Salmon, and let it boyl something more than an hour, or until you think it is enough; then take it up, and dish it in your Charger on Sippets; and having your fryed Collops of Salmon, very thin, garnish it all about, and on the top of your Salmon; you must have ready fryed some toasts picked at both ends; stick them all full with Oysters fryed in Batter, and prick the other end of the toasts, upon the back and upper side of the Salmon, then lear it all over with drawn butter, and if you please a little Vinegar; so prick on and garnish it with bay leaves.

To Roast a Pike.

YOu must lard him very well (being salted) all over with Pickle Herring, and season him with falt, a little beaten Pepper, Nutmeg, and some minced Time: if you have two, you may put one on the one side the spit, and the other on the other side; with two or three sticks on each side your Pikes, to splinter them together and bind them over with packthred, and let them roast, sometimes letting the back stand towards the fire, and sometimes the sides, not turning them as you do flesh, unless you see occasion to keep them from burning; then dissolve half a dozen Anchovies in a little Butter, and paste them therewith; after they are half roasted, put down two sticks of Oysters, betwixt each Oyster a bay leaf; let there be a dish under them to

catch

catcht that which they are basted withal, with a little Claret wine, Oyster liquor, minced time, and a grated Nutmeg; when your Oysters are ready, draw them into your dish, taking out the bay leaves, and put in an Onion cut in halves, and let them boyl on the fire, then take up your spit, and cut your strings, that you may lay the brown side of your Pike upwards, (or if you can his back) then put a ladle of drawn butter to your lear and oysters, and pour it over your Pikes, and garnish it all over with Lemmons : your more safe way, is, to order it after the same manner aforesaid, to put him in a dish, and bake him in an Oven; and the same form you put him in, you may shift him into your dish you send him up in, and so lear him as before, and garnish him with fryed bay leaves.

To roast Eeles.

WHen they are flead, cut them to pieces, about four inches long, dry them, and put them into a dish; mince a little Time, two Onions, a piece of Lemmon Pill, a little Pepper beaten small, Nutmeg, Mace and Salt, It being all exceeding small, strow it on your Eeles with the yolks of two or three eggs, so mingle in the seasoning all together with your hands: then having a small spit, (otherwise take a couple of square sticks made for that purpose) spit through your Eel cross wayes, and put a Bay leaf between every piece of Eel, tying your sticks on a spit, let them be roast; you need not turn them constantly, but let them stand until they hiss, or are brown, so do them on the other side; and put the dish underneath (which the Eel was in with the seasoning) to save the gravie, baste it over with drawn Butter, put a little Claret wine, minced Oysters, a grated Nutmeg, and an Onion, with some drawn butter; give it one boil up, and dish up your Eel with your lear over it.

To

To roaſt Porpus.

TAke a Joll of Porpus, ſtick it with Sage and Roſemary all over, and lard it very thick with the back of Pickle herring, then ſplit it if it be too big; ſplit it, ſo faſten it on your ſpit with tape, baſte it over with the yolk of an egg: and whilſt it is moiſt, ſtraw on minced Onions and Time together; boyl three or four Onions ſliced thin in a little Claret wine, and put in two or three Anchovies, and beaten Pepper; you muſt keep your Porpus baſted with butter; and when it is roaſted and brown enough; then put a ſpoonful or two of muſtard and vinegar to your aforeſaid ſawce, as it boyls, and ſhake it with a ladle of drawn butter; ſo diſh up your Porpus, and pour on your Lear; forget not to ſeaſon it with ſalt, before you put it to the fire.

To roaſt a Carp.

TAke a great live Carp, and when it is ſcaled and drawn, make a little hole in the belly, and dry up all the blood, both within and without, then take two handfuls of your aforeſaid Chewit meat, adding to it a handful of grated bread, a little cream, the yolks of three eggs, with the white of one, put to it one handful of Sugar, make it into a pretty ſtiff body, and force your Carps belly full of the ſaid meat, and put it upon a ſpit: otherwiſe you may bake it in an Oven, upon two or three croſs ſticks in a braſs diſh; when it hath been in the Oven a while, turn it, and let the gravy run into the diſh, when its enough, diſh it on ſippets, and add to the gravie of the Pike, a little Oyſter liquor, and drawn butter; let your lear be thick: ſo garniſh your Pike with ſmall fiſh fryed, and ſhell fiſh, ſo pour on your Lear.

To

To Roast a Salmon whole.

Take a Salmon and draw it at the gills, scale, wash and dry it; then lard it all over with pickle Herring, or a fat salted Eele; take two or three handfuls of parboiled Oysters, season them with grated bread, a handful of sweet herbs, four or five hard eggs, an Onion, minced all together, add to it Cloves, Mace, Ginger, Nutmeg, Pepper and Salt, mingle these together, and put them into the belly of the Salmon, at the gills; then lay them in an earthen pan, fit for him to lie in, on sticks in the Oven; put therein a little Clarret-wine, baste over your Salmon well with butter, before you put him in; and when it is enough, draw it, and thicken your Lear with your gravy that comes out with him, and some of the spawn of the Salmon boiled and beaten, or with the meat of a Crab or Lobster, so pour on your Lear, with drawn Butter on the top, and stick it all over with toasts, and Bay-leaves fryed: you may open his belly and take forth the Oysters, and garnish about him also; your safest way to keep him from breaking; is to turn him round in a dish and bake him.

How to Spitchoock an Eele.

Take a fair Eele, and split him in the back close to the bone, from the head to the tail, but not through the belly; scour him well with Salt, and wash him, lay him up, and dry him, and cut the bone through all along the back, that it may have no strength to double up the Eele, when it is on the Gridiron; then cut him (if he be large) in six pieces; wash him over in the inside whth Butter, and sprinkle on Salt, and a little minced Time; your Gridiron being very hot upon the coales, lay him on with the inside downwards, and when he is broyled on that side, turn him, and let him broil on the skinny side very well; so dish him up, and pour all over

The whole Body of Cockery Diſſected. 141

over him drawn Butter, Vinegar, and a grated Nutmeg, garniſh him round with Bay-leaves.

There is ſome fiſh which is hard to broil, that I have often ſeen to drop through the Gridion, done by them who thought ſcorn to be taught; therefore I ſhall give ſome general rules for thh broiling of theſe, as Whitings, Haddocks, young Codds, Herrings, or Makeril, *&c.*

For Boylnig.

IN the firſt place be ſure your Gridiron be exceeding clean; Secondly, let it be exceeding hot, and waſh the bars with butter; then let your moſt rottenſt fiſh be very dry, waſhed over with Butter, and extreamly ſalted over that; then put the back of your fiſh to the fire-ward, upon the ſalted ſide, until your Gridiron be full; then butter them over the upper ſide, and ſtrow them well with Salt, then turn them (when they are brown enough on the other ſide) and put them over a hot fire again: the fire being thus hot, and ſo ſalted, it will bind the fiſh together, ſo that it will not break; when you take them up, you may put a plate on the top of them, and turn them thereon, as you turn a Tanzie

To broyl Flownders or Plaice.

You muſt ſcorch them over on both ſides, and broil them as aforeſaid, and let your Lear be Butter and Vinegar, or you may take a ricker if you pleaſe) you may ſplit Salmon Peels, or Trouts, and obſerve this way of broiling; if you ſend the out ſide upward, it will ſeem two fiſhes for one; if the other ſide upmoſt, it will ſhew handſom and yellow; ſo with a ladleful of drawn Butter, a little Vinegar and Nutmeg, is a lear for the ſaid fiſh; ſtrow in all over with Parſlee fryed
green;

green; all thefe fryed and broyled fifh, do many times help forth, for want of other difhes in the fecond courfe; therefore have I made mention of them to that purpofe, by which rules you may be enabled to underftand the nature, and how to order moft kinds of fifh.

How to fry a difh of Maids.

FIrft skin them, then half boyl them in water and falt, let your water boyl very fierce when pou put them in, then take them forth and dry them very well, and flower them; then make a batter of about a dozen yolks of eggs, (with three whites amongft them) a fpoonful of flower, a little Nutmeg, Ginger and Salt; then take a handful of Parflee boyled green and minced very fmall, beat all thefe together with a little Sack, let it be a thick batter; fet on your pan with clarified Butter, dip your Maides in your batter, and when your pan is hot, put them in, and fry them as crifp and brown an you can (do not over charge your pan) fo done, difh them up, and let their Lear be Butter, Vinegar, Nutmeg, beaten together, with the livers of the faid fifh, ftrow them all over with Parflee fryed green.

To fry a difh of Ling for firft courfe.

WHen you boyl Ling for dinner, you muft fave a Joll, and at night when it is cold and congealed together, you may cut it out in Collops as broad as your thumb or finger, then having your yolks of eggs beaten, and your pan hot with clarified ftuff, dip your Ling in your eggs, and charge your pan; (otherwife flower your Ling well, and fry it without eggs) then difh up your Ling, and having about a dozen potched eggs, butter your Ling all over with drawn butter, and lay on your potched eggs upon your Ling, fo cover it and fend it hot to the Table; this may as well be done with Oyl, to them which love it.

The whole Body of Cookery Diſſected. 143

How to Frigacy or Butter Crabs or Lobſtors.

TAke out all the meat in the ſhells, and break the Claws of your Lobſter, and take out the meat, mince it, or ſlice it, and put it into the other; add to it a ſpoonful or two of Claret-wine, a little Fennel minced, and a grated Nutmeg; let it boyl up, then put in a little drawn Butter, a little Vinegar, and the yolk of an egg, if it be not thick enough; if there are Lobſters, you may diſh them up with ſippets round in ſaucers, on a plate garniſh them with Fennel and Bay leaves; or you may diſh them in a diſh with ſippets: if they are Crabs, put it in the ſhell it was taken out, and garniſh it round with their Fins, ſtick them with toaſts, and to them only ſhould you add a little Cinamon and Ginger beaten in the buttering.

How to Frigacy Shrimps, Perriwinkles, Pranes, Crawfiſh, &c.

TO theſe you muſt put a little Claret wine, an Onion or two cut in pieces, a couple or two of Anchovies, and a faggot of ſweet-herbs; ſtew them or any one of them up together with a little Ginger and Nutmeg; toſs them up with the yolk of an egg, a little Vinegar and drawn butter; you may put them into little Coffins, like Hearts or Diamonds, to garniſh a Bisk or Olue; otherwiſe to be diſhed upon ſippets, for a ſecond courſe diſh.

A Phraiſe of Cockles.

TAke your Cockles, boyl them, and pick them out of the ſhells, waſh them clean from gravel, then break a dozen eggs, with a little Nutmeg, Cinamon and Ginger, and put your Cockles therein, and beat them together with a handful of grated bread, and a quarter of a pint of Cream, then put Butter into your Frying-pan,

pan, and let it be hot, as for eggs, and put in the Phraife; fupply it with Butter in the fide of the pan, and let the thin of the eggs run ftill into the middle, till it moves round, and when it is fryed on that fide, butter your plate, and turn it, and put it into your pan again, and fry the other fide brown; then take it forth and difh it, and fcruife on the juice of Lemmons, and ftrow on Ginger and Cinamon, and fend it up; you may green it with the juice of Spinnage, and cut it out into quarters, and garnifh your fifh of either fort; thus may you fry Pranes, Perriwinkles, or other fhell fifh.

How to broyl Oyfters.

SEt your great Oyfters, then take a little minced Time, grated Nutmeg, and grated bread, and a little Salt, put this to your Oyfters, then get fome of the largeft bottom fhells, and place them on your Gridiron, and put two or three Oyfters in each fhell; then put fome Butter to them, and let them boyl on the fire, till the lower fide is brown, fupplying it always with melted Butter; when they are brown to your mind, then feed them with white-wine and fome of their own liquor, with a little grated bread, Nutmeg and minced Time, fo let it boil up again; then add fome drawn Butter to thicken them, and difh them on a difh and plate; but if you have Scollups fhells, it is the beft way to broyl them in.

To Broyl Scollups.

FIrft boil your Scollups, then take them out of the fhells and wafh them, then flice them, and feafon them with Nutmeg, and Ginger, and Cinamon, put them into the bottom of your fhells again, with a little Butter, white-wine and Vinegar, and grated bread; let them be broiled on both fides: if they are fharp, they ought to have a little Sugar added to them: for your

matter

matter of the fish is sweet; but you may do them another way with Oyster liquor and gravy, and Anchovies, minced Onion and Time, with the juice of a Lemmon in them. I have done them both ways, but the sweet and sharp is the more natural way.

How to bake certain Fish.

To bake a Carp two ways.

SCald your Carp, and season him with a little Pepper, Cloves, Mace, Ginger and Salt; your Coffin being made fit for him; (if you have two, you must make your Coffin for one to turn one way, and the other another way) put therein two or three Onions cut in halves, a handful or two of Oysters, seasoned with Time, being added to the aforementioned spices; then put in the yolks of three or four hard Eggs with Butter thereon, and close up your Pie; when it is baked, let your Lear be drawn butter and a little Gravy drawn from the meat with Claret-wine, beaten up with the yolk of an Egg; put it in at the funnel of your Pie, shake it together, and so dish it up; if you cut it up, you may take out the Onions; some do bake them sweet, being thus seasoned with Raisons and Currans, Dates and Pruens, with a sweet and sharp Lear with Butter, Vinegar, Sugar, and the yolks of two or three eggs beaten.

To make an Eele Pie.

YOur Eeles must be flead, washed, and cut in pieces as long as your finger: put to them a handful of sweet herbs, Parflee minced with an Onion; season them with Pepper, Salt, Cloves, Mace and Nutmeg; and having your Coffin ready made, of good hot Butter Paste, put all over them a handful or two of Currans, and a Lemmon cut in flices, then put on Butter, and clofe your Pye; when it is baked, add to it a Lear made with a little Vinegar and White-wine, beaten up with the yolks of a couple of eggs, and a little drawn Butter, put this in at the funnel of your Pye, and fhake it together upon your Plate.

To bake a Turbet.

YOur Turbet being wafhed and drawn, and the fins barbed round about, fcorch him on both fides, feafon him very well with fweet herbs, Cloves, Mace, Nutmeg, Pepper and Salt on the under fide; feafon him in the fcorches (in the upper fide) only with Cloves, Mace, Nutmeg, and Salt; then make your Coffin in the manner and form of a Turbet; dry him in your Oven, then take him forth, and wafh him in the infide with the yolks of eggs, and ftrow the bottom over with a minced Onion, and half a dozen Anchovies, then put in your Turbet, with the backfide downward; and having fome fmall forced-meat balls of fifh, put round about by the fides, and put Oyfters and the refufe and liver all over him on the top, and the yolks of fix hard eggs, with good ftore of Butter, and put him in the Oven; fee that you fupply him with Butter in the baking; let the bottom of your Oven be very hot, that he may boyl up to the top; when he is baked, make your Lear with White Wine, Vinegar, Oyfter liquor; let it be hot, and beat it up with the yolks of three or four eggs, and put it to your Turbet, fhaking it together that it mingle with your Butter; put it in the Oven again for a little while, and then difh it up; garnifh it on the top with fryed Oyfters, and ftick it all over with toafts, putting drawn Butter on the top; having a Cut dryed in on a bottom of a difh, lay it on your Pie, and fend it up.

The whole Body of Cookery Diffected.

To bake a Salmon Pie to be eaten Hot.

TAke the tayl of a whole Salmon, cut off by the fins, so that you spoyl not the Joll; then cut it in Collops quite through both sides, Chine and all, until you have cut it down to the Tail, then Butter your Collops over and Salt them, and half broyl them on both sides on a hot Gridiron; then take them off, and having a Coffin ready, set and dryed in an Oven, that may be big enough to contain the said Collop: and having a handful of sweet Herbs, a little Fennel, an Onyon, with a handful of Oysters, all minced exceeding small, take out your dryed Coffin, wash the bottom thereof with the yolks of eggs, and see that it may not run; then take a handful of the said herbs (being seasoned with Cloves, Mace, Ginger, Nutmeg, Peper and Salt) and strow them over the bottom of your Coffin; then lay in your greatest Collops first, and strow them over with your sweet herbs and seasoning, and prick on seasoned Oysters all over, with sliced Lemmon: then lay on your smallest pieces on them, and do by them as before to the greater; so put on butter, and put it into the Oven, that it may boyl; then having your Lear, (with a little Wine, Oyster liquor beaten in with the yolk of an Egg) also ready to boyl, put it into your Pie, and let it only boyl up in the Oven: this done, take it out, and shake it together with a little drawn Butter, strow it over with the yolks of hard Eggs minced small, and send it up with a Cut thereon.

To bake a Joll of Ling in a Pie.

LEt your Ling be almost boyled, then season it with Pepper only (the skin being first taken off) strow the bottom of your Coffin with an Onion or two minced small, close your Pie and bake it: then take the yolks and whites of about a dozen Eggs, not boyled altogether

together hard, mince them small with your knife, and put them into drawn Butter, toss them together, draw your Pie, and pour in this Lear of Eggs all over, and shake it together: so put on your lid, and dish your Pie.

Another way.

SEason it, and put it into the Coffin, as aforesaid, lay on sliced Ginger and large Mace, close it up, and put a funnel thereon, put it in the Oven until the sides and bottom be hardened, then draw it, and fill it with Oyl, so that it may boyl to the top of the Ling; then put it in again, and let it remain until it is baked: draw it and cut it up: beat three or four spoonfuls of Mustard, with some of the said Oyl, or others, and pour therein, shaking your Pie, that it may mingle altogether.

To bake a Pike in a Coffin.

WHen he is washed and drawn, lard him with pickle Herring, mince a good handful of sweet herbs one Onion, and a handful of Oysters, with a little Lemmon pill: put to them some Pepper, Salt, Cloves, Mace, Nutmeg: wash over your Pike with the yolks of Eggs, both the inside and outside, and season him with the forementioned minced Ingredients: (being before scorched on both sides) then having your Coffin ready (in the form of a Pike) lay him in, with a little forced meats round about him, and scraped Horse Raddish, with a handful or two of Grapes all over him, put on Butter and close him: when he is baked, lear him with White wine, Vinegar, drawn Butter, and the yolk of an Egg: put it in, shake them together, and let it stand a little while in the Oven. If you would have him richly baked, you may add Oysters and Shell-fish, yolks of hard Eggs, Lemmon, Anchovies and gravie to your Lear.

To

To bake a Lump in a Coffin.

YOu muſt flea him, and cut all the fiſh from the bones in pieces about the bigneſs of your two fingers, ſeaſon it with minced Time, ſweet herbs, Cloves, Mace, Ginger, Salt and a little Pepper, with a handful of grated bread: your Coffin being made, ſtrow in the bottom thereof one handful of the ſeaſoning, and put therein your Collops of Fiſh: and put on them pieces of Marrow, Oyſters, the yolks of hard Eggs cut in halves, with ſliced Lemmon; lay on the top of that more ſeaſoning, lay over the reſt of your fiſh, and ſupply them with the Ingredients (in order before mentioned, with a few ſmall balls of forced Fiſh upon the top of them, put on butter enough to bake it, and cloſe up your Pie, and put it into the Oven, and when it is baked, put in a Lear of Whitewine, Oyſter liquor, drawn butter, and the yolk or two of an Egg: cut up your Pie, or put it in at the funnel, and ſhake it about, ſo ſerve it up.

To bake Flounders or Plaice.

WHen they are drawn and waſhed, fin them and ſcorch them, feaſon them with Pepper, Salt, Mace and Nutmeg, mince an Onion and ſtrow in the bottom of your Coffin, then put in your Plaice, lay on them ſome Lobſter cut in pieces, the yolks of hard eggs, and a handful of Grapes if you have any, then put on Butter, cloſe your Pie, put him into the Oven and bake him; let your Lear be a little White-wine Vinegar, boyled Parſlee minced ſmall, the Carkaſe of a Lobſter, drawn Butter, and the yolk of an Egg, all which put into your Pie when it is baked, and ſhake it together, and ſerve it up.

To bake an Oyster Pie.

TAke a good handful of Parflee, Time, VVinterfavoury, an Onion or two, mince them very fmall, put them to a little grated Bread, Cloves, Mace, Nutmeg, Salt and Peper beaten, feafon your great parboyled Oyfters, and put them into your Coffin; put on them fome blanched Chefnuts, and a Potatoe boyled and cut in pieces, with the yolks of hard Eggs cut in halves; if it be not a fafting day, you may add marrow, fo put over it fome fliced Lemmon, large Mace, Butter, and clofe up your Pie, and bake him; you muft put them in a thin Coffin, for a little more than half an hout will be a fufficient baking for them; when it is enough, lear it with Oyfter liquor, White-wine, the yolk or two of an Egg, and drawn Butter: cut up your Pye and put it in: fhake it together, and let it ftand a little in the Oven, and ferve it up.

To make a Batylle of Pye of Fifh.

YOu muft fet a large Coffin, cut with Battlements, and fet forth round the Coffin, with as many Towers as will contain your feveral forts of Fifh; you may fet it in the infide alfo, from one bending to another, for partitions, to lay your feveral Fifh with their Lear afunder: dry your Coffin well, and wafh it over in the infide with the yolks of Eggs: flower it in the bottom to foder it: then whatever Fifh you have prepared before for your Pie, muft be either broiled or fryed brown: in the middle of your Pye, you may put the head of a Salmon cut off beyond the gills, forced and baked in an Oven: bake the heads likewife of your other Fifh, that they may ftand upon forced meat bottoms, then difh up all your fifh in order, every fort one oppofite to another, placed in the feveral partitions, and having ready your Oyfters, Cockles, Perriwinkles and
Pranes,

The whole Body of Cookery Dissected.

Pranes, being boyled up in Lears (as you have been formerly taught) and thickened up with drawn butter, pour it over your Fish, and garnish on your shell-fish all over and let the forced heads stand over the battlements: If your Pie be full of Lear, you may let it stand in the *Oven* to keep warm: when you send it away, pour on Lear on the top, garnish it with fryed Oysters or Lemmon, or what you please.

You may make the like partitions upon a sheet of Paste in a dish, with a standing Battlement set round the brims: in which partitions you may dish up all manner of shelled Fish, and send them severally to the Table with their distinct lears.

To make Peteets of Shrimps or Pranes.

WHen you have made your little Coffins like Hearts, Diamonds, round, or how you please: you may fry up your shelled fish, with the yolks of Eggs, Cinamon, Ginger, Nutmeg, Cloves and Mace beaten together, and when they are crisp and brown, fill your dryed Coffins with a lear made with a little Claret-wine, drawn Butter, and Oyster-liquor, beaten up with the yolk or two of an Egg: so put it to your Fish, and let it stand in the Oven until you dish it up.

By these rules in boyling, broyling, roasting and baking of those varieties of Fish beforementioned, the ingenuous Practitioner may know the nature, and how to order and dress any other.

To Marrinate a Carp, to be eaten hot or cold.

TAke a large Carp, scaled, scoured and washed clean from the slime, split him through the head down the back, dry him with a cloth, sprinkle him with Salt, and flower him dry: let your pan be hot, full with oyl or clarified Butter: fry him away very crisp and brown, put him in a broad pan with as much White-wine

wine as will cover him, with some fried Bayleaves and Rosemary, a faggot or two of sweet herbs, with some sliced Ginger, Nutmeg, Cloves, Mace, whole Pepper, Salt, and a sliced Lemmon; so you may dish it up with some of the liquor, garnish it with Bay-leaves and Lemmon, with your spices all over it.

To Hash a Carp.

TAke a good male-Carp or two, scale and scrape off the slime with your knife; when you open them, wash out the blood with a little White-wine, cut off the heads, then take all the flesh from the bone, and cut it in pieces as big as the top of your thumb; you may cut after the same manner a fat Eel amongst it; then take about a pint of White-wine, or Claret-wine, put to it a faggot or two of sweet herbs, a quartered Nutmeg, Ginger, Mace, a couple of whole Onions, and two or three Cloves of Garlick; when all these ingredients have boiled a little while in the wine, take them out, then add to your Wine half a pint of Oyster liquor, a piece of Butter, and the blood of your Carp you saved before; and when it boils very fast, put in your Hash of Carps and Eel, with about a pint of Oysters; add to it Salt, a grated Nutmeg, and two or three Anchovies, and let it boil as fast as it can until it is enough, and crisp; then beat up the yolks of two or three eggs, with a ladleful of drawn butter to thicken it, so dish it upon sippets, and stick it with toasts fried stiff, with fried Oysters over them.

A Frigacy of fresh Salmon.

TAke a tail of fresh Salmon, and cut it out in pieces as long as your thumb, not altogether so thick; take sweet Margerum, Time, Parslee, a little Fennel, and mince it exceeding small; season it with Salt, small Pepper, Cloves, Mace, Ginger, and Nutmeg

The whole Body of Cookery Diſſected. 153

Nutmeg beaten; put all theſe to your pieces of Salmon, with the yolks of eight eggs, mingle it all well together, your pan being full of liquor and hot, put it in with two or three hands, becauſe you muſt part it one from another, that it fries not in lumps: when it begins to turn brown, and is about half fried, put out your butter from it, and put in about half a pint of White-wine, as much Oyſter liquor, a pint of ſet Oyſters, with a little minced Time, Nutmeg, three Anchovies, an Onion or Onion or two whole: when it is enough, beat the yolks of two or three eggs with a little of the liquor, put it it, and keep it ſhaking together, let it be thick, ſo diſht in upon ſippets, and put drawn butter over it: you may garniſh it with Shell-fiſh, ſliced Lobſter, or fried Oyſters: ſet it on the coals, and grate a Nutmeg over it; if none be offended with fleſh, you may add half a pint of gravy to this Lear.

To Frigacy great Plaice *or Flounders.*

RUn your knife all along upon the bone, on the black ſide of your Plaice: then raiſe the fleſh on both ſides from the head to the tail, and take out the bone clear; then cut it down the middle, where the bone went, and likewiſe croſs-ways, that it may be in Collops the length of half the breadth of the Plaice about two inches broad: it being very well dried from the water, and ſprinkled with ſalt, and flowered very dry, fry it away in a very hot pan of Clarified ſtuff, ſo that it may be very criſp, take it out of the pan, keep it warm in an Oven, or by the fire: make clean your pan, and put into a ladleful of butter, a little white-wine, ane oyſter liquor, the meat of the ſhells of a Crab or two, with about a pint of Oyſters, half of them minced, a little minced Time, a grated Nutmeg, with two or three Ancoeies; let all theſe ſteſh up together in your pan, then put in your fried Plaice,

and

and toss them up all together, dish them on sippets, and pour over all your Lear: garnish them with the yolks of hard Eggs minced, and slices of Lemmon: After this manner you may do Trouts, Salmon, Pikes, Mullets, Bace, or any firm fish, you may also make them green as well as yellow, because of having varieties of colours, as well as tastes at your Table.

To make Chewits of Salmon.

YOu must first broyl half a dozen slices of Salmon cut off from the Tail; when it is above half broyled, and cold, you may mince it with a handful of set Oysters, and some Marrow; then mince a little Time, Parslee, sweet Margerum very small, with a few Chesnuts, Pistaches, and a piece of a Lobster: put all these together, and season them with Cloves, Mace, Nutmeg, Cinamon, Ginger and Salt; so you may fill your small Chewits, and bake them in an Oven, and when they come forth, lear them with Gravy, Oyster liquor, and a little drawn butter; this will serve to garnish your Bisk Pye, or other boyled or baked meats of Fish.

To broyl a Carp.

LEt your Carp be scaled, washed and scoured clean from the slime and blood, then scorch it on both sides and wash it over with Butter, and season it in the scorches with Time, Nutmeg and Salt: then put it on your Gridiron, and broyl it softly over Charcoals: keep it basting whiles it is thereon (you may also broyl some Collops of Salmon with it) then set upon the coals in a stewing dish, a quarter of a Pint of Claret-wine, a little Oyster liquor, a few minced Oysters, and hard Eggs, with a handful of Pranes: when your Carp or Carps are broyled, dish them up, and garnish them with fryed Collops of Salmon and pour on your Lear (being thick) with a ladleful of drawn butter.

To

To force an Eele.

Scour great Eeles with Salt, and flea them, with the head and part of the Nose unto the skin, then cut the bone from your Eele, and mince your Eele or Eeles very small, with a handful or two of Oysters: mince likewise a handful of Parslee and Time, with a few other sweet Herbs, and a great Onyon: season it with Peper, Salt, Cloves, Mace, Ginger and Nutmeg: put to it a good many bits of butter, and make it up into a Body with the yolks of raw Eggs: then fill your Eele-skins down to the Tail, and sew them up to the head, sew up the slit of the belly towards the head, and the head and neck together: fill them not too full for fear they should swell, and break in the boyling: turn them round, as you do a Salt Eele, and boyl them: you may aftetwards broil them if you please: and send them up garnished with Bay-leaves, for a second course dish: or you may cut them in pieces for the garnishing of other Fish; otherways you may almost boyl them; when they are first fleaed, and season them with the aforesaid Seasoning, but very high like a Saffage: only add more to them some Sallet Oyl in the mixing; fill them as before, and dry them in your Chimney: when they are enough, you may slice them out, and eat them with Oyl and Vinegar: you may do Salmon or other Fish after the same manner in Eele-skins.

BOOK

BOOK XIV.

Contains several sorts of hot baked Meats of flesh.

To bake a Gammon of Bacon, to be eaten hot, with the Ingredients.

Take a Westphalie Gammon of Bacon, and boil him down, take off the skin, season him with Pepper, and a little minced Sage; stick him with Lemmon peel in the upper side; then having a Coffing of hot buttered paste, (something high) put him in the middle thereof; take a dozen of Pigeons, and as many Lamb-stones, and Sweet-breads, of each: season them with Pepper, Salt, Cloves, Mace; lay your Pigeons round about the Gammon, and your Lamb-stones and Sweet-breads round on the top of it; lay over it large Mace, few sweet herbs minced, and put on butter all over; the Gammon being tenderly boyled before, will be fully baked with the Pigeons and Sweet-breads: close up your Pye, and let it have a gentle soaking; your crust need not be very thick for so much baking as your Ingredients will ask; when he is enough, let your Lear be Claret wine, boyled up with two or three Onions, a faggot of sweet herbs, with half a handful of sage boyled and minced, a little strong broth, and drawn butter thickened up with the yolk of an egg; when you dish up your Pye, cut it open, pour in your lear, and shake it about, put on your lid again, and serve it.

To make a Pye of Mutton

Cut out a Loyn of Mutton in steaks, cut away the chine bone as much as you can, beat them flat with the back of your Cleaver, season them with Pepper, Salt, and minced Time, and put them into your Pye, Close it up, and bake it, then take half a handful of Capers, and as much Sampier, mince them with an Onion small, boyl them up in a little Claret wine, put to them two or three Anchovies, a grated Nutmeg, a little gravy, so thicken it with the yolk of an egg, and a little drawn butter; when your Pye is enough, take it out, and cut it up, and pour in your lear all over your steakes, and turn them in your Pye that the lear may mingle with them

Another way.

Let your meat be cut forth, and seasoned as aforesaid, adding some Cloves, Mace, Nutmeg beaten with an onion or two minced, so fill your Coffin, and put on it a handful or two of Raisons, and some Cabbage Lettice, if it be at that time of the year, and when it is closed and baked, take a little strong broth, and White wine, with a little Vinegar, the yolk or two of an egg, and drawn butter; this beat up together for your lear: so open your Pye, pour it in, shake it together, put on your Lid, and serve it: if you please, you may season it only with Pepper and Salt, putting in a little Claret wine, when it is half baked, and so it is a good plain way, and savory meat.

For a sweet Lamb Pie.

Cut out your Loyn or Leg of Lamb, season it in little pieces, with a little small Pepper, some Salt, Cloves, Mace, Nutmeg, and minced Time; your Coffin being made, put in your Lamb, strow on a handful full of Currans; lay over it all some small balls of sweet forced meat (in the winter time, take boyled Potatoes cut in pieces, and quartered dates, a little Orangado, and Citern, But in the Summer some pieces of Artichokes, Grapes, or hard Lettice) put in some blades of large Mace, and close up your Pye, let your lear be Sugar and Verjuice beaten up together, with the yolks of two Eggs, and a ladle of drawn Butter: put it in your Pye, when it is baked, shake it together, put on your lid, and serve it.

Another way for a savoury.

SEason your Lamb with Pepper and Salt, a little Cloves, Mace, and Nutmeg, with Time minced, put into your Coffin, with a few Lambstones and sweet breads, seasoned with your Lamb, with as many Oysters, and savoury forced meat balls, so put on butter, and close up your Pye: let your lear be three or four Anchovies dissolved in a little Claret wine, add a little Oyster liquor, Gravy, and a grated Nutmeg, beat it up with the yolk of an Egg, and a little drawn Butter; when your Pye is enough, take it out, pour in your lear, and shake it together.

Another way.

SEason it as aforesaid (you may put in some Artichokes or hard Lettice in your Pye if you please) then take a little strong broth, a little White wine, and chop in the tops of two or three bunches of Sparragras being boyled before, and some green boyled Parslee minced, add to this a ladleful or two of drawn Butter and a grated Nutmeg: and when your Pye comes out of the Oven, pour it all over the meat thereof, and shake it about.

To bake a Hen to be eaten Hot.

PArboyl your Hen, then cut off the legs and wings as when she is carved ; cut off the Merry thought, & through the breast bone, so also the carkass, that she may be handsom to lie in the pie ; break the bone, season her with a little pepper and Salt, Cloves and Mace ; then put her into your Pie, with some pieces of Lambstones Sweet breads, and Sassages, with a few Oysters between with hard Eggs and a couple of Onyons cut in halves, so put on butter, and close up your Pie: when it is baked, let your lear be a little Claret wine, strong broth, beaten up with the yolk of an egg, a grated Nutmeg, and drawn butter ; pour it into your Pye, and shake it together.

How to bake an Hen another way.

CUt her to pieces, and let your seasoning be a little Pepper, Salt, Cloves, Mace, minced Time, (Nutmeg) and other sweet herbs: your Hen being thus in pieces, season it therewith : put in the yolks of three or four Eggs, and mix them up altogether, then season some thin slices of fat Bacon, with minced Sage and Pepper, so lay your meat in order into your Pie, with a piece of Hen, and a slice of Bacon, until it be all in: put over it some savoury forced meat about the bigness of a VValnut, with a little sliced Artichoke between ; so sprinkle over your meat with a handful of stript Barberries, put butter in your Pye, and close it up : and when its half baked, put in a ladle of Claret wine and set it into the Oven until it is enough: draw it and cut it up ; if it be too thin, beat up the yolk of an Egg with some of its own liquor ; put thereon a ladleful of drawn butter, shake it together, and put on the lid again.

Another

Another way to bake a Hen in a Patty Pan.

TAke a young Hen or two, and let them be almoſt boiled or roaſted, then take all the fleſh from the bones (but not very clean) and cut it all in ſlices, ſeaſon it with ſome Time, Parſlee, ſweet Margerum, and an Onion minced very ſmall, with a little Cloves, Mace, and Nutmeg beaten; then having a ſheet of fine paſte driven out for your patty pan, put your bones in the bottom, and your ſliced meat on the top; put over butter, and cloſe your patty with another ſheet of paſte; then ſet on your pan on a few embers, and ſome coals on the lid, by ſupplying it with freſh coals at top and bottom, you may bake it as well as in an Oven; when it is baked, take about eight eggs and break them in a diſh, and butter them on the fire; when they are thick, put to them ſome Claret-wine, and ſtrong broth; add to them a handful of Parſlee boiled green, and minced ſmall; ſtir a all together with a ladle of drawn butter; caſt your patty into a diſh, and cut up the lid; ſtir up all the meat from the bottom, that you may take out bones; then put in your Lear of eggs (before provided) and mingle them all together with your knife or ſpoon; then quarter your Lid, and cut it into eight parts, and put it round your patty; then ſtick up your bones in the middle of your meat, garniſh it with quartered Oranges, and ſend it up.

To bake a Capon or Turky in a Patty pan.

TAke a cold Capon or Turky that hath been roaſted before, and ſlice it thin from the bones; ; (preſerve your ſtraight thighs and pinnions) take alſo three ſweet breads, and as many Lamb-ſtones, with two handfuls of Oyſters cut in pieces as big as a Wallnut, ſeaſon your meat with Cloves, Mace, Nugmeg, and Salt, with a little minced Time, ſweet Margerum, and Pennyroyal;
your

your patty pan being covered with a sheet of paste, lay in your bones in the bottom, strow in a minced Onion; so lay your Capon or Turky over the bones, and on the top of that your Lamb-stones, sweet-breads and oysters; and between all about two handfuls of Chesnuts blancht, strow it over with Pine Apples and Pistaches, so put butter on the top, and close your patty; and when it is baked, put in a Lear made with Claret-wine, a little strong broth, gravy, drawn butter, two or three Anchovies dissolved, with a grated Nutmeg: if it be not thick enough, beat in the yolks of two eggs: Cast your patty forth into the dish, cut it up, pour in your Lear, and shake it together, lay on slices of Lemmon, and cut the lid into eight parts, and set it up round the patty.

How to season and bake a Pasty of Venison.

WHen you have ordered your side or hanch of Venison by taking out the bones and sinews, and the skin on the fat, season it with Pepper and salt only, beat it with your rolling pin, and proportion it for your pasty, by taking away from one part, and adding to another; your paste being made with a peck of fine flower, and about four pound of butter, and a dozen eggs, work it up with cold water into as stiff a paste as you can; drive it forth for your pasty, let it be as thick as a mans thumb, roll it upon a rolling pin, and put under it a couple of sheets of Cap-paper, well flowred; then your white being already minced and beaten with water, proportion it upon your pasty, to the breadth vnd length of your Venison: so lay on your Venison on the said white, wash it round with your feathers, and put on a border: season your Venison at the top, and turn over your other leaf of paste, so close your pasty; then drive out another border for the garnishing the sides up to the top of the pasty; so close

M   it

it up together with your rolling pin, by rolling it up and down by the sides and ends: and when you have flourisht your garnishing, and edg'd your Pasty, vent it at the top; and indore it with butter, set it into the Oven, it will ask five or six hours baking, according as it may be; when its enough, draw it, and put it on your Pasty Plate.

Another way to bake Venison, to be eaten hot.

Raise a Coffin of hot butter past, it may be four square; put in your Beef-fuet smally minced in the bottom of your Pye, and having your Venison cut, flasht, and proportioned for your Pye, season your Venison with some Pepper beaten small, with Cloves, Mace, Cinamon, Ginger and Nutmeg beaten, with a handful of Salt; put it into your Coffin, with some butter on the top of it, to make it smooth for your lid, and close it; this Pye must be of a good thickness; when it is baked, take it forth, cut it up, and put in about a quart of Gallendine ur Venison sauce, more or less, as you see fit: so shake it together; this Pye ought to have six hours baking, because it ought to be very tender.

To make a Battlely, or Bisk Pyes in the Spring.

You may make your Coffin round, or Castle fashion; you must take of these several sorts of Meats, or Ingredients for your Pye, according to the bigness thereof: take four small Chickens, four Pigeons, a couple of young Rabbets, half a dozen Quails, two pair of Lamb-stones, and as many Sweet-breads, three Pallets sliced, season them all with a little small Pepper beat, Cloves, Mace, Nutmeg, Salt, and some minced Time: you must also have some Sastages ready, with some savoury forced meat, and a handful or two of parboiled Oysters, (unless it be after *April*: if in *May*,

Shell-

Shell-fifh will come in feafon,) firft take your Rabbet being cut in pieces (and feafoned as aforefaid) and put it in the bottom of your Pye with fome flices of Bacon ; you may cut your Chickens and Pigeons in halves ; lay on half a Chicken, then half a Lamb-ftone, then half a Pigeon, then a Sweet-bread; do fo with your forced meat Balls, fo your others, until they are equally difperft one amongft another: ftrow on your fliced Pallets all on the top, with a handful of Oyfters or Sherdoons, with the marrow of three marrow bones, wrapt up in the yolks of eggs, and a handful or two of blanched Chefnuts, with a few Pine Apples and Piftaches ; put in three or four halves of Onions, lay butter over all, and clofe your Pye ; when its enough (baked) draw it; let your *L*ear be White-wine, diffolve therein three or four Anchovies beat up with the yolks of eggs, and ftrong broth, and drawn butter, cut up your Pye, put it in, and fhake it together ; garnifh it with your Sprigs of Pafte dried: Now if you were to make this Bisk in harveft, then you muft take in the ftead of Spanifh Potatoes, Skerrets, Chefnuts, Oyfters, Sherdoons, with many fuch Ingredients, which we make ufe of in the Winter, and coming in of the Spring: In the room of them we have Artichokes, Sparragrafs, Colliflowers, Cabbage, Lettice, and many other herbs (Ingredients) which the garden doth afford ; as alfo certain wild fowl do come in, as Partridge, Quail, Rail, Puetts, *&c.* And in Autumn, inclining to Winter, you have all manner of wild fowl comes in the room of your Rabbets, Chickens, Pigeons, and fuch fowl as you had before ; you muft likewife then make ufe of all fuch Ingredients you left off withall in the beginning of the Spring ; As to pickle Roots, Chefnuts, *&c.* fo let Reafon rule you to make ufe of thofe things, as the feveral times and feafons do produce, and you fhall not err.

To make a Sherdoon Pye in the Spring.

THere is a thistle which hath a root like an Artichoke and must be boyled, and ordered accordingly: when its boyled, you may season it with Cinamon, Ginger, and beaten Nutmeg; you must take the marrow of four Marrow bones, season them with Cinamon, Sugar, the yolks of three or four eggs, and grated bread. A thin coffin being ready, put in your Sherdoons, so wrap the marrow in the yolks of eggs, and put it into the pye, with a handful of dates, and lay on it some sliced Lemmon, large Mace, put your Butter on, so close it, set it in the Oven: when its enough, draw it, cut it up, and let your lear be Sack and drawn butter.

To make a Lumber Pye.

TAke a pound and half of Beef suet, and as much of a leg of Veal parboyled: mince it together, then take a few sweet herbs, as Time, Winter Savoury, sweet Margerum, and a good handful of Spinnage: mince all these together with a Pippin or two, and two or three handfuls of grated bread, a little Rose water, and as many yolks of eggs, with the whites of two, as will make it into a tender moist forced meat: add to it a pound of Currans, season it with Nutmeg, Ginger, Cloves, Mace, and Salt: then having your Coffin made put it in, all about it equally, then having the marrow of two or three Marrowbones seasoned with Cinamon, grated bread, and yolks of eggs, lay it on your forced meat; put on it sliced Orangado, dryed Cittern, Ringo Roots, candyed Ginger, preserved Barberries, and Dates, put also Sugar to your Lumber meat, lay on butter, and close it up: when its baked, let your lear be Verjuice and Sugar beaten up in two yolks of eggs: open your pye, put it in, and shake it: scrape on Sugar and serve it.

To make a diſh of Chewits.

TAke a Neats tongue that's tenderly boyled, elſe parboyled Veal, mince it, put to it as much Beef ſuet, two or three Pippins, about a dozen of Dates, an Orangado-pill, let them be all finely minced and mingled together, ſeaſon it with Cinamon, Ginger, Nutmeg, Cloves, Mace, Carraway ſeeds, ſalt, and a little Roſe-water and Sack, and having your Coffins ready made, with a high one in the middle, and half a dozen hearts and diamonds round about, mingle your meat with a pound or two of Currans, or as many as you ſhall think to be enough, according to the quantity of your meat: Fill your pyes, and cloſe them, they will ask about an hours baking: when they are baked, ſcrape on ſugar, and ſend them up: you may make good minced pyes after the ſame manner, with good cleanly tripe, adding Raiſons of the Sun to your ordinary minced pyes.

To make an Ox cheek Pye.

TAke a young Ox cheek, and boyl him pretty tender; and when he is cold, ſlice him out from the bones like a haſh, put to it a handful of minced ſweet herbs, and an Onion with them, ſeaſon it with a little ſmall Pepper, Salt, Cloves, Mace and Nutmeg; put it into your Coffin, with a few Pallets ſliced and ſeaſoned, & ſome balls of ſavoury forced meat, put in two or three whole Onions, with butter, and cloſe it up; when it is baked, put in a lear of Claret wine, Vinegar, and a little Sugar, beaten up with the yolks of two eggs.

To make a Calves head Pye.

YOu muſt cleave your Calves head, waſh the cheeks very well; and when its almoſt boyled, and cold, take it from the bones; cut it in pieces about the bigneſs of a great Oyſter, then take a pretty quantity of Time, ſweet

sweet Margerum, Rosemary, Parslee: mince them all small together, and put it to your meat, with a little Pepper, Salt, Cloves, Mace and Nutmeg, season some slices of Bacon cut very thin, with Pepper and Sage; season also a handful of Oysters with the seasoning appertaining to the Calves-head, your Coffin being made, put in your meat, with the Bacon and Oysters all over it; slice on Lemmon, and put on a handful of Barberries, with butter over it, so close your Pye; make a lear with a little gravy, drawn with Claret-wine, and beaten up thick with two yolks of eggs, and a little drawn butter: when it is baked, cut it up, and pour your lear all over: Put on your lid, and serve it up.

To make a Neats-Tongue Pye, to be eaten hot.

TAke a couple of Neats-Tongues, and almost boil them, then blanch them, and cut out the meat at the butt-ends, as far as you can, not breaking it out of the sides; put a little suet to the said meat you cut out, a few sweet herbs, and Parslee, minced altogether very small, season it with a little Pepper, Salt, Cloves, Mace, Ginger, and a handful of grated bread, a little Sugar, and the yolks of three or four eggs; mould it up into a body, season your tongues in the inside, and outside, with your seasoning aforesaid, and wash them within with the yolk of an egg, and force them, where you cut forth the meat, and make small forced meat balls of the residue: then having your Coffin made in the form of, a Neats-Tongue Pye, lay them in, with the balls round them: put on Dates and sliced Lemmon, with butter on the top, close it up: when it's baked, put in a lear of a thin Gallendine or Venison sauce, shake it together, and send it up.

To make a Chicken Pye for the Winter.

TAke half a dozen, or eight small Chickens; when they are scalded, drawn, and truss for baking, season them with Cloves, Mace, Nutmeg, Cinamon, and Salt; wrap up part of the seasoning in butter, and put it in their bellies: your Coffin being made, lay them in, put over and between them some pieces of marrow, quartered Dates, pieces of Spanish Potatoes boiled, with a sliced Lemmon, and half a handful of Barberries stript; so put on butter, and close up your Pye: let your lear be made with White-wine, Sugar, a grated Nutmeg, and beaten up with the yolk of an egg, and a little drawn butter; when your Pye is ready, cut it up, and pour it over; shake your Pye well together, and cover it, you may put Suckets and Chesnuts in it if you please.

Another way.

VVHen you have truss, and seasoned your Chickens with Pepper, Salt, Cloves, Mace, and Nutmeg beaten, mince a good handful of Parslee, a little Time, and wrap it up in a piece of butter, with some of the seasoning aforesaid, and stuff the bellies of your Chickens; so lay them into your Coffin prepared for them, strow over them some Lemmons cut like Dice, and half a handful of Grapes, with some pieces of boiled Artichokes, and hard Cabbage of Lettice, so put butter on it, and close it up; when it is ready, put in a lear of White-wine and gravy, beaten up thick with a little drawn butter, and the yolk of an egg, and a grated Nutmeg, shake it together, and serve it up.

Another way.

YOur Chickens being seasoned as aforesaid, you may if you please cut them in halves or quarters, and put

put them into your Coffin ; so may your pye be the larger, and the lower when its baked (plain) take a little Verjuice, white wine, and a handful of parslee boyled green and minced, with a bunch or two of Sparragrass boyled, and cut in pieces an inch long : when your lear boyls, put this all in together with some sliced Artichoke, grated Nutmeg, a little Sugar, and drawn butter, beaten up thick with the yolk of an egg ; when your pye is ready, pour your lear all over your Chickens, and shake it together, thus you may bake Rabbets.

To make a Calves head Pye.

YOu must boyl and blanch your Calves feet, and when they are cold, mince them with half the quantity of beef suet, with a handful of good sweet herbs, Parslee and Spinnage minced, put to them a good quantity of Currans, some Cloves, Mace, Cinamon, Ginger, Nutmeg, Sugar and Salt, with a little Rose water ; your Coffin being ready, put in your minced meat, put over it Dates, sliced Lemmon, and a little Butter, close it, and bake it ; when its enough, let your lear be Verjuice, Sugar, grated Nutmeg, beaten up with the yolk of an egg, a little Rose water, put it into the pye through the funnel, and let it soak together in the Oven until you serve it up.

To make an Olive Pye.

CUt thin collops off a piece of the butt end of a leg of Veal, as many as you judge will fill your Coffin : hack them very thin with the back of your knife, season them with a little Pepper, Salt, Cloves, Mace, Nutmeg and Ginger, wash over your Collops on the upper side with your feathers dipt in the yolks of eggs ; then mince a good handful of all manner of sweet herbs, especially, Time and Parslee, with some Spinnage ;

mince

mince likewife as much Beef fuet very fmall, put to it a good handful of Currans, the yolks of about eight hard eggs minced, with a little Orangado, feafon all this together, (as you did the Collops) fprinkle it with Rofe water, and put it on your Collops ; fo roll them up very hard with the forced meat within them, and lay them in your Coffin, ftrowing your forced meat that is left, all over it ; then according to the feafon of the year you may put on Artichoke bottoms, hard Cabbage Lettice, or Endive fcalded, elfe Chefnuts or Dates: put butter on your pye, clofe it, and bake it : let your lear be White wine, Verjuice and Sugar beaten up with the yolk of an egg, and drawn butter, put it in at the funnel when your pye is enough, and let it ftand in the Oven until you fend it up.

To make an Artichoke Pye.

BOyl the bottoms of about eight or ten Artichokes, fcrape them, and make them clean from the core ; feafon them with Cinamon, Sugar, Nutmeg, Salt, with a little fmall Pepper ; take the Marrow of four Oxbones, feafoned with the like feafoning, (except Pepper) lay your Artichokes in the Coffin prepared, then lay your Marrow all over them, being wrapt up in the yolk of an egg, and grated bread, that it may not melt ; you may alfo boyl the ftalkes of your Artichokes (near the bottoms) and feafon the pith thereof, as aforefaid, cutting them about three inches long, and put them in with your Marrow, and put amongft it quartered Dates, fliced Lemmon, and large Mace, fo put on Butter and clofe your Pye ; let your lear be White-wine, and Sack, with a little Sugar, beaten up with the yolk of an egg and drawn butter; when it is enough, put it in at the funnel, fhake it together, fcrape on Sugar, and garnifh it, and fend it up,

To

To make a Skerret Pye.

BOil your biggest Skerrets, blanch them, season them with Cinamon, beaten Nutmeg, Ginger and Sugar; your Coffin being ready, lay in your Skerrets; season also the Marrow of three or four bones, with Cinamon, Sugar, a little grated bread, with the yolks of three or four raw eggs, put on your Marrow, with the yolks of eight hard eggs cut in halves, a handful of blanched Chesnuts, and a few quartered Dates; lay Butter over your Pye, and close it; let your lear be Butter, Vinegar, and Sugar, with a little Sack, and the yolk of an egg; when your Pye is baked, put it in, shake it together, so scrape on Sugar, and garnish it.

To make a Potato Pye.

BOyl your Spanish Potatoes (not overmuch) cut them forth in slices as thick as your thumb, season them with Nutmeg, Cinamon, ginger, and Sugar; your Coffin being ready, put them in, over the bottom, add to them the Marrow of about three Marrow-bones, seasoned as aforesaid, a handful of stoned Raisons of the Sun, some quartered Dates, Orangado, Cittern, with Ringo-roots sliced, put butter over it, and bake them: let their lear be a little Vinegar, Sack and Sugar, beaten up with the yolk of an Egg, and a little drawn Butter; when your pye is enough, pour it in, shake it together, scrape on Sugar, garnish it, and serve it up.

To make Marrow Pasties to fry.

TAke the Marrow of four bones, throw it into a Bason of water, and let it drain in a Cullender; let the pieces be as big as the top of your thumb, put them into a deep dish, with the rest of your small Marrow: mince a little Orangado, Cittern and Dates exceeding small: take two handfuls of grated bread, and put

put it all into the difh with your Marrow, with about a fpoonful or more of Sugar : Seafon it with a good quantity of beaten Cinamon, Salt, a grated Nutmeg, and a little Ginger, with a little Sack and Rofe-water; break to it the yolks of half a dozen eggs, fo mix it altogether; if it be too thin, put it on the coals, keeping it ftirring with a fpoon, that the eggs may congeal it together, take it off the coals; your pafte muft be made with fine flower, cold butter, and yolks of eggs : make it very rich, then drive out thin fheets, put them on papers, and lay on your Marrow in pieces, that your Pafty may be four or five inches long, and three or four inches broad; then lay on of your grated bread, and your other ingredients, over all your Marrow, to congeal it together; wafh it in the clofing with yolks of eggs, turn over your fheet, and clofe him as you do a Pafty, Jagging of him round with your Jagging-iron, fo do by the reft : mingle your Marrow, eggs and bread proportionably together ; your pan being ready, full of Clarified ftuff, when it is hot prick your Pafties, and put them into your pan, holding it high from the fire, becaufe they are apt to burn; they ought to boyl at the top, as well as at the bottom, and to be turned two or three times in the frying; when they are enough, take them up with your flice, and place them on your plate; (fix or eight will make a fair difh) fcrape on Sugar and ferve them up. After this way you may do it with flices of Artichokes cut thin, in the bottom, under your Marrow, and at the top likewife : the fame may be done with Potatoes in the Winter.

To make egg Pyes.

YOu muft make your pafte pretty rich with the yolks of eggs, your butter muft be melted, and well mixed with your flower and eggs; your water to bring it into a pafte muft be hot, but not boyling hot

hot, so make it up into a pretty stiff Paste; you must drive it out into borders, and cut your sets even at the bottom, and jag it in the edges, then set it round on a bottom, that it may contain in the inside the bigness of a Goose egg, and about the height of four inches; about a dozen or sixteen will make a handsom dish; Jag them round at the foot, when they are set to the bottom, then take the yolks of about twenty eggs boiled hard and minced very small, with a little Orangado, Cittern and Dates likewise minced, put it into a dish, with the yolks of about six eggs, and the whites of three, beat it all together with half a pint of Cream, and let there be another pint heating on the fire, and when it is almost scalding hot, beat it in by little and little into the afore-mentioned Composition; if it thickens too much, add more Cream, season it with Rose-water, Sugar, Cinamon, Nutmeg, and a little Salt; put a little Marrow into all your Pies, and set them in the Oven, so fill them with a little ladle; let your stuff be so thin, that it may run like a Pancake-batter; they will ask about a quatter of an hours baking; when you dish them, stick them with Cittern, and strow them over with small Biskets, scrape on Sugar, and send them up. Note, that the Coffins must be dried a little in the Oven before they are filled.

To make a Trotter Pie, and Taffaty-Tarts.

YOu must make a Coffin with hot buttered paste, about the height of the Crown of a hat, and as small in circumference, fill it with sliced Pippins, close it without Sugar; if you mistrust it will fall, pin a paper about it, and put it in the Oven a baking; you must roll out sheets for your Taffaty-Tarts, with such paste as you had for your Marrow Pasties; it must be exceeding thin, and four square, your Apples may be cut throughout your Pippin, as thin as you can cut them, paper your

your sheets of paste, and lay on your Apples in one end, only leave a place to close; lay on the slices of your Apples in the form of a little square Trencher in length, but not in breadth by two inches ; strow on a little Orangado, or minced Orange-pill, between every laying of Apples, build them up about four stories high, after the same manner : lay on the top thin slices of Orangado and Cittern ; cover them flat over with powdered Sugar, and wet them with your wetting-brush round in the closing ; then turn over your sheet of paste, as you do a Pasty, and close them firmly ; jag them squarely off at the ends and sides, as many as you make ; prick and indore them with Butter, so bake them in a moderate Oven ; when they are almost baked, you may take them out, and ice them if you please ; when your Pye is enough, take him forth, put him on a plate, and cut up the lid, put in Butter, Rose-water and Sugar ; when he is dished, put round about him your Taffatie-Tarts, then hang three Esses of paste on your Pye, and put on them a cut garnish; you may garnish your Tarts with dryed Cittern, Orangado, or what other preserves you please ; scrape on Sugar, and send them up.

To make an Orangado Pye.

YOu must make a handsom thin Coffin, with hot buttered paste, then slice your Orangado and put over the bottom thereof; quarter some Pippins and cut them in halves, so that it may be cut in eight parts, and lay them over your Orangado ; then put on more Orangado on the top of them, and pour on them some sirrup of Orangado, and Sugar on the top, so close your Pye ; when it is baked, scrape on Sugar, and serve it up.

Another

Another way.

YOu may make your Paste with fine flower, and a few yolks of eggs, and a little Milk ready to boil; work up your flower and eggs together, and bring it afterwards into a stiff paste with your Milk; roll it out in sheets, and cut out your Patterns four square, let them be about twelve inches long, and six inches high, roul them thin by degrees from the foundation upwards, and cut Battlements on the top; then with your iron, or penknife, you may carve them in what garnish, form or fashion you please; but in all the Tower, from the foundation, &c. you must carve it; then bring up your pattern to a circumference, close it together, and set it on a bottom, so it will be like a Tower, you may make as many as you will in the form thereof, with an high one in the middle, that it may be after the likeness of a Castle; then dry them in an Oven, put them on a dishing-plate; you may put what suckets and sweet meats you will within, but hang and garnish it in every one of your cuts and holes, and on all your Battlements, with Orangado cut in pieces, so garnish your dish with sweet meats and suckets.

A hot baked meat of compounds.

TAke part of a leg of Lamb, and cut it into thin slices, make forced meat of the other part of it; then take two or three Chickens, and as many Pigeons, cut them in pieces, also take Quails, Larks, or other small fowl; season it all severally by it self, with a little Pepper small beaten, Cloves, Mace, Nutmeg, and Salt; take likewise a handful of sweet herbs and Parslee, a little Beef-suet, and a handful of Currans, mince all these finely together, with a handful of grated bread; season them as the meat, aforesaid, and knead them up with a little Butter into a ball; your aforesaid collops being opened,

opened, spread it on them; and roul them up into little Collers; you may make a Pye in the fashion of a Battalia, or a round Pye very large, but not high, then distribute all your Lamb in the bottom of your Pye, with your pieces of Chickens and Pigeons betwixt your Collops, and lay over that your Larks and Quails, &c. with your forced meat balls as big as a Walnut, between your fowl, as also the bottoms of Artichokes boyled Sparragrafs, Lettice or Grapes, in the Summer-feafon, otherwife Chefnuts, Dates, Skerrets, Potatoes, Pine-Apples, Piftaches; feafon fome thin flices of Bacon with Pepper, Nutmeg, Time, and a little Sage, and put it all over your Pye in the vacant places, also fome Lamb-ftones, fweetbreads, Marrow, and the yolks of hard eggs; you may take but a few of all thefe ingredients, left your Pye be very big : put butter on your Pye, clofe him and bake him; for your Lear, diffolve two or three Anchovies in White-wine, a little ftrong Broth and Gravy, with a grated Nutmeg, and a little drawn butter beaten up with the yolks of two eggs; when your Pye is baked, put in your Lear and fhake it together; if you pleafe, you may put Oyfters in it; this is a baftard Bisk Pye.

To make a Pigeon Pye.

TRufs your Pigeons to bake, and fet them, and lard the one half of them with Bacon, mince a few fweet herbs and Parflee with a little Beef-fuet, the yolks of hard eggs, and an Onion or two; feafon it with Salt, beaten Pepper, Cloves, Mace, and Nutmeg; work it up with a piece of butter, and ftuff the bellies of your Pigeons, feafon them with fome falt, fmall Pepper, a little Cloves, Mace, and beaten Nutmeg, take alfo about four fweet-breads, as many Lamb-ftones, feafoned as aforefaid, with a few flices of Bacon, (but omit Salt in your Bacon) you may make a round Coffin, and put

in

in your Pigeons, and your Lamb-ftones, fweet-breads and Bacon, between and about them, you may put in alfo Artichoke bottoms, or what other dry ingredients of that nature, becaufe your Pye is of a lufcious fat; put Butter in your Pye, and clofe it up; you may put in a little White-wine, beaten up with the yolk of an egg, when it comes out of the Oven, for your Lear.

Another way.

WHen they are truffed, feafon them with falt, a little fmall Pepper and Nutmeg; put in their giblets, with fome Butter, fo clofe up your Pye, and bake it; then take up a good handful of Parfley boiled and green, an handful of fet Goofberries and Grapes, half an handful of boiled Barberries, two or three bottoms of boiled Artichokes fliced; let your Parfley be minced fmall; put all thefe together into a Pipkin, with a quarter of a pint of White-wine and ftrong broth; put to it a Ladleful or two of drawn Butter: when your Pye is baked, cut it up, and pour your Lear all over, fhaking of it well together: in the Winter you may ufe Potatoes, or Skerrets in this Pye.

To make a Kid Pye.

TAke a Kid, and take out moft of the bones, preferving the meat in form; what bones you take not out, break them, then fet your Kid, and lard him with Bacon; beat him down, that he may lie as low as poffible, with his back upwards in the Pye, then feafon him with a little falt, Cloves, Mace, Nutmeg, Cinamon and minced Time; proportion a Coffin according to his form, and lay him in; in the Winter time take Spanifh Potatoes half boiled, and fliced Dates, Raifons of the Sun ftoned, and put all over him, with a few preferved Barberries, a little Orangado and Cittern, lay on fome large Mace & Buter, & clofe it up; make your Lear of of a quarter of a pint of White-wine, as much Sack, boyled up with a little Cinamon, Nutmeg, grated bread, two or three spoonfulls of Verjuice, a little Sugar, with a ladleful or two of drawn Butter: when your Pye is baked and dished, cut it up, and pour on this Lear, shake it together, and serve it up.

Another way.

WHen you have truffed, boned, and larded him, as aforesaid, season him with Salt, small Pepper, Cloves, Mace, Nutmeg and minced Time, put him into a Coffin, aud lay Butter thereon, close him and bake him; then take a quart of set Oysters, dryed with a cloath, flowered and fryed brown: then put out the butter they were fryed in, and put to them half a pint of White-wine, half a pint of their liquor, an Onion minced exceeding small, with a little Time, a grated Nutmeg, and a handful of green Parsle, boyled and minced, with a few Barberies; when it boyls up together, beat it thick with the yolk of an egg, and a ladleful of drawn Butter, dish up your Pye, and cut it up; pour on your Lear, with your Oysters all over your Kid, so put on your lid and serve it up; this will serve towards, or in the Spring: the other sweet way in *December*, or when Kids are very young.

Two other wayes.

YOu may cut a quarter, or what you please out in steaks, and season it with sweet spice, as Cinamon, Cloves, Mace, Nutmeg, Ginger, adding a little Salt, and bake it with fruit or suckets, as Rasons, Currans, Dates, Orangado, Cittern, &c. your Lear must be Verjuice, White-wine-Vinegar, Sugar, beaten up with two yolks of eggs.

If you would have it baked savoury, season it with Pepper, Salt, Cloves, Mace, Nutmeg, and minced Time;

time; let your Lear be a little strong Broth, White-wine, gravy, and drawn Butter, with a handful of Oysters minced; if you please, you may put in a handful of boyled Parsle minced also.

To make a Pasty of an old Goat.

TAke the hind quarter of a fat Goat, bone and skin it, cut it with your knife four square, fit for a Pasty; beat it well with a Rolling-pin, season it with Pepper, Salt, minced Time, and Nutmeg, (let it look gray with Salt) then let it soak all night in its seasoning, with Red-wine, or Claret, then bake it as you do a Venison Pasty, with minced Beef suet: then break the bones all to pieces with a Cleaver, and put them into a Pipkin, with some other pieces of meat, and put to them a pint of Claret-wine, and a little strong Broth, and cover your Pipkin close with a sheet of course Paste, and bake them in the Oven with your Pasty; when your Pasty is very tender, or enough, draw it and set it on a dish, and plate, and fill it with your liquor powred from your bones out of your Pipkin, and send it up: It will not be known from Venison, by the generality of men, either in taste or colour.

To make a Lamb-Pasty.

BOne your Lamb, skin it, and cut it forth four square, in the manner of a Pasty: season it with Salt, Pepper beaten small, Cloves, Mace, Nutmeg, and minced Time: let your Paste be rich cold buttered Paste: lay your Lamb upon minced Beef-suet, and put on an high border about it, then turn over your sheet, close, finish and bake your Pasty; when it is baked and drawn, put in a Lear of White-wine, Sugar, Vinegar, beaten up with the yolks of two or three eggs; if you wold have it savory and not sweet, add the more spice in the seasoning, and let your Lear be only gravy, or the baking of of bones, and some meat, in Claret wine, as before: this you may observe in all other baked meats, betwixt the Lears of sweet and savoury.

To bake a Fawn, or young Roe.

YOu must bone him, set and lard him with Bacon, season him with a little small Pepper, Salt, Cloves, Mace and Nutmeg: then you may make a Coffin according to the form of a Roe: or you may set your border round about him, head and all being proportioned, and so close it on the top of the back, or where the ridge-bone of your Roe should be: else do it after your own fancy, (for that is not my work intended) when it is baked, cut it up, so as you may put in your Lear, and close it handsome again: let your Lear be Claret-wine grated bread, a good quantity of beaten Cinamon, Vinegar and Sugar boyled up together; put in a ladleful of drawn Butter, and pour it all over your Fawn or Roe, and shake it together: let not your Lear be so thick that it will not run over your meat; if you would have it savory, you must bake your bones with Claret wine, and so fill it as before directed.

To make Pasties of Pies to fry.

YOu must order your Rice, and season it as aforesaid, then drive out thin sheets of cold buttered Paste; and lay on a spoonful of Rice: It must not be so thin as to run it self, but put it all abroad square about four inches in breadth, and five inches in length: then having the Marrow of two Bones, cut in pieces, about the bigness of a Nutmeg, seasoned with Cinamon and Nutmeg, mingled with the yolk of one or two Eggs: stick this on your Pasty all over your Rice, then lay on another spoonful of Rice all over your Marrow, wash it round about with the yolks of eggs, and close your Pasty, Jagg it round: you may make a dozen or twenty in a dish, or what number you please; and fry them in a Kettle, or pan full of stuff, as you fry Fritters: remember to prick them, and fry them very soberly, that the Marrow may be fryed through, yet not burned: stick them with Lozenges, or sprigs of Past, scrape on Sugar, and serve them for second Course.

BOOK XV.

Contains all manner of Tarts, and made Dishes.

How to make a Bacon Tart.

YOu must take some fat clear Bacon that is not rusty, and scrape it with your knife, until you have the quantity of a pound or upwards, throw it into fair water: after its well soakt, drain it out, and put it into a stone morter, and beat it with a wooden pestle; then put to it some Orangado, and dryed Cittern sliced; put to it some Rose-water, two handfulls of grated bread, eight eggs, casting away four whites; a pint and half of Cream; season it with sugar, cinamon, ginger, nutmeg, and a little salt; beat it all together well, and when your coffin, or coffins are made, and a little dryed in an Oven, you may put it in and bake it, and serve it up, with a cut, & wafers on it.

To make an Almond-Tart.

TAke about one pound of sweet Almonds, being blancht, and watred for a while, beat them in a stone Morter, with a little Rose-water, and when they are well beaten, beat them in again with a little cream, and put on about a quart of cream on the fire, and put them therein; keeping them stiring that it doth not burn

burn to: let them boyl (with three or four sticks of Cinamon, large Mace, and a grain of musk tyed with a thred) untill it grows thick, then take it off the fire, and beat in the yolks of about six eggs, with the whites of three; so season it with Sugar, a little Orangado sliced, and Cittern; your Coffin or Dish being ready, put it in, and bake it.

To make a Pine-apple Tart.

Beat two handfulls of Pine-Apples, with a pricked Quince, with the palp of two or three Peppins, when they are well beaten, put to them half a pint of Cream, a little Rose water, the yolks of half a dozen eggs, with a handful of Sugar, if it be thick you may add a little more Cream to it: so having your thin low Coffins for it dryed, fill them up: and bake them: You may garnish them with Orangado, or Lozenges: of Sugar past, or what else you please.

Another Tart of Pistaches.

You must beat your Pistaches Kernels (about the quantity of two handfuls) in a morter, with the quarters of about four Pearmains, adding to them a preserved Quince, preserving all the Cock-treads of your eggs, and eight yolks, with almost a pint of Cream, mingle it altogether well in a morter, with Sugar and Rose water perfumed with Ambergreece, and Musk, remember that your quarters of Pear-mains, were first boyled, before mixt with the rest of your Ingredience: It must be filled into thin shallow Coffins, about two Inches high: You may either fry or bake them, otherwise you may bake them open: Your Coffins being dryed, you may stick them over with sliced pistaches, so scrape on Sugar.

To make a Spring Tart.

You may gather the leaves of Primroses, Violets, Strawberries, with a little young Spinnage, or all other

182 *The whole Body of Cookery Diſſected.*

other buds that are not bitter, boyl them in a little milk, then put them forth into a Cullender, and preſerve your milk for another uſe: chop your herbs very ſmall, and boyl them up again in Cream; take as many yolks of eggs, with two or three whites, as will make your cream into a thick body, after it is off the fire: if it be not thick enough with your herbs, put in a handful of grated Naple Bisket, colour it all green with the juice of Spinnage, ſeaſon it with Sugar, Roſe-water, Cinamon, Nutmeg, and a little Salt: you may bake it in a diſh, on a ſheet of paſte croſs-barred over, with puff-paſte, ſo garniſh it with Lozenges.

To make a Cowſlip Tart.

YOu muſt take the bloſſoms, of at leaſt a Gallon of Cowſlips, mince them exceeding ſmall, and beat them in a morter, put to them a handful or two of grated Naple-Bisket, about a pint & half of Cream, ſo put them into a skillet, and let them boyl a little on the fire, take them off, and beat in eight eggs with a litle cream, if it doth not thicken, lay it on the fire gently until it doth, but take heed it curdles not, ſeaſon it with ſugar, roſewater; and a little ſalt; you may bake it in a diſh, or little open Tarts, but your beſt way is to let your Cream be cold before you ſtir in your Eggs.

To make a Cheeſe Tart.

TAke about three quarters of a pound of old Cheeſe of Parmyzant, and grate it; put it into a ſtone mortar: with about a dozen eggs: caſting away ſix of the Whites; put therein half a pound of ſweet butter melted, with ſome Ginger, Cinamon, grated Nutmeg, and Salt; with a penny Manchet grated: ſeaſon it with ſugar and roſe-water: then beat into it ſo much Cream, that it may be as thin or thinner than batter for Fretters, you may make it in a diſh on a ſheet of paſte, otherwiſe wife you may dry your Coffins, and put it in with your Ladle: and put over it crofs bars of puff-pafte, fo bake it, and garnifh it.

To make a Prewen Tart.

STew a pound and half of Prewens, in as much Claret wine as will cover them, and when they are tenderly done, ftrain them through a bolter or thin ftrayner, rub them all to pieces with your hands, and pour in fome of the liquor they were ftewed in to wafh the Prewens from the ftones; fo that which remains in the bolter, or ftrainer, fhall be nothing but the skin or ftone thereof; fet your difh with the palp of the Prewens, on a Chaffin-difh of coales, with a little whole Cinamon, Large Mace, with a little Orangado and Cittern minced, feafon it with fugar, Rofe-water, beaten Cinamon and Ginger, let it boyl up until it be thick together: then take out your whole fpice; you muft make your Coffin about an inch and half high: And fet it in corners, in what form you pleafe, either in fix, eight, or twelve; when its dryed in an Oven put in your Tart ftuff, plaining it all over with a fpoon, put it into the Oven, and let it ftand a little; when you take it forth, ftick it with fugar, lozenges, and ftrow it over with fmall bisket red and white, fcrape on fugar.

To make Cheefe Cakes.

PUt Runnet to three Gallons of Milk, that it may be a tender Curd; run it through a thin ftrayner, when its come and gathered, fcruife, or prefs out the Whey, as well as you can poffible, put it into a deep difh, or bafon, put to it about a pound of fweet butter melted, a matter of fourteen eggs, cafting away half the whites, feafon it with Cinamon, Ginger, Cloves, Nutmeg, fugar, fufficient to fweeten it, with a little falt; with Orangado, and Cittern minced, with Rofe water, and a handful of grated bread or Naple Bisket, mix it all well together, if it be too ſtiff, add a little ſweet Cream, let it not be too thin to beat down the ſides of your Cakes; then make your paſte with the yolks of eggs, melted butter, and warm milk with a handful of fine powdred Sugar; roll out your paſt very thin, and jagg out your patterns, by a large round Trencher; and paper them; then put on your ſeaſoned Curds by ſpoonfuls; and turn up the ſides on it in four, ſix, or eight Corners, bake them in a quick Oven, but not too hot, they will ask but a quarter of an hours time baking: You may bake them on ſheets of paſte in a pattee pan, elſe in ſet Coffins.

To make a diſh of Puffs.

TAke Cheeſe-curds, as before, to the value of three pints, mix with them a good handful of flour dryed in an Oven, put to them ſix eggs, caſting by the whites of four, with about a quarter of a pound of butter in little bits, ſeaſon them with Cinamon, Ginger, and a little Salt; mix them together with your hand very well; then take vvhite paper buttered over, ſo lay on your curd by ſpoonfuls; bake them in an Oven, as before; vvhen they are enough, take them off the papers, put them into a diſh; and vvaſh over their upper ſide vvith butter, ſcrape Sugar upon them, and ſet them into the Oven again; and when they are vvell dryed, put into them Roſe vvater, drawn butter and Sugar; ſo toſs them up together, then diſh them up, and put to them the ſaid lear, and ſcrape Sugar over your diſh; you may alſo make them green, another vvay; throw a handful of ſpinnage into boyling vvater, that it may be very green, take it up, and vvring the vvater clean out of it, mince it exceeding ſmall; and put it to your Curd, ſeaſoned as aforeſaid, ſo bake them and ſerve them up as before.   *To*

To bake a set Custard.

YOu may make your Custard paste of fine flower, and put in the yolks of a few Eggs; but let them be well mingled; then make up your paste (with milk almost ready to boyl) let it be very stiff; and mould it very well; then drive forth your pattern; let your border be very thin, raised about three inches high, and when it is footed round cut off your border; (if you make a great Custard, you may raise two large borders) drive out your bottom very thin; and when it is papered, form your Custard upon it, in the best fashion you can; then wet it round with a feather, between the bottom and foot, and set it; jagg off the Paste round by the foot, and prick your Custard in the bottom; then take a pottle of Cream, and let it heat on the fire; beat a dozen of eggs with a little Cream, and strain it through a strainer, to take forth all the Cock treads; then beat it into your Cream, being blood-warm; you may put Raisons, Dates, and Currans in the bottoms of your Custards, and put them into the Oven to dry; then season your stuff with Sugar and Rose-water, and stir it together on the fire, but let it not be but little more than blood-warm; stir it together, and fill your Custard with your ladle: with this stuff your may make Dowcets; this is only to teach them which are ignorant, for every Cook is expert in this, and commonly make their paste with boyling water and flour: take heed your Oven be not too hot.

To make Tarts of the Jelly of Pippins.

FOr making of your Jelly of Pippins, you must take of your fairest Apples, pared, quartered, and cored; for every pound of them, take three quarters of a pound of fine Sugar, put them into a stew-pan, and almost cover them with clear Spring-water, put to them three

three or four sticks of Cinamon, cover your pan very close with a lid, set them upon Charcoals, and let them boyl up softly, until they come to a colour; see that your fire be not too fierce, and stir them somtimes that they do not burn; when they are enough, they will look as red as Ruby, and clear as Crystal, then take them off the fire, and put them in a dish; when they are cold, you may fill them into Coffins dried, like Hearts or Diamonds: and stick them with Orangado and Cittern, and serve them up as a dish, or garnish other rich Tarts or baked meats with them: you may also put them on thin sheets of rich Paste, and make them little in the manner of Taffaty-Tarts.

To make a Goosberry Tart green, and clear as Christal.

MAke the Coffins of your Tarts, and put powdered Sugar all over the bottom; then take your fair round Goosberies, and fill your Coffins with them, laying them in one by one: put sugar on the top of them, so lay on another laying, then cover them with sugar: let your lids be carved at the top, so close your Tarts, and give them a quick baking; so will they be green and clear: In the same manner must you bake Codlins, after you have made them green, by adding to them good store of sugar, and cutting the lid on the top: by a contrary way, must you bake Cherries, or whatsoever you will have red, as Currants, Rasberries, Straberries, Pippins or Quinces, *&c.* you must allow to them sugar sufficient, as before, but bake them close without cutting the lids, and let them bake soberly, giving them soaking enough, and they will be red.

To make Puff-Paste.

TAke a pottle of flour, and the whites of six eggs, make it up into a Paste, with cold water, let it not be very stiff: when it is well wrought, roll it forth four square

square into a sheet, as thick as your finger, then take three pound of Butter, and beat it well with a rolling-pin, then lay it on in slices, all over your Paste, about as thick as your finger, and strow a little flour all over; then roll up your sheet of Paste like a Coller, with the Butter within, scruise and close it at both ends with your rolling-pin; also scruise it all along the roll of paste, and roll it broad and long wayes, then clap up both ends, and make them meet in the middle, one over another, and fasten it down again with your rolling pin, rolling it forth every way, as thin as it was at the first, when you laid on the butter; then flour your board well underneath, and spread it over with butter, roll it up, and work it, as before: thus do three or four times, until your three pound of Butter be gone: in the summer you must make this Paste in the morning, with the stiffest butter you can get, and lay it in a cold place, until you make use thereof: in the winter time you must beat your butter very well, otherwise it will be harder than your Paste, and break holes through it.

To make a laid Tart for Preserves.

TAke a sheet of puff-paste, being rolled forth, about an inch thick, and as broad as a large Pie-plate (or as you please) put it on a large sheet of white paper, and carve it with your pen-knife, in what form or fashion you please, either like four flowerdeluces, or in the fashion of a tree with limbs and branches; then take it on your pasty-peel, and put it into your Oven, not too hot nor two cold; when it is baked, take it forth, and wash it over with a little butter; scrape on sugar, and let it dry a little longer in the Oven, dish it upon a dishing Plate, and place on your Preserves all over the limbs or branches of your Tart, and your suckets and dryed sweet-meats.

To

To make a Warden or Pear-Pye.

FIrst bake your Wardens, or Pears in an Oven, with a little water and a good quantity of Sugar, let your pot be close covered with a piece of dough: let them not be fully baked by a quarter of an hour: when they are cold, make an high Coffin, and put them in whole, adding to them some Cloves, whole Cinamon, Sugar, with some of the liquor they were baked in, so close it and bake it.

To Bake a Quince Pye.

CUt your Quinces from the Core, and fill your pye, lay over it sliced Orangado, and pour into it the sirrup of Barberries, Mulberries, Orangado, and put on good store of Sugar, with two or three sticks of Cinamon; so close and prick it, but give it as little vent as you can: you may also bake them whole, after you have cored them with your coring iron, and pared them very thin; when they are placed in your pye, fill the vacant place where your core was taken out, with the sirrup of Orangado; they ought to have as much Sugar to them as their weight, but not if you have store of sweet sirrup.

To make a Pye with whole Pippins.

YOu must pare and core your Pippins, and when your Coffins is made, take a handful of sliced Quinces, and strow over the bottom thereof; then place in your Pippins, and fill the core holes with the sirrup of Quinces, and put into every one a piece of Orangado, so pour on the sirrup of Quinces over your Apples, with Sugar, and close it; these pyes will ask good soaking, especially the Quince-pye.

A

A set Tart.

YOu may make your paſt rich, put in good ſtore of yolks of eggs, and warm milk, but not too much Butter, and drive out a ſheet of paſte very thin; let your borders alſo be driven out in lengths (thin) but ſo as they will ſtand; cut out your borders through your ſheet an inch and half high; Jagging out one length with your Jaggin-iron, and another with your knife; then take the center of your bottom, and ſet up a tower of about three or four inches high, then ſet your proportions round about, ſome Hearts, and ſome Diamonds, to ſet the outward circumference in what form or figure you pleaſe: when you have pricked and dryed it, you may fill it with your Sweet-meats, Jellies, Leaches, &c. as for example, pour in Chriſtal Jelly into an Heart, and alſo into the oppoſite: Leach into another, and alſo into the oppoſite: ſo two of each ſort, one oppoſite to another, in all your figures.

RARE

RARE RECEIPTS IN COOKERY

Part II.

To make a Bisk divers wayes.

TAke a Rack of Mutton and a Knuckle of Veal, put them a boyling in a Pipkin of a gallon with fome fair water, and when it boyls fcum it, and put to it fome Salt, two or three blades of large Mace, and a Clove or two, boyl it to three pints, and ftrain the meat, fave the broth for your ufe, and take off the fat clean.

Then boyl twelve Pidgeon-Peepers; and eight Chicken-peepers, in a Pipkin of fair water, falt and a piece of interlarded Bacon, fcum them clean, and boyl them fine, white, and quick.

Then

Then have a roaſt Capon minced, and put to it ſome gravy, Nutmeg and Salt, and ſtew it together, then put to it the juyce of two or three Oranges, and beaten butter, &c.

Then have ten Sweet-breads, and ten Palats fry'd, and the ſame number of Lips and Noſes, being tender boyled, and blancht, cut them like Lard, and fry them, and put away the butter, and put to them gravy, a little Anchovi, Nutmeg, and a little Garlick, or none, the juyce of two or three Oranges, and Marrow fry'd in Batter, with Sage leaves, and ſome beaten Butter.

Then again, have ſome boyl'd Marrow, and twelve Artichokes, Suckets, and Peaches finely boyl'd and put into beatten Butter, ſome Piſtaches, boyled alſo in ſome wine and gravy, eight Sheeps tongues larded and boyled, and one hundred Sparragraſs, boyled, and put into beaten Butter or skirrets.

Then have Lemons carved, and ſome cut like little dice.

Again, fry ſome Spinnage and Parſle &c.

Theſe foreſaid materials being ready, have ſome French bread in the bottom of your diſh; then diſh on it your Chickens and Pidgeons, broth it, next your Quails; then Sweet-breads, then your Palats, then your Artichokes or Sparragraſs, and Piſtaches; then your Lemon, Pomgranat, or Grapes; Spinnage and fryed Marrow; and if yellow Saffron or fryed Sage, then round the center of your boyled meat, put your minced capon, then run all over with beaten butter, &c.

1. For variety, clarified with yolks of eggs.
2. Knots of Eggs.
3. Cocks Stones.
4. Cocks Combs.
5. If white, ſtrained Almonds with ſome of the broth.   6. Gooſ-

6. Gosberries or Barberries.
7. Minced meat in balls.
8. If green, juyce of Spinnage ſtamped with Manchet.
2. Garniſh with boyled Spinnage.
10. If yellow, yolks of hard eggs ſtrained with ſome broth and Saffron; and many other varieties.

To boyl a Capon in Rice.

BOyl a Capon in ſalt and water, and if you like it, you may put into a fair cloth a handful of Oatmeal; then take a quarter of a pound of Rice, and ſteep it in fair water, and ſo half boyl it: then ſtrain the Rice through a Cullender; and boyl it in a Pipkin, with a quart of Milk: put in half an ounce of large Mace, half a pound of Sugar: boyl it well, but not over thick: put in a little Roſe-water, blanch half a pound of Almonds; and beat them in a Morter with a little Cream and Roſe-water very fine; ſtrain them in a Pipkin by it ſelf; then take up your Capon; and ſet your Almonds a little againſt the fire: garniſh your diſhes as you think fit, and lay in your Capon, and put your Rice handſomly thereon, then broth up your Rice.

A Bisk another way.

TAke a Leg of Beef cut into two pieces, and boyl it in a gallon, or five quarts of water, ſcum it, and about half an hour after, put in a knuckle of Veal, and ſcum it alſo, boyl it from five quarts, to two quarts, or leſs; and being three quarters boyled, put in ſome ſalt, Cloves and Mace: being through boyled, ſtrain it from the meat, and keep the broth for your uſe in a Pipkin; then take eight Marrow bones clean ſcraped from the fleſh, and finely cracked over the middle; boyl in water or ſalt three of them; the other reſerve for garniſh to be boyld in ſtrong broth and laid on the top of the

Bisk, when dished; again, boyl your fowl in water and salt, Teals, Partridge, Pigeons, Quailes, Larks, Plovers; then have a joynt of Mutton made into balls with sweet Herbs; Salt, Nutmegs, grated bread; Eggs, Suet, a clove or two of Garlike, and Pistaches boyled in broth; with some interlarded Bacon, Sheeps tongues larded and stewed, as also some Artichokes, Marrow, Pistaches, Sweet-breads and Lamb-stones, in strong broth, and mace, a clove or two, some white-wine and strained Almonds, or with the yolk of an Egg, Verjuice, and beaten butter and sliced Lemon, or Grapes whole; then have fryed Clary, and Pistaches in yolks of Eggs; with carved Lemons all over.

To boyl a Leg of Mutton the French fashion.

TAke a fair Leg of Mutton, and a piece of suet off the Kidney cut in long slices as big as ones finger, then thrust your knife into the flesh of your Leg, down as deep as your finger is long; and thrust into every hole a slice of the said Kidney suet, but take heed one piece touch not another, boyl your Leg well, but not too much, then put half a pint of the broth into a Skillet or Pipkin; and put to it three or four blades of whole Mace, half a handful of Barberies, and Salt, boyl them until the broth be half boyl'd away; then take it off the fire, and strait before the broth hath done boyling, put in a piece of sweet butter, a good handful of French capers, and a lemmon cut in square pieces like dice, with the rind on, and a litle Sack, with the yolks of two hard Eggs minced, lay your Leg of Mutton with the fairest side upward upon sippets in your garnished dish: having all these things in readiness to put into your aforesaid broth, when it comes boyling off the fire, then pour it on your Leg of Mutten hot.

To boyl Partridges.

Take three Partridges, put them into a Pipkin, with as much water as will cover them, alſo take three or four blades of Mace, one Nutmeg quartered, five or ſix whole Cloves, a piece of ſweet Butter, two or three manchet toaſts toaſted brown, ſoak them in a little ſack, or Muſcadine, ſtrain it through a canvas ſtrainer with ſome of the broth, and put them into the Pipkin with your Partridges; boyl them very ſoftly; often turning them until your broth be half conſumed, then put in a little ſweet butter and ſalt. When your broth is boyled, garniſh your diſh with a ſliced Lemon, and the yolk of a hard Egg minced ſmall; then lay on ſmall heaps between the ſlices of Lemon; and place your Partridge in your garniſht diſh, on ſippets; and your broth hot on them; lay upon the breaſts of your Patridges, round ſlices of Lemon pared; mince ſmall and ſtrow on the yolk of a hard Egg; prick over all their breaſts five or ſix wing feathers, and ſerve them up; after this manner you may boyl young Turkies, Pheaſants, or Pea-Chickens, Wood-cocks, Quails, &c.

Capons in Pottage in the French faſhion.

Take two Capons, draw and truſs them, parboyl them, and fill their bellies with Marrow, put them in a Pipkin with a Knuckle of Veal, let them boyl together; when they are half boyled, with ſtrong broth, if you have it, then put in your Lamb-ſtones and Sweet-breads; ſeaſon it with Cloves, Mace, and a little ſalt, a Faggot of ſweet Herbs and an Onion; let it boyl gently until all is enough; take heed you boyl them not too much; in the interim, make ready the bottoms and tops of four rolls of French bread, put them a drying in a fair diſh, wherein you put the Capons, ſet it on the fire, & lay over them, ſome ſtrong broth;

broth; with a ladleful of gravy, cover it, until you dish them up; then dish up your Capons, with your Knuckle of Veal between them, garnish your Capons with Sweetbreads and carved Lemon; and your Veal with slices of Bacon fryed up with the yolks of Eggs, and pour on it strong broth and gravy, with a little drawn Butter, and serve it up.

To make a boyled meat, much like a Bisk.

TAke a Rack of Mutton, cut it in four pieces, and boyl it in three quarts of fair water in a pipkin, with a faggot of sweet herbs bound up close; scum your broth, and put in some salt, about half an hour after, put in three Chickens, scalded and trust, with three Partridges boyled in water; the blood being well soaked out of them, putting to them three blades of large Mace; then have all manner of sweet herbs, finely picked, being minced; and before you dish up your boyled meat, put them to your broth, and let them have four or five walms, and take for the top of your boyled meat, a pound of interlarded Bacon cut in thin slices, put them in a pipkin, with the Marrow of six bones, twelve bottoms of young Artichokes, six Sweet-breads of Veal, strong broth, Mace, Nutmeg, with Goosberries or Barberries; Butter and Pistaches; these being all ready, garnish your dish with Artichoke, carved Lemon, Pistaches, Grapes, and large Mace; your sippets being finely carved, with slices of French bread in the bottom of your dish, dish up your Mutton three pieces round about, and one piece in the middle, with your three Chickens between the three pieces of Mutton, and your Partridge in the middle, pour on the Broth with the herbs; then put on your pipkin over all; it being Marrow, Artichokes, and the other ingredients with sliced Lemons, Barberries, and drawn Butter over all; your sippets round the dish, &c.   *To*

Rare Receipts in Cookery. 197

To boyl a Neck, Loyn, or Chine of Mutton, or a Neck, Leg, Fillet, Knuckle of Veal, Leg, or Loyn of Lamb.

Cut any of thefe meats in fo big pieces, as that two or three of them may ferve in a difh, and put them into a pot, with fo much water as will cover them; if you have one neck of Mutton or Veal, you may take ten fprigs of Winter-favory, and as much of Time, adding to them twelve great Onions, if they are fmall take the more: grate to them half a penny loaf, with half an ounce of Cloves and Mace, and one handful of Spinnage, a little Salt and Parflee (if in the Spring or Summer, otherwife Capers and Sampier) let it boyl moderately, until it be half confumed: when you take it off, add a little Vinegar and drawn Butter; but you muft note, not to let your Spinnage and Parflee to have above a quarter of an hours boyling: you may difh it in as many difhes as you pleafe, and ferve it hot to the table.

To boyl a Chine of Veal whole, or in pieces,

Boyl it in ftrong broth, with a faggot or two of fweet herbs, a piece of Bacon: and when its above half boyled, put in Capers, a little large Mace, whole Pepper, fome Salt and Oyfter liquor, your Chines being well boyled, have fome ftewed Oyfters by themfelves, with fome Mace and whole Onions, Vinegar, Butter, and Pepper, &c. then have Cucumbers boyled by themfelves in water and falt, or pickled Cucumbers boyled in water, putting thereto, beaten Butter, and Cabbage, Lettice, being parboyled: then difh your Chines on fippets, broth them, and put on your ftewed Oyfters, Cucumbers, Lettice, and parboyled Grapes, or fliced Lemon, and run it over with beaten Butter.

To bake a Pig to be eaten cold, called a Mare-maid Pye.

TAke a Pig, flea it and quarter it, bone it; take also a good Eele fleaed, split, boned, and seasoned with Pepper, Salt, and Nutmeg: then lay a quarter of your Pig in a round Pye, and part of the Eele on that quarter; then lay on another quarter on the other, and then more Eele, and thus keep the order until your Pye be full; then lay a few whole Cloves, slices of Bacon, and Butter, and close it up, bake it in a good fine Paste; being baked and cold, fill it up with good sweet Butter.

Another way.

SCald it and bone it, being first cleansed, dry the sides in a clean cloth, and season them with beaten Nutmeg, Pepper, Salt, and chopt Sage; then have two Neats tongues, dryed well, boyled and cold, slice them out all the length, as thick as half a crown, and lay a quarter of your Pig in a square or round Pye, and slices of the Tongue on it: then another quarter of Pig and more tongue, thus do for four times double, and lay over all, slices of Bacon, a few Cloves, Butter, and a Bay-leaf or two, then bake it, and being baked, fill it up with good sweet Butter; make your Paste white of Butter and Flour.

To bake Steaks the French way.

SEason your Steaks with pepper, nutmeg, and salt lightly, and set them by; then take a piece of the leanest of a leg of Mutton, and mince it small with some Beef-suit, and a few sweet-herbs, as tops of time and penny-royal, grated bread, yolks of eggs, sweet cream, raisons of the sun, &c. work altogether, and make it into little balls, and roles, put them into a deep round Pye on the Steaks, then put to them some butter, and
sprinkle

sprinkle it with verjuice, close it and bake it; when its enough, cut it up, and liquor it with the juice of two or three Oranges or Lemons.

A Pudding stewed between two dishes.

TAke the yolks of three eggs, and the white of one, half a dozen spoonfuls of sweet cream, a nutmeg grated, a few cloves and mace, a quarter of a pound of beef-suet minced small, a quarter of a pound of currans, temper it like a pudding, with grated bread, and a spoonful of rose-water; then take a Caul of Veal, cut it in square pieces like trenchers, lay three spoonfuls of your batter on one side, then roll it up in the Caul, pin on one side, over another with two small pricks, and tye each end with a thred; you may put two, or three, or four of them in a dish; then take half a pint of strong mutton broth, and half a dozen spoonfuls of vinegar, three or four blades of large mace, and an ounce of sugar, make this broth to boyl upon a chaffin-dish of coals, and then put in your pudding when it boyls, cover it with another dish, and let it stew a quarter of an hour loger, turn them for burning; then take up your pudding, and lay it on sippets, and pour the broth upon the top, garnish your dish with the core of a Lemon and Barberies; serve them hot, either at dinner or supper.

To make French Puffs with green herbs.

TAke spinage, parsle, endive, a sprig or two of savery; mince them very fine, season them with nutmeg, ginger, and sugar, wet them with eggs according to the quantity of herbs more or less, then take the core of a Lemon cut in round slices very thin; put to every slice of your Lemon a slice of this stuff, then fry it with sweet Lard, in a frying-pan, as you fry eggs, and serve them with sippets or without, sprinkle them either with white wine or Sack, or any other wine, faving Rhenifh wine, ferve them either at dinner or fupper.

To Bake all manner of Land-fowl; as Turkey, Buftard, Peacock, Crane, &c. to be eaten cold.

TAke a Turkey and bone it, parboyl and lard it thick, with great lard, as big as your little finger, then feafon it with two ounces of beaten Pepper, two ounces of beaten Nutmeg, and three ounces of Salt; feafon the fowl, and lay it in a pye fit for it, put firft Butter in the bottom, with fome ten whole Cloves, then lay on the Turkey, and the reft of the feafoning on it; lay on good ftore of Butter, then clofe it up, and bafte it, either with Saffron-water, or three or four eggs, beaten together with their yolks; bake it, and being baked and cold, liquor it with Clarified Butter, &c.

To fry Sheeps-tongues, Deers-tongues, or Calves-tongues.

BReak three or four eggs, with Nutmeg, Cinamon, Sugar, and Salt, peel your tongues, and flice them in thin flices, put them into your eggs; and when your frying-pan is hot with Butter and fweet Lard, cut the core of a Lemon in fmall pieces like Dice, and put it into your Eggs and Tongues, but not before you are ready to put your meat into the pan, for then it will make them curdle, and fry them in fpoonfuls like eggs, on both fides; the leaft burning takes away all the good tafte of the other things; fry them, and difh them on fippets, or upon thin Manchet-toafts, fryed with fweet Butter; let your fauce be Sack or White-wine, fweet Butter and Sugar, heat it hot, and pour it on the top of your Tongues, fcrape on Sugar, and fend it hot to the Table.

To

To bake a Pig to be eaten hot.

FLay a small fat Pig, cut it in quarters, or in smaller pieces, season it with Pepper, Ginger, and Salt, lay it into a fit Coffin, strip and mince small a handful of Parslee, six sprigs of Winter-savoury, strow it on the meat in the pye, and strow upon that the yolks of three or four hard eggs minced, and lay upon them five or six blades of Mace, a handful of clusters of Barberries, a handful of Currans well washed and picked, a little Sugar, half a pound of sweet Butter, or more, close your pye, and set it in an Oven, as hot as for Manchet, and in two hours it will be baked; draw it forth, and put in half a point of Vinegar and Sugar, being warmed upon the fire, pour it all over the meat, and put on the pye-lid again; scrape on Sugar, and serve it hot to the table.

To bake all manner of Sea-fowl, as Swan, Whopper, to be eaten cold.

TAke a Swan, bone, parboyl, and lard it with great lard; season the lard with Nutmeg and Pepper only; then take two ounces of Pepper, three of Nutmeg, and four of Salt; season the fowl, and lay it in the pye with good store of Butter, then close it up in Rye-paste, or Meal course bolted, and made up with boyling liquor, and make it up stiff; or you may bake them to eat hot, only giving them half the seasoning; you may bake them in earthen pans, or pots, for to be preserved cold, they will keep longer: In the same manner you may bake all sorts of wild-Geese, tame-Geese, bran-Geese, Muscovia-Ducks, Gulls, Shovellers, Herns, Curlews, &c. In baking of these fowl to be eaten hot, for the garnish, put in a big Onion, Goosberries, or Grapes in the pye, and sometimes Capers or Oysters, and liquor it with Gravy, Claret, and Butter.

To Harſh a Carp.

TAke a Carp, ſcale and ſcrape off the ſlime with your Knife, wipe it with a dry cloth, bone it and mince it with a freſh-water Eele; being fleaed and boned, ſeaſon it with beaten cloves, mace, ſalt, pepper, and ſome ſweet-herbs, as time, parſle, and ſome ſweet-Marjoram minced very ſmall; ſtew it in a broad-mouthed pipkin, with ſome claret-wine, gooſberries, or grapes, and ſome blanched cheſnuts: being finely ſtewed, ſerve it on carved ſippets about it, and run it over with beaten butter, garniſh the diſh with ſtale grated manchet ſearſed, and ſome fried Oyſters in butter, Cockles or Prawns; ſomtimes for variety, uſe piſtaches, Pine-apple ſeeds, or ſome blanched Almonds, ſtewed amongſt the haſh, or ſparragraſs, or artichokes boyled, and cut as big as Cheſtnuts, and garniſh the diſh with ſcraped Horſe-radiſh, and rub the bottom of the diſh in which you ſerve the meat, with a clove or two of Garlick, ſomtimes mingle it with ſome ſtewed Oyſters, or put to it ſome Oyſter-liquor.

For the Stock for Jelly.

TAke two pair of Calves-feet finely cleanſed, the fat and great bones taken out and parted in halves; being well ſoaked in fair water for twenty four hours, and often ſhifted; boyl them in a braſs pot or pipkin cloſe covered, in the quantity of a gallon of water, boyl them to three pints, then ſtrain the broth through a clean ſtrong Canvas, into an earthen pan or baſon; when it is cold, take off the top, and pare off the dregs off the bottom; put it in a clean well-glazed pipkin of two quarts, with a quart of white-wine, a quarter of a pint of cinamon-water, nutmeg & ginger-water, as much of each, or theſe ſpices ſliced; then have two pound of double refined ſugar, beaten with eggs in a deep diſh

or

or bafon. Your Jelly being new melted, put in the eggs with fugar; ſtir all the aforeſaid materials together, and ſet it a ſtewing on a ſoft Charcole-fire, the ſpace of half an hour or more; being well digeſted, and clear run, take out the bone and fat, of any meat for Jellies; for it doth but ſtain the ſtock; and make it, that it will never be white and pure clear.

To make a Jelly as white as Snow, with Jordan Almonds.
TAke a pound of Almonds, ſteep them in cold water, till they will blanch, which will be in ſix hours; beat them with a quart of Roſe-water, then have a decoction of half a pound of Izing-glaſs, boyled with a gallon of fair ſpring-water, or elſe half Wine; boyl it till half be waſted, then let it cool, ſtrain it, and mingle it with your Almonds, and ſtrain with them a pound of double refined ſugar, the juice of two Lemons, put Saffron to ſome of it, and make ſome blew, red, yellow, green, or what colour elſe you pleaſe; and caſt it into Lemons or Orange-Rhindes, &c. ſerve of divers of theſe colours on a diſh or plate.

To make ſome Kickſhaws in Paſte, to fry or bake in what form you pleaſe.
MAke ſome ſhort puff-paſte, roll it thin, if you have any molds, you may work it upon them with the pulp of Pippins, ſeaſoned with Cinamon, Ginger, Sugar, and Roſe-water; cloſe them up and bake them, or fry them; Or you may fill them with Gooſberries, ſeaſoned with Cinamon, Sugar, Ginger, and Nutmeg; roll them up in yolks of eggs, and it will keep your Marrow, being boyled, from melting away: Or you may fill them with Curds, boyled up with whites of eggs and cream, and it will be a tender Curd; but you muſt ſeaſon the Curd with parboyled Currans, three or four ſliced Dates put into it, or ſix bits of Marrow,

row, as big as half a Walnut, put in some small pieces of Almond-paste, Sugar, Rose-water, and Nutmeg. And this will serve for any of these Kick-shaws, either to bake, or for a Florentine in Puff-paste; any of these you may fry or bake, for dinner or supper.

To make a Pottage.

TAke Beef Palats that are tenderly boyled, blanched, and sliced; put to them a piece of good middle Bacon, and five or six sweet-breads of Veal; let these boyl together in a deep dish with strong Broth, put to them a handful of Champignions, a great Onion or two, about six Cloves, a little large Mace, and a faggot of sweet herbs; when it is almost boyled, add to it a pint of Gravy, a grated Nutmeg, season it with Salt; make ready a dish with your tops and bottoms of French bread sliced: put Gravy thereon, and set your dish on the coals; add Chesnuts to your Broth, you must have in a Pipkin by, with the Marrow of three bones stewed in strong Broth, with the bottoms of three or four Artichokes cut in pieces; when all is enough, dish up a round piece of your Bacon upon sippets, in the middle of your dish, and your sweet-breads and palats round about, with your other Bacon in slices; then dish up your Marrow, Artichokes, and Chesnuts, all over that, so pour over your Broth; and scruise on two or three Lemons.

To make a small Bisk of flesh roasted.

TAke half a dozen of Chicken peepers, and as many squob Pigeons, scalded, drawn, trust, and set, lard the one half of them, or any other such like fowl, as Larks, Quails, &c. then take Lambstones blancht, also Cocks combs and stones, with Ox palats tenderly boyled, and cut three inches in length and breadth, lard them exceeding thick with small lard, also take slices of of Bacon, and great Sage leaves; spit your fowl on a small spit, with one of your slices of Bacon and Sage between each fowl, as also a piece of palat; thus do until all your fowl, Bacon, and palats are spitted; parboyl likewise some great Oysters, and lard them with a small larding prick; also lard your Sweet-breads and Lamb-stones; & spit them with slices of Bacon between each of them; then season your Oysters with grated Bread, Nutmeg, and Time, a little Salt; and when your Sweet-breads are almost roasted, broach your Oysters upon square rods, and tye them on the Sweet-breads, baste them with the yolks of Eggs beaten with a grated Nutmeg, and let them roast together; then take your Cocks combs and stones, (being tenderly boyled) and fry them, being dipt in yolks of Eggs: also fry the bottoms of Artichokes, and Marrow in Eggs; put all these in a deep dish with a pint of Gravy, on a heap of coals, (only the Artichokes and Marrow by themselves with a little drawn Butter) add to them Oyster liquor, Claret wine, grated Nutmeg, with some Anchovies dissolved, a handful or two of Mushrooms, some Chestnuts, and Pistaches; when your Range is ready, baste up your birds, and dish them into the middle of your dish; then dish two rows of your palats (opposite one to another) from your Chickens towards the dish brim; so with your Sweet-breads in two parcels crosing them; also your Lamb-stones & Oysters, thwarting in two parcels opposite likewise; these eight parcels will cover your dish from the fowl to the brim; let your Bacon be garnisht over the whole; then take your other ingredients in the lear, and garnish over your fowl, and the rest with your Artichokes, Marrow, Pistaches, and Chestnuts over all; then add a little drawn Butter, and the juice of two or three Lemons to your lear, and pour it over all; garnish it with Lemon and Bay-leaves fryed, and send it to the table hot: this dish is for your second course.

A

A Jelly for service of several colours.

TAke four pair of Calves feet, a knuckle of Veal, a good fleshy Capon; and prepare those things, as is said in the Chryſtal Jelly; boyl them in three gallons of fair water, till ſix quarts be waſted; then ſtrain it into an earthen pan, let it cool; and being cold pare the bottom, and take off the fat on the top alſo; then diſſolve it again into broth, and divide it into four equal parts, put it into four ſeveral pipkins, as will contain five pints each pipkin; put in a little ſaffron into one of them; into another Churcenela beat with Album, into another Turnſole; and the other his own natural white; alſo to every pipkin a quart of white Wine, and the juice of two Lemons; then alſo to the white Jelly, one race of Ginger pared and ſliced, and three blades of large Mace; to the red Jelly, two Nutmegs, as much in quantity of Cinamon; alſo as much Ginger to the Turnſole; put alſo the ſame quantity, with a few whole Cloves; then to the amber or yellow colour, the ſame ſpices and quantity; then have eighteen whites of Eggs, and beat them with ſix pound of double refined Sugar, beaten ſmall and ſtirred together, in a great Tray or Baſon with a Rolling-pin, divide it into four parts into the four pipkins, and ſtir it to your Jelly, broth, ſpice, and wine: being well mixed together with a little Musk and Ambergreaſe: then have new bags, waſh them firſt in warm water, and then in cold, wring them dry, and being ready ſtrung with pack-thread, and ſticks, hang them on a ſpit by the fire, from any duſt, and ſet new earthen pans under them, being well ſeaſoned with boyling liquor: Then again ſet on your Jelly on a fine Charcoal fire, and let it ſtew ſoftly the ſpace of an hour, or almoſt; then make it boyl up a little, and take it off: being ſomewhat cold, run it through the bag twice or thrice, or but once if it be very clear: into the bags of colours

colours put in a sprig of Rosemary, keep it for your use in those pans, dish it as you see good, or cast it into what mould you please: As for example, these, Scollop shells, Cockle shells, Egg shells, half Lemon or Lemon-peel, Wilks, or Winkle shells, Muscle shells, or moulded out of a Butter squirt: or serve it on a great dish and plate, one quarter of white, another of red, another of yellow, the fourth of another colour, and about the sides of the dish Oranges in quarters of Jelly, in the middle a whole Lemon full of Jelly finely carved, or cast out of a Wooden on Tin mould, or run it into little round glasses, four or five in a dish, or silver trencher plates, or glass trencher plates.

To bake Apricocks green.

TAke young green Apricocks, so tender, that you may thrust a pin through the stone, scald and scrape the outside, oft putting them in water as you peel them, till your Tart be ready, then dry and fill the Tart with them, and lay on good store of fine Sugar, close it, and bake it, scrape on Sugar, and serve it up: before you close it, cut your lid in branches, or works, that it may look somewhat open, and it will look the greener.

To make an Oatmeal Pudding.

STeep Oatmeal in warm Milk three or four hours, then strain some blood into it of fish or flesh, mix it with Cream, and add to it suet minced small, sweet herbs chopped fine, as Time, Parslee, Spinnage, Succory, Endive, Straw-berry-leaves, Violet-leaves, Pepper, Cloves, Mace, fat Beef-suet, and four Eggs, mingle all together, and so bake it.

To make an Oatmeal Pudding boyled.

TAke the biggest Oatmeal, mince what herbs you like best, and mix with it, season it with Pepper and Salt;

Salt; tye it ſtrait in a bag; and when it is boyled, butter it and ſend it up.

Oatmeal Puddings, otherwiſe of fiſh or fleſh blood.

TAke a quart of whole Oatmeal, ſteep it in warm Milk over night, and then drain the groats from it, boyl them in a quart or three pints of good Cream; then the Oatmeal being boyled and cold, have Time, Penny-royal, Parſlee, Spinnage, Savory, Endive, Marjorum, Sorrel, Succory, and Strawberry-leaves, of each a little quantity, chop them fine, and put them to the Oatmeal, with ſome Fennel-ſeeds, Pepper, Cloves, Mace, and Salt, boyl it in a Napkin, or bake it in a diſh, Pye, or Guts; ſometimes of the former Pudding you may leave out ſome of the herbs, and add theſe, Penny-royal, Savory, Leeks, a good big Onion, Sage, Ginger, Nutmeg, Pepper, Salt, either for fiſh or fleſh dayes, with Butter or Beef-ſuet, boyled, or baked in Diſh, Napkin, or Pye.

To make white Puddings an excellent way.

AFter the Hogs humbles are tender boyled, take ſome of the Lights with the Heart, and all the fleſh about them, picking from them all the ſinewy skins, then chop the meat as ſmall as you can; and put to it a little of the Liver very finely ſearſed, ſome grated Nutmeg, four or five yolks of Eggs, a pint of very good Cream, two or three ſpoonfuls of Sack, Sugar, Cloves, Mace, Nutmeg, Cinamon, Carraway-ſeed, a little Roſe-water, good ſtore of Hogs fat, and ſome Salt, roll it in rolls, two hours before you go to fill them in the Guts, and lay the Guts in ſteep in Roſe-water, till you fill them.

To make an Italian Pudding.

TAke a fine Manchet, and cut it in ſquare pieces like Dice, then put to it half a pound of Beef-ſuet minced ſmall, Raiſins of the Sun, Cloves, Mace, minced Dates,

Dates, Sugar, Marrow, Rose-water, Eggs, and Cream, mingle all these together; put them in a buttered dish, in less than an hour it will be baked; when its enough, scrape on sugar and send it up.

To make Metheglin.

TAke all sorts of herbs, that are good and wholesom, as Balm, Mint, Rosemary, Fennel, Angelica, wild Time, Hyssop, Burnet, Agrimony, and such other field herbs, half a handful of each, boyl and strain them, and let the liquor stand until the next day; being setled, take two gallons and half of Honey, let it boyl an hour, and in the boyling scum it very clean, set it a cooling as you do bear, and when it is cold, take very good Barm, and put it into the bottom of the Tub, by a little and little as to Bear, keep back the thick setling that lyeth in the bottom of the vessel it is cooled in : when it is all put together, cover it with a cloth, and let it work very near three dayes; then when you mean to put it up, scum off all the Barm clean, & put it up into a vessel; but you must not stop it very close in three or four dayes, but let it have some vent to work, when it is close stopped, you must look often to it; and have a peg on the top to give it vent, when you hear it make a noise, as it will do, or else it will break the vessel, somtimes make a bag, and put in good store of sliced Ginger, some Cloves and Cinamon, boyled, or not.

How to make Ipocras.

TAke of Grains half a dram, take of Cinamon four ounces, of Ginger two ounces, of Nutmeg half an ounce, of Cloves, Mace, of each a quarter of an ounce; bruise all these well in a morter, and infuse them in a gallon of white-wine, four or five dayes, the vessel being close stopt, then put to it a pound and half of sugar; when the sugar is dissolved, put to it half a pint of rose-water,

water, and as much Milk, let it ſtand a night, and then let it run through an Ipocras bag; then may you put it in a fine new runlet, if you purpoſe to keep it; or if you ſpend it preſently, you may put it into certain pots for the preſent.

To Jelly Lobſters, Crawfiſh, or Prawnes.

TAke a Tench and ſplit him from the head to the tail, taking out the gills, and waſh him in four or five waters very clean from the blood; ſet as much water on, as will conveniently cover him, in a broad pan, preſſing him down with a diſh or plate; let your liquor be ſeaſoned with ſalt, wine-vinegar, cloves, mace, ginger, quartered nutmeg, five or ſix Bay-leaves, a faggot of ſweet herbs bound up together (obſerve to let your liquor boyl with the fore-named ingredients, before you put in your Tench) it being boyled take it up, and waſh off all the looſe ſcales; then ſtrain the liquor through your Jelly bag; and put to it a piece of Izing-glaſs; being firſt waſht and ſteept for that purpoſe; boyl it very cleanly, and run it through a Jelly bag again; then having your ſhell fiſh, lay them in a clean diſh, the Lobſters being cut in ſlices, and the Crawfiſh, Prawns and Shrimps whole, run this Jelly over them; you may make this Jelly of divers colours to garniſh your diſh.

To Stew Crabs.

YOur Crabs being boyled, take the meat out of the bodies of barrels, and ſave the great claws and the ſmall legs whole to garniſh your diſh; ſtrain the meat with ſome Claret-wine, grated Bread, Wine-Vinegar, Nutmeg, Salt, and a piece of Butter; ſtew them together a quarter of an hour, on a ſoft fire in a Pipkin, and being ſtewed almoſt dry, put in ſome drawn Butter, the yolk of an Egg, a grated Nutmeg, with the juice of

Oranges

Oranges beat up thick; then diſh the legs round about them; put the meat into the ſhells and ſerve them.

To force Crabs.

TAke ſo many Crabs as you pleaſe, take the meat out of the Claws, and mix it with the meat of the body, the skin and ſtrings thereof pick out; and take ſome Pine-apples, Piſtaches, and Artichoke bottoms minced with the body of an Eele half boyled, but not very ſmall, with the meat of the claws before you mix it, as alſo a handful of Oyſters; put to it a little grated Manchet, Nutmeg, Cinamon, Ginger, and Salt, with a Lemon cut in Dice, with the yolks of two or three raw Eggs, and a quarter of a pound of Butter in ſmall bits; make up this into a reaſonable ſtiff force meat, and force your ſhells, make the reſt into ſmall balls; and put them into a deep tin diſh, and bake them gently in an Oven; let your meat in your ſhells be a very tender meat; when they come out of the Oven, add to them ſome drawn butter, and the juice of Oranges and Lemons, diſh them with your forced balls round about them, ſtick them full of picked ſprigs of Paſte about four inches long, and ſtick upon your ſprigs fryed Oyſters, ſo ſend them for a ſecond courſe.

To make water Leach.

TAke a pound of ſweet Almonds, blanch them in blood-warm water, and throw them into cold water; beat them in a Morter with Roſe-water, and when they are beaten to an Almond-paſte, put a pint of Roſe-water more to them, and a pottle of fair ſpring water; and about a quart or more of Rheniſh-wine: ſet theſe together in a skillet on a heap of Charcoals; then add to it about half a pound of Iſinglaſs, being before pulled to pieces and ſteeped in fair water for the ſpace of two hours; put to it ſome whole Cinamon, large Mace, let

let it boyl about an hour keeping it ſtirring, then ſtrain it into a Baſon through a piece of Tiffany; ſeaſon it with ſugar, roſe-water; and a little oyl of cinamon, nutmeg, cloves and mace, with a grain of musk tyed up, then ſet it on the fire again; you may take out ſome in a ſaucer to try its ſtrength; if it be too ſtrong, you muſt add Reniſh-wine; if too weak, boyl it longer with Iſinglaſs; you may add alſo ſome juice of Lemons; ſtrain it again when it is boyled enough, run it into what colours you pleaſe.

To make a boyled Pudding.

TAke two grated penny loves, and as much flour dryed in an Oven, ſeaſon it with Cinamon, Cloves, Mace, Nutmeg and Salt; put to it four Eggs, caſting away two of the whites; temper it with ſweet Cream; put to it a handful or two of Raiſins, as many Currans, with about half a pound of Beef-ſuet minced very ſmall; let it not be ſo thin, that the Raiſins and Currans fall to the bottom; ſo waſh over a double cloth with Butter, and put it into a baſon or skillet; gather it together, and tye it cloſe, only give it a little liberty to riſe, let your water boyl before you put it in.

Another way.

TAke a pint and half of Cream; and boyl it up with ſome beaten Cinamon and Nutmeg; and when it is cold, beat to it ſix Eggs, caſting away the whites of three, ſeaſon it with ſugar, roſe-water and ſalt; then cut two penny loaves in ſippets, and butter over a cloth as before, and put it in a Baſon, ſpread the ſippets all over the bottom of your Baſon, as alſo the ſides, that the cloth may not be perceived: then ſtrow on a handful of minced Marrow, and Dates not very ſmall; then pour a ladleful of Cream or two all over, and lay it over with ſippets again, then ſtrow a handful of Marrow

row and Dates as before, ſo do until all your cream and eggs is in: then lay it all over with ſippets on the top, and waſh them well over with butter: ſo gather up your cloth and bind it, when your pot boyls put him in.

A baked Pudding after the Italion faſhion, correſted.

TAke a penny white loaf or two, and cut it in the manner of dice: put to it half a pound of Beef-ſuet minced ſmall, half a pound of Raiſins of the Sun ſtoned, a little Sugar, ſix ſliced Dates, a grain of Musk, the Marrow of two bones, ſeaſon it with Cloves, Mace, Nutmeg, Salt and Roſe-water, then beat three Eggs with about half a pint of Cream, and put it to your bread and other Ingredients, and ſtir it together ſoftly that you break not the Bread, nor Marrow: then ſlice ſome thin pieces of Apple into the bottom of your diſh, that you bake it in, and put your Pudding thereon: bake it in an oven not ſo hot as for Manchet: when its enough, ſtick it with Cittern, and ſtrow it with Sugar.

To blanch Manchet in a frying-Pan.

TAke twelve Eggs, caſting by the whites of ſix, beat them in three quarters of a pint of Cream: put to it almoſt a penny Manchet grated, a little Sugar, Cloves, Mace, Nutmeg, and a little Roſe-water, beat all theſe together, and fry it in ſweet Butter, as you fry a Tanſy; when it is fryed, waſh it over with a little Sack and the juice of a Lemon, then turn it out on a Plate, diſh it, ſcrape on ſugar, and ſend it up.

Another way.

GRate four Manchets, and put them in a diſh with ſix Eggs, two quarts of Cream, Cloves, Mace, Roſe-water, Salt, Sugar, with a handful or two of Currans, and a pound of Beef-ſuet minced, with a handful

ful of Dates fliced, all manner of good fweet herbs minced and ftamped with a handful of fpinnage, ftrain out the juice of them, add thereunto Cinamon and Nutmeg, beat all thefe together, put Butter in your difh with fippets thereon, fo put your Pudding therein and bake it.

To boyl Pidgeons the French Fashion.

TAke your Pidgeons, fet and lard them, put them into a Pipkin with fo much ftrong broth as will cover them; when they are fcummed, put to them a faggot of fweet herbs, fome large Mace, a handful of Capers, and Raifins of the Sun fhred fmall, fix quartered Dates, a piece of Butter, with the yolks of three hard Eggs minced, with a handful of Grapes or Barberries, then beat two yolks of raw Eggs, with Verjuice and fome of your broth, a ladle of drawn Butter, and a grated Nutmeg: fo difh it on fippets, and lay it round with flices of Bacon.

To boyl Mullet, or Pike with Oyfters.

TAke a fair Mullet or Pike, trufs it round, and fet on a pan of water, ftrow into it a handful of falt, and a handful of fweet herbs, make your water boyl, tye your Mullet or Pike in a fair cloth, and put him in your boyling liquor, with a pint of white wine Vinegar, let your fifh boyl leifurely until it fwim, take the liver and a pint of Oyfters, with their liquor and a little White-wine, three or four blades of Mace, and a little grofs Pepper; boyl all thefe by themfelves, when they are enough, ftrain the yolks of three or four Eggs with half a pint of Sack; add to it a ladleful of drawn Butter, then difh up your fifh on fippets, pour on your broth and Oyfters all over; you may add roafted Chefnuts and Piftaches, fo garnifh it over with fryed Oyfters; ftick it with Toafts and Bay-leaves; and ftrow all over your difh hard Eggs minced.

To

Rare Receipts in Cookery.

To boyl Carps an honourable way.

TAke two live Carps, or as many as you intend to boyl, knock them on the head, open them in the bellies, and draw them clean; take heed you break not the gall, wash out the blood with a little Clarret wine and save it; salt them well on the bellies; and save the scales, as whole as you can on them; set on your pan with fair water, and about a quart of Vinegar, a faggot or two of sweet herbs, half a dozen cloves of Garlick, sliced Ginger, large Mace, and quartered Nutmegs, and a handful and half of Salt, with a Lemon or two cut in slices; when your pan boyls, put in your Carps upon your false bottom, and whilst they boyl, make your sawce after this manner: take the body of a Crab or two, and put it into a deep dish, put to it the blood of your Carp and Claret wine (before named) with two or three Anchovies, a little Time and Fennel minced exceeding small, some Oyster-liquor, Vinegar and Salt, and half a dozen Oysters minced; let this stew up altogether, and be ready with your Carp; if it be thick, you may add Claret-wine, or Gravy, if none be offended; when it is enough, grate a Nutmeg into it; and beat it up with the yolk of an Egg, and a little drawn Butter, & put it into half a dozen large Saucers; it ought to be but little thinner than Mustard; then take up your Carps being quick boyled, and dish them on a large Dish and Plate, garnish the brims thereof, and underneath with Fennel, Flowers, or Orenge peel minced, garnish your Carps with Oysters fryed up in Eggs, and put your sawcers on your dish round your Carps, and serve it up.

Another way to boyl a dish of great Flownders.

WHen your Flownders are drawn, scotch them on the black side very thick, and put them into a

great

great Diſh, pour on Vinegar, and ſtrow them over with a handful of Salt, and when your pan boyles ſeaſoned as before, lay in your Flownders on your falſe bottom with their white ſides downwards; they will be boyled with about a dozen walms; take them up, diſh them in a large diſh on ſippets, with the black ſide upwards, and pour on drawn Butter all over them, grating on a Nutmeg, and ſcruiſe in a Lemon or two; ſo garniſh it with Lemon and ſend it up.

To make a Haſh of Partridges or Capons.

TAke twelve Partridges and roaſt them, and being cold mince them very fine, the brawns and wings, and leave the legs and rumps whole, (to be carbonadoed) then put ſome ſtrong Mutton broth to them, or good Mutton gravy, grated Nutmeg, a great Onion or two, ſome Piſtaches, Cheſnuts and Salt, then ſtew them in a large earthen Pipkin, or Sawce-pan, ſtew the Rumps and Legs by themſelves in ſtrong broth in another Pipkin, then have a fine clean diſh, then take ſome light French bread chipt, and cover the bottom of your diſh, and when you go to diſh your Haſh, ſteep the bread with ſome mutton broth, or good mutton gravy; then pour the Haſh on the ſteeped bread, lay the legs and the rumps on the Haſh, with ſome fryed Oyſters, Piſtaches, Cheſnuts, ſliced Lemon, and Lemon-peel, yolks of Eggs ſtrained with the juice of Orange, and beaten Butter beat together, and run over all; garniſh your diſh with carved Oranges, Lemons, fryed Oyſters, Cheſnuts and Piſtaches; thus you may Haſh any kind of Fowl, whether water or land.

A rare Frigaſy.

TAke ſix Pigeons, and as many Chicken-peepers, being clean drawed, ſcald and truſs them, head and all on, then ſet them, and have ſome Lambſtones and
ſweet-

Rare Receipts in Cookery. 217

sweet-breads blanched, parboyled, and sliced, fry most of the sweet-breads floured, have also some sparragrafs ready; cut off the tops an inch long; the yolks of two hard eggs, Pistaches, the Marrow of six Marrow-bones, half the Marrow fryed green, and white batter; let it be kept warm till it be almost dinner-time, then have a clean frying-pan, and fry the Foul with sweet Butter; being finely fryed, put out the Butter, and put to them some roast Mutton-Gravy, some large fryed Oysters, and some Salt; then put in the hard yolks of Eggs, and the rest of the sweet-breads that are not fryed, the Pistaches, Sparragrafs, and half the Marrow, then stew them well in the frying-pan, with some grated Nutmeg, Pepper, (a Clove or two of Garlick if you please) a little White-wine, and let them be well stewed; then have ten yolks of eggs dissolved in a dish, with Grape-verjuice, or Wine-vinegar, and a little Mace, and put it to the Friggasy; then have some slices of light bread in in a fair large dish set on coals, with some good Mutton-gravy, then give the Frigasy two or three walms on the fire, and pour it upon the sops in your dish; garnish it with fryed sweet-breads, fryed Oysters, fryed Marrow, fryed Pistaches, sliced Almonds, and the juice of two or three Lemons.

To make a Bisk of Carps and other several Fish.

MAke the Carbolion for the Bisk, of some Jacks or small Carps, boyled in half white-wine and fair spring-water, some Cloves, Salt, & Mace, boyl it down to a Jelly, strain it, and keep it warm for to scald the Bisk, then take four Carps, four Tenches, four Perches, two Pikes, two Eeles flayed and drawn, the Carps being scalded, drawn & cut in quarters, the Tenches scalded and left whole, also the Perches and the Pikes all finely scalded, cleansed and cut in twelve pieces three of each side, then put them into a large stew-pan, with three

quarts

quarts of Claret-wine, an ounce of large Mace, a quarter of an ounce of Cloves, half an ounce of Pepper, a quarter of an ounce of Ginger pared and sliced, sweet herbs chopped small, as stripped Time, Savory, sweet Marjoram, Parflee, Rosemary, three or four Bay-leaves, Salt, Chesnuts, Pistaches, five or six great Onions; and stew all together on a quick fire: Then stew a pottle of Oysters, the greatest you can get, parboyl them in their own liquor, cleanse them from the dregs, and wash them in warm water from the grounds and shells: put them into a Pipkin with three or four great Onions pilled: then take large Mace, and a little of their own liquor, or a little Wine-vinegar or White-wine: next take twelve Flownders, being drawn and cleansed from the guts, fry them in clarified Butter, with an hundred of large Smelts; being fryed stew them in a stew-pan, with some Claret-wine, grated Nutmeg, sliced Orange, Butter and Salt: then have an hundred Prawns boyled, picked, and buttered, or fryed: next bottoms of Artichokes, boyled, blanched, and put in beaten Butter, grated Nutmeg, Salt, White-wine, Skirrets and Sparragrass, in the aforesaid sauce; then mince a Pike and an Eele, cleanse them, and season them with Cloves, Mace, Pepper, Salt, some sweet herbes minced, some Pistaches, Barberries, Grapes, or Goosberries, some grated Manchet and yolks of raw Eggs: mingle all the aforesaid things together, and make it into balls, or force some Cabbage-Lettice: and bake the balls, in an Oven: being baked, stick them with Pine-apple seeds, and Pistaches, as also the Lettice: then all the aforesaid things being made ready, have a clean large dish, with large sops of French bread, lay the Carps on them, and between them, some Tench, Perch, Pike and Eele, and the stewed Oysters all over the other Fish: then the fryed Smelts and Flownders over the Oysters; then the balls, and Lettice, stuck with Pistaches, the Artichokes,

chokes, Skirrets, Sparragrafs, buttered prawns, yolks of hard Eggs, large Mace, fryed Smelts, Grapes, sliced Lemon, Oranges, red Beets or Pomgranats; broth it with the lear that was made for it, and run it over with beaten Butter.

To dress Eggs in the Spanish fashion.

TAke twenty eggs fresh and new, and strain them with a quarter of a pint of Sack, Claret, or Whitewine, a quartern of Sugar, some grated Nutmeg, and Salt, beat them together with the juice of an Orange, and put to them a litle musk, or none; set them over the fire, and stir them continually, till they be a little thick, but not too much; serve them, with scraped Sugar, being put in a clean warm dish, on fine toasts of Manchet, soaked in juice of Orange, or Sugar, or in Claret, Sugar, or White-wine, and shake the Eggs with Orange-Comfits, or Muskadines, Red and White.

To dress Eggs in the Portugal fashion.

STrain the yolks of twenty eggs, and beat them very well in a dish, put to them some musk and rosewater, made of fine sugar, boyled thick in a clean skillet, put in the eggs and stew them on a soft fire; being finely stewed, dish them on a french plate, in a clean dish, scrape on sugar, and trim the dish with your finger. Other wayes, take twenty yolks of eggs, or as many whites, put them severally into two dishes; take out the Cocks treads, and beat them severally for the space of an hour; then have a sirrup made in two several skillets, with half a pound a piece of double refined sugar, and a little musk, and amber-greafe, bound up close in a fine rag; set them a stewing on a soft fire till they are enough on both sides; then dish them on a plate, and shake them with preserved Pistaches, Muskadines, white and red; and green Citron sliced; put
into

into the whites the juice of Spinnage to make them green.

To dress Eggs called in French Ala Augenotte, or the Protestant way.

BReak twenty eggs, beat them together, and put to them the pure Gravy of a leg of mutton, or the Gravy of roast Beef, stir and beat them well together, over a Chaffindish of coals, with a little salt: add to them also juice of Orange and Lemon, or grape-Virjuice, then put in some mushrooms well boyled and seasoned; Observe as soon as your eggs be well mixed with the Gravy and other Ingredients, then take it off the fire, keeping them covered awhile, then serve them with grated Nutmeg over them.

To dress Eggs in fashion of a Tansey.

TAke twenty yolks of eggs, and strain them on flesh-days, with about half a pint of Gravy, on fish-dayes with Cream and milk; add salt and four mackaroons small grated, as much bisket, some rose-water, a little sack or claret, and a quarter of a pound of suger, put these things to them, with a piece of butter as big as a walnut, and set them on a Chaffin-dish, with some preserved Citron, or Lemon grated, or cut in small pieces, or little bits, and some pounded Pistaches, being well buttered, dish it on a plate, and brown it with a hot fire-shovel; strow on fine sugar, and stick it with preserved Lemon-pill in thin slices.

To dress Poacht Eggs.

TAke a dozen of new laid eggs, and the meat of four or five Partridges, or any roast Poultry, mince it as small as you can, and season it with a few beaten cloves, mace, and nutmeg; put them into a dish, with a ladleful or two of pure mutton Gravy, and two or three

Rare Receipts in Cookery.

three Anchovies diffolved; then fet it a ftewing on a Chaffin-difh of coals; being half ftewed, as it boyls, put in the eggs one by one; and as you break them, put by moft of the whites, and with one end of your egg-fhel, put in the yolks round in order, amongft the meat; let them ftew till the eggs be enough, then put in a little grated Nutmeg, and the juice of two Oranges, put not in the feeds, wipe your difh, garnifh it with four or five whole Onions, boyled and broyled.

To butter Eggs upon Toafts.

TAke twenty eggs, beat them in a difh with fome falt, and put Butter to them, then have two large rolls or fine manchets, cut them in toafts, and toaft them againft the fire, with a pound of fine fweet butter, being finely buttered, lay the toafts in a fair clean difh, put the eggs on the toafts, and garnifh your difh with pepper and falt, otherwayes half boyl them in the fhells; then butter them, and ferve them on toafts, or toafts about them: To thefe eggs, fometimes ufe musk and Ambergreafe, and no Pepper.

An excellent way to Butter Eggs.

TAke twenty yolks of new laid or frefh eggs; put them into a difh with as many fpoonfuls of Jelly, or mutton Gravy without fat, put to it a quarter of a pound of fugar, two ounces of preferved Lemon-pill, either grated or cut in thin flices, or very little bits, with fome falt, and four fpoonfuls of Rofe-water, ftir them together on the coals, and being buttered, difh them; put fome musk on them, with fome fine fugar; you may eat thefe eggs cold, as well as hot, with a little cinamon water, or without: Otherwayes, drefs them with claret-wine, fack or juice of oranges, nutmeg, fine fugar, and a little falt, beat them well together in a fine clean difh, with carved fippets and candid Piftaches ftuck in them.

To

To make Cheese-cakes.

FOr your Coffins, take half a pound of Floure, a quarter of a pound of fine Sugar beaten in a morter, two spoonfuls of Rose-water, three or four yolks of eggs; make this into a paste, with cold butter, and two or three spoonfuls of milk; roll it into sheets as broad as Trencher-Plates, and cut them round with a Jagging iron; then take three pints of tender Cheese-curds, made of new milk, pressed exceeding dry from the whey; put to them about twelve yolks of eggs, and three whites, one pint of thick Cream, a pound of fine Sugar, some Nutmeg and Cinamon beaten exceeding small, otherwayes oyl of the same; three spoonfuls of Rose-water, and as much or more of Sack; beat all these together, by adding a pound of sweet Butter melted, and so much grated Naples bisket or Mackaroons, as will bring it into such a body, that when you lay it with your spoon on your sheets of Paste, it will not so run abroad, as to beat down the sides; fill your sheets with three or four spoonfuls of each, or at your pleasure; raise them and close them at the corners, and give them a quarter of an hours baking in a gentle Oven, you may infuse musk or ambergrease in them if you please; if this be too thin, so that it will run abroad, set it on a heap of Charcoals, and harden it, but always keep it stirring, for it must be cold before you use it.

To make Dowsets.

TAke two quarts of sweet Cream, and infuse a Nutmeg or two cut in pieces, two or three sticks of Cinamon, and blades of large Mace, set it for some time upon the coals, but boyl not your Cream at all; then take fourteen eggs, casting by ten whites, and beat them to your Cream blood-warm, then run it through

through a ftrainer, and beat to it about half a pound & upwards of white fugar, four fpoonfuls of Rofe-water, if you pleafe a little oyl of Cinamon and Nutmeg; you may colour fome of your ftuff with Cowflips, Spinnage, Violets, or Gillyflowers, and fo have your varieties at your Feaft; your Coffins are ufually after the manner of high cups, about four or five inches high; fome bake them in little cups of Chainy; about eight, ten, or twelve in a difh is enough; you may ftick your white ones with a fliced Citron, and your coloured with fliced Almonds, and fo ferve them up.

How to make a congealed meat, to be eaten cold.

TAke a Calves head and parboyl it, then cut off all the meat from the bones and mince it fmall, feafon it with minced Sage, Time, and other fweet herbs, and fome Onion with them, as alfo beaten Pepper, Cloves, Mace, Nutmeg, Anchovies, minced, and a reafonable quantity of falt; then take a narrow pot or pitcher fomthing high and fmall, and put in two handfuls of the meat into the bottom of the pot; then ftrow in a little Bacon thereon cut in dice, then put in two handfuls more, as alfo minc'd Bacon thereon, till all the minced Calves-head is in the pot; cram it in hard, and ftop the pot with a cork & a cloth, and let it boyl in a pot up to the neck, for the fpace of fix or feven hours, then take it off, let it ftand tell it is cold, and then break the pot, and the congealed colour will be fitting to be fent to the Table whole, or to be fliced forth for fecond courfe; thus may you do Calves-feet, or Cow-heels, feafon it high with minced herbs, falt, fpice and bacon.

How to congeal a Turkey or Capon.

PArboyl either, and take the flefh from the bones and mince it, the blackeft flefh by it felf, and the whiteft by it felf; then take a great Onion, a little Horfe-Raddifh,

Raddish, and a little Time minced small, season it with this, as also Mace, Nutmeg and Salt, with a handful of fat bacon cut smaller than Pease, and a handful of Westphalia-Bacon minced small, mingle all these together with your flesh, only the white by it self, and the black in another parcel; then put a handful or more into a Pitcher or narrow Pot, as aforesaid, then put a handful of the black flesh on it, and then the white again, so do till all be rammed into the Pot, then having a quart of White-wine and nine Anchovies, with two ounces of Izing-glass, boyled to the consuming of half a pint thereof, strain it into the Pot to your aforesaid Ingredients, and stop it close with a cork and a cloath, and boyl it in a pot of water, your Pitcher standing up to the neck, for the space of six hours; when it is cold, break your pot, and it will be in a Coller; you may slice it, or serve it whole in a Coller; if you have three little pots, you may divide it in three, and so serve it in three little Collors at a Feast; these kind of meats ought to be seasoned high.

How to make small Pindents to fry for first Course.

TAke one pint of Flour, and as much grated bread, eight Eggs, cast away the whites, or five thereof, beat it to a thick batter, with Cream, Rosewater and Sack; season it with beaten Cinamon, Ginger, Nutmeg and Mace, put to it a handful of parboyled Currans, and a handful of minced Marrow, if not Beef-suet, add Salt, then let your pan be hot with clarified Butter or sweet suet, then drop it in by spoonfuls, and when they are fryed on both sides, dish them up on a dish and plate, and scrape on sugar: you may add a handful of sugar to the batter.

How

How to make rich Pancakes.

TAke a pint of Cream, and half a pint of Sack, and the yolks of eighteen Eggs, and half a pound of sugar, season it with beaten Cinamon, Nutmeg, Mace, beat all these together for a good space, then put in as much flour as will make it so thick as it may run thin over the pan; let your pan be hot, and fry them with clarified Butter; this sort of Pancakes will not be crisp, yet it is counted a rare way amongst the Gentry.

Another way to make them crisp.

TAke the said ingredients, only put no sugar into your batter, and put in but fourteen eggs, cast away the whites of nine; let it be as thin as it can run, fry them crisp, and strow sugar on them when you send them up.

How to fry a leg, breast, or neck of Lamb.

BOne your Lamb, and parboyl it, then slice it in thin pieces, and take about six yolks of eggs, put to them Time, sweet Marjoram, and Parsley minced small, and a grated Nutmeg, and a little Mace beaten, add Salt, and beat it all together with your yolks; let your pan be hot with clarified Butter, and dip your slices of Lamb into your eggs and herbs, and fry it softly: when it it fryed enough on both sides, put in a little Whitewine, Gravy, and strong Broth, beaten with the yolks of two eggs, a sliced Nutmeg, the juice of a Lemon, and some drawn Butter, shake it till it boyls in your frying-pan, and pour it into your dish upon sippets; if you love it sweet and sharp, add to your Lear Whitewine, Sugar, and Vinegar, instead of strong Broth.

How to make a green Frigasy of Chickens.

TAke four Chickens, and boyl them almoſt enough, then cut them in pieces, then take a good handful of Parſlee ſcalded green, and mince it ſmall, and put it into the yolks of eight eggs, put to it ſome minced Time and grated Nutmeg, your pan being hot with clarified Butter, dip in your pieces of Chickens into the green batter, and put them into the frying-pan, and when they are fryed gently on both ſides, put to them a Lear of White-wine, beaten with three yolks of eggs, and Parſlee boyled green, minced ſmall, with a Lemon cut dice wayes, and a little Sugar and Vinegar, and keep them ſhaking in the pan till they boyl; then put them into a diſh, and ſerve them up upon ſippets; you may add Gooſ-berries or Grapes to them in the ſummer ſeaſon, and in the Winter Skirrets or Potatoes over them.

A fryed meat in haſte for the ſecond courſe.

TAke a pint of Curds made tender of morning Milk, preſſed clean from the Whey, put to them one handful of flour, ſix eggs, caſting away three whites, a little Roſe-water, Sack, Cinamon, Nutmeg, Sugar, Salt, and two Pippins minced ſmall, beat this all together into a thick batter, ſo that it may not run abroad; if you want wherewith to temper it, add Cream; when they are fryed, ſcrape on Sugar, and ſend them up; if this curd be made with Sack, as it may as well as with Rhennet, you may make a Pudding with the whey thereof thus.

How to make a Pudding with Whey.

PUt into a quart of Whey one pound of Butter, one penny roll cut very thin in ſlices, a ſtick or two of Cinamon, ſome large Mace, and let it boyl all together half

half a quarter of an hour, then cool it, and beat to it ſix eggs, caſt away three whites, you may add Almonds beaten, Dates cut in quarters, Marrow, Sugar, Roſe-water and ſalt butter; your diſh having a garniſh about the brims, it will take a quarter of an hours baking; when you make Sack and Pottage, as is taught in my firſt Book, you may make uſe of the Whey thereof, if you make not a Cawdle with it, as you may do if you pleaſe.

How to make Apple-pyes to fry.

TAke about a dozen Pippins, pare them, cut them, and almoſt cover them with water, and almoſt a pound of Sugar, let them boyl on a gentle fire, cloſe covered, with a ſtick of Cinamon, minced Orange pill, a little Dill-ſeed beaten, Roſe-water; when this is cold and ſtiff, make it into a little paſty with rich paſte.

How to make a boyled meat, a forced meat, a diſh of Collops, and a roaſt meat, and a baked meat, of a leg of Veal, with ſome other ſmall ingredients.

FIrſt, for your boyled meat, take a ſmall knuckle of the ſaid leg, and about a pound of good middling Bacon, take off the rhine and the inſide, and cover both in a little pot with ſtrong Broth, when it boyls and is ſcummed, put to it two whole Onions, and a good faggot of ſweet herbs, a little whole Pepper and large Mace, when it is almoſt boyled, take an handful of Spinnage, as much Lettice and Parſlee, and hack it three or four times over with a knife, and put it into your Broth and Meat, add ſome minced Time and ſweet Marjoram, let them have a quarter of an hours boyling, when it is enough and ſeaſoned with Salt, beat to it the yolks of three eggs, and diſh the Knuckle of Veal on ſippets, and cut the Bacon round about, and over it, then pour on your broth and herbs on the meat, garnish your dish with Lemon and serve it up; in the Winter time you may make Barley broth of the said Knuckle, and leave out the Bacon.

Then split your Fillet of Veal down by the bone, and of the sinewy part make two or three large Collops, as broad and as long as half a sheet of white-paper, by beating of them thin with a Cleaver; then cut two dishes of Collops very thin, and hack them more thin with the back of a knife; take half these Collops, and fry them brown in clarrified butter, then put them into a Pipkin with strong broth, Claret-wine, Gravy, two Anchovies, a handful of Oysters, two Onions, a faggot of sweet herbs or time minced, stew them up together; when they are enough, add a grated Nutmeg and drawn Butter, and dish them upon sippets.

For the roast Olives, take the other half, the thin Collops being spread abroad, season them with Cloves, Mace, Nutmeg and Salt, then take a good handful of sweet harbs, parslee and spinnage, mingled together with a piece of beef suit, the yolks of hard Eggs, put to it a handful of Currans, & season it with Cloves, Mace, Nutmeg beaten, salt and a little sugar; so put the yolks of four new Eggs, and lay part thereof upon all the Collops, and roll them up close; so spit them cross wayes on a small spit, and let them roast with a dish under them, having therein the rest of the herbs, if any left, put a little Claret-Wine and Vinegar into the said dish; when your Olives are roasted, draw them into the said dish, and set them on a tapitt of Coles, and let them boyl, then put to them a ladleful of drawn butter, let your sauce be sharp sweet, by adding a little sugar, dish them up, and pour the sauce over them, and garnish them with Lemon.

Then

Then take the reſt of the meat undiſpoſed of, and the pieces that you could not well cut in Collops, & parboyl it, and mince it with more Beef-ſuet than it ſelf contains to, alſo three Pippins, ſome Dates, a little Orangado, ſeaſon it with Cloves, Mace, Nutmeg, Cinamon, then take the one half of this minced meat, and add Sugar, Roſewater, and a handful of Currans thereto, of this meat make one dozen of ſmall Petetes, about the bigneſs of a Gooſe egg, cloſe them and bake them, and when they are baked, put to them Verjuice, Sugar, beaten up hot with the yolk of an egg, ſo ſcrape on Sugar, and ſerve them up to the Table.

For your forced meat, take the reſt of your minced meat, and mingle it with a good handful of ſweet herbs, Spinnage and Sives, a little Bacon minced, then put a little Sugar and Vinegar, the yolks of half a dozen hard eggs, and as many raw eggs, ſo make it up into a body very tender, with grated Bread, and lay it all over your three large Collops, and roll them up cloſe, bake them in an Oven, and when they are baked, ſlice them out into a diſh, add Butter, Vinegar, and Gravie, to the liquor that they were baked in, for their Lear; ſo have you five diſhes, boyled, fryed, roaſted, baked and forced.

A Fridayes *diſh made with Barley.*

TAke a quarter of a pound of perled Barley, & boyl it untill it begins to break, then put it into a Cullendor, and ſet on your skillet with other liquor, and when it boyls, put in the Barley again, and let it boyl till it be very ſoft, then ſtrain the water from it, then take a quarter of a pound of blanched Almonds, & beat them in a Morter, when they are almoſt beaten, beat your Barley with them, then put to it ſome of the ſaid liquor, a little Sack, Roſe-water, ſeaſon it with Sugar, Nutmeg, Cinamon, and boyl them well together on a Chaffin-dish of coals, when you send it up, add a ladleful of drawn Butter, scrape on Sugar.

For a Friday, to make a dish of fryed toasts.

Take a stale two penny loaf or two, and cut them in round slices throughout the loaf, soak them in Sack and strong Ale on the one side, then dry them on a pye-plate on that side, do so to the other side, then take the yolks of a dozen eggs beaten, seasoned with Nutmeg and Cinamon, dip your toasts therein, your pan being hot with clarified Butter, put them in and fry them brown on both sides, and dish them up, and pour on them Butter, Rose-water, and Sack drawn together, so scrape on Sugar.

Another Friday, or Lent dish.

Take a pint of flour, put to it three yolks of eggs, a little Butter, a little Sugar, Cinamon beaten, and Nutmeg grated, & make it into a stiff paste with Cream & Rose-water, then Roll them out into very thin ropes, and gage them round your pan, being hot with clarified Butter: fry them quick away, but burn them not; take them up, and let them dry, then dip them in the yolks of eggs, being seasoned with Cinamon and Nutmeg, and fry them of a good yellow colour, and dish them, scrape on Sugar.

A second course-dish in the beginning of the Spring.

Take of Primrose-leaves two handfuls, & boyl them, scruise the water from them, & mince them small, three Pippins, season it with Cinamon, put to it half a handful of dry flour, and the yolks of eight eggs, only two whites of the same, mingle this together, adding a little Sugar, Cream, and Rose-water, your stuff must be thick that it run not abroad, your pan being hot with clarified Butter, drop them in by less than spoonfuls,

Rare Receipts in Cookery. 231

fulls, and fry them on both sides as crisp as you can, dish them, and scrape on sugar.

To make a made dish.

Take a quarter of a pound of Almonds, and beat them small, and put in Rose-water in their beating, that they may not oyl, strain them into Cream, then take Artichoke bottoms and Marrow, your Cream being boyled with Dates, Sugar, whole Cinamon, large Mace, and Nutmeg, cool your Cream, and beat in the yolks of four eggs, then pour in your Cream into a dish, garnished with Paste on the brims, put on your Artichokes and Marrow, and bake it for a quarter of an hour, you must take out the whole spice.

An excellent way how to broyl Eeles.

Take the great Eeles, such as you spitchcock, or others, and flea them, and cut them into lengths about four inches, and scotch your pieces very thick with your knife, then baste them over with Butter in the scotches, then having one Onion minced small, with more Time than it, a little small Pepper, Nutmeg and salt, cast all this to your Eeles, and rub it into the scotches, your Gridiron being very hot, lay it on, and let it broyl softly; for your sauce, take a little Oyster-liquor, boyled with Time, Nutmeg and drawn butter; otherwise drawn butter it self.

How to butter a dish of eggs with Anchovies.

Break your twenty Eggs into your Butter in a dish, as at other times, and set them on coals, then take eight Anchovies, and dissolve them in six spoonfuls of white-Wine, and pour them into your Eggs, then having one handful of Pistaches beaten small in a Morter, put them into your eggs with a quarter of a pint of

Mut-

Mutton Gravy, if you pleafe, you may leave out your White-wine, and diffolve your Anchovies in Mutton Gravy, let not your eggs be too ftiff; then having a difh full of toafts cut in large fippets, lay your eggs by fpoonfuls on the toafts, or elfe difh them other wayes, with the toafts about them, and on the brims of the difh.

How to fry a difh of Cheefe.

TAke a quarter of a pound of good Cheefe, or Parmyzant, and grate it, put to it a little grated bread, a few Caraway feeds beaten, the yolks of as many eggs as will make it into a ftiff batter, fo that it will not run, fry it brown in Butter, and pour on drawn Butter with Claret-wine when they are difhed.

How to broyl a leg of Pork.

TAke part of the Fillet, and skin it, and cut it into thin Collops, then hack them thinner with your knife, then take Sage, and a little Time minced exceeding fmall, with a little fmall Pepper and Salt, and ftrow over them; then put them upon your Gridiron, fo ftrow the other fide with your feafoning, and broyl them on both fides; for their fauce, take Muftard, Vinegar, Sugar, and drawn Butter, fo put your Collops thereon.

How to roaft the faid Collops.

WHen they are cut and hacked, as aforefaid, then take one handful of fweet herps, with fome Sage and Spinnage, mince them fmall with Beef-fuet, and a little flack of the Hog, feafon this with Mace, Nutmeg, Pepper beaten, and Salt, fo ftrow it all over your Collops, and roll them up, and fpit them as you do Olives; make fauce with the faid herbs, with Muftard, Butter and Sugar; when they are roafted, draw them and difh them. *How*

How no make a Palate Pye.

TAke one fat Capon or Fowl, and cut him into small pieces, season him with Mace, Nutmeg, minced sweet herbs, and a little salt, and put this in the botton of your Coffin, then take two dozen of Larks, or other small fowl, and force them with the aforesaid seasoning, adding the yolks of three eggs, with some Bacon minced, and force them, filling their bellies, and lay them in upon your Capon in the Coffin, then season half a dozen Lambs sweet breads, being cut in pieces, and if in the season, some stones, and boyled Palates sliced, and hard eggs, place all these between, with some forced meat balls, as big as the yolks of eggs, and also yolks of eggs boyled hard, and according to the season Artichokes, or Oysters in Winter; close your pye with Mushrooms in it, and butter, and make a Lear of strong Broth, Gravy, Anchovies, or as rich as you can with a hogo.

Very

Very rare and moſt choice
RECEIPTS
For all manner of
Preſerving, Conſerving, and Candying, &c.

To Preſerve Pippins.

TAke and ſlice them round, as thick as half a Crown, and ſome Lemon-pill (in ſlices) amongſt them: Or elſe cut like Orange-pill, or ſmall Lard; being boyled and cut in the ſame manner; then make the ſirrup weight for weight, that being well ſcummed clean, and clarified, put in your Pippins, and boyl them up quick; to a pint of water add a pound of Sugar; or a pint of Claret or White-wine; ſo you may make them of different colours.

Another way.

TAke three pints of Conduit-water, nine ſpoonfuls of Roſe-water, two pound, or more, of Sugar, boyl all together, ſcum it clean, then pare and core them, if you intend to keep them long; weigh them, after they are ſo done, and unto every one of your Apples, add a pound

pound of fugar; but if you keep them not long, put in as many as your firrup will boyl; and let them feeth (being often turned) about three hours or more; when they are enough, the firrup will be like a Jelly: After this way you may Preferve all forts of Apples.

Another way to Preferve them Green.

TAke them when they are fmall, and green off the tree, and pare four or five of the worft, cut them all to pieces, boyl them to pap in a quart of fair water, then pour the liquor from them into a bafon, and put to them one pound of refined Sugar, add to this as many green Pippins, unpared, as your liquor will cover; let them boyl foftly; and when they are enough, or as tender as Codlings, take them up, and peel off the outermoft white skin, then will they be green, boyl them again in your firrup, until it be thick, for your keeping all the Year.

To Preferve Apricocks.

TAke of Apricocks and Sugar, of each one pound; clarifie your Sugar with a pint of water, and when it is made perfect, put it into a preferving-pan, together with your Apricocks, fo let them boyl gently; when they are enough, and your firrup thick, pot them, and keep them for your ufe: In the like manner you may do your Plumb, or Pear.

Another way.

TAke them when they are green and young, that you may thruft a needle through ftone and all, but all other Plumbs muft be taken green, and at the higheft growth; then put them into indifferent hot water to break them, let them be clofe covered therein, until it will come off with fcraping, all this while they will look yellow; then put them into another skillet of hot water, and

and let them there remain until they turn perfect green; then take them out and weigh them, and add to them the like quantity or more, of the best refined Sugar, with the white of an egg: So keep it preserved for your use.

Another way to Preserve them Ripe.

STone and weigh them with the like quantity of Sugar; pare them, and strow on the Sugar; let them remain together, until the moisture of the Apricocks hath dissolved the sugar, and are come to a sirrup; then set them on a soft fire, but have a care they boyl not, until your sugar be all melted; then boyl them a pretty pace for half an hour, keeping them stirred in the sirrup; then set them by for two hours, and boyl them again until your sirrup be thick, and your Apricocks look clear; Boyl up the sirrup higher, then take it off; and when it is cold, put in your Apricocks into a Glass, or Gally-pot; being well closed up, keep them for your use.

To Preserve Pippins Red.

TAke of the best coloured Pippins, being pared, with a Pearcer, bore a hole through them; then make sirrup for them, as much as will cover them; so let them boyl in a broad preserving pan, put into them a piece of Cinamon-stick; so let them boyl close covered very leisurely, turning them very often, or else they will spot, and the one side will not be like the other; let them thus boyl, until they begin to Jelley, then take them up and pot them: You may keep them all the year for your use.

To Preserve Pears.

TAke them when they are new gathered, being sound and mellow, put them into your pot with a laying of Vine-leaves dryed in the bottom thereof, then put a laying of Pears, and on them another of leaves, so do until your pot be full; then put in some old wine, with a weight on the top of your pot to keep them down, that the Pears swim not, and so Preserve them.

Another way for white Pippins.

TAke fair large Pippins after *Candlemas*, pare them, and bore a hole through them, as you did before for the red; take a weak sirrup, and let them boyl until they be tender; then take them up and boyl your sirrup a little higher, and put them up in a Gallypot, let them stand all night, and the next morning the sirrup will be somewhat weaker; then boyl the sirrup again to its full thickness, so pot them for your use all the year; if you would have them to have a more pleasant taste than the natural Pippin, put in one grain of Musk, and a drop of Chymical oyl of Cinamon, and that will give them a pleasant taste.

To Preserve Medlars.

TAke the weight of them in Sugar, adding to every pound thereof, a pint and half of fair water, let them be scalded therein, till their skin will come off; then take them out of the water, and stone them at the head; then add your Sugar to the water, and boyl them together; then strain it, and put your Medlars therein, let them boyl apace, until it be thick; take them from the fire, and keep them for your use.

To Preserve Peaches.

TAke a pound of your faireſt and beſt coloured Peaches, and with a wet linnen Cloth wipe the white hoar of them; parboyl them in half a pint of White-wine, and a pint an half of running-water, and being parboyled, peel off their white skin; then weigh them, and to every pound of Peaches, add three quarters of a pound of refined Sugar, diſſolved in a quarter of a pint of White-wine; boyl it almoſt to the height of a ſirrup a quarter of an hour, or more, if need ſhould require, ſo put them up, and keep them all the year for your uſe.

Another way.

TAke your Peaches, and put them into ſcalding hot water, till you can pull off the skin; then take your Roſe-water and Sugar, and boyl it until it be thick; then put your Peaches therein one by one, ſtrowing on Sugar; and as they melt, ſtrow on Sugar about four or five times more, and let them boyl, with a ſoft fire, until they be tender; Obſerve to keep them covered while they boyl, then take them out, and preſerve them for your uſe.

Another way.

TAke a dozen or twenty young Peaches, part them in two, and take out the ſtones; then take as much Sugar as they weigh, with ſome Roſe-water, put in your Peaches, and make a ſirrup, that it may ſtand and ſtick to your fingers; boyl them ſoftly a while, then lay them in a diſh, and let them there ſtay for two or three dayes; then ſet your ſirrup on the fire, boyl it up, put in your Peaches, and ſo preſerve them for your uſe.

To Preserve Quinces.

TAke of Quinces a pound, and core them; parboyl and peel off the outermoſt white skin, weigh and add to them a pound of refined Sugar; then cover, and boyl them over a gentle fire, adding to them a ſtick or two of good Cinamon, cut in ſmall pieces; and ſo ſtir them continually, that they may be well coloured on every ſide; and when the ſirrup is come to the height of a perfect Jelly, then take them off the fire, for the higher your ſirrup is, the better will your Quinces keep.

Another way to preſerve them white or red.

PAre and core your Quinces, that muſt be white; put them in fair water two or three hours, take the weight of your Quinces in Sugar, put them in as much water as will make the ſirrup to cover them; let your ſirrup boyl, a little before you put your Quinces in; after let them boyl apace, until they are tender and clear; then take them out, and boyl the ſirrup by it ſelf a little while; when they are cold, put them into your Pots or Glaſſes for your uſe; if you would have them red, put them into your Sugar raw, cover them cloſe, and boyl them ſoftly until they be red; they muſt not at all be put in cold water.

To perſerve Goosberries.

TAke of the largeſt of your Goosberries, but not through ripe, pick all the ſtalks from them, waſh them clean, take a pound, ſet them on the fire until they be hot, then take them off, and let the liquor run from them, then take ten ounces of hard Sugar, and four ounces of Sugar-Candy, clariſie it with a pint of water and the white of an egg, and boyl it to a thick ſirrup, then put in your Goosberries, let them boyl a
walm

Rare Receipts in Preserving.

walm or two so, betwixt hot and cold put them up, and keep them all the year for your use.

Another way.

TAke your Gascoyn Goos-berries, which are of the largest sort, set a pan of water on the fire, and when it is luke-warm cover them close, keep them warm half an hour; then have other water as aforesaid, put them into that, after the same manner coddle them three times over in hot water, until they look green; then pour them into a sieve, extract all the water from them, then add as much clarified Sugar as will cover them, let them simper leisurely close covered, which will make them look as green as Leek-blades; let them stand so for an hour, then take them off the fire, and let the sirrup stand until it be cold; then warm them once or twice, take them up, and let the stirrup boyl by it self; so pot and keep them for your use.

Another way.

TAke of your biggest Goos-berries, with their stalks on; then prick three or four holes in each of them; take to every pound of Goos-berries a pound of Sugar, and lay the most of your Sugar in the bottom of your preserving-pan, lay your Goos-berries one by one thereon, then strow more Sugar on them, to each pound of Goos-berries add four spoonfulls of water, set them on a Chafin-dish of hot embers, let them stand uncovered a pretty while before they boyl, but not too long, for it will make them red; let them not seeth too fast, put the rest of the sugar upon them as they boyl, and it will keep them from breaking; when they are enough, put them up for your use.

R   *To*

To preserve Mellacatons.

STone and parboyl them in water, then peel off the outward skin; they will boyl as long as a piece of Beef, therefore you need not fear the breaking of them; when they are boyled, make a sirrup of them, as you do of other fruit, and keep them all the year.

To preserve Damsins.

TAke those which are large and well coloured, but not through ripe, then they will break; pick them clean and wipe them one by one; weigh them, and to every pound of Damsins, you must add a pound of *Barbary* Sugar that is white and good, dissolved in half a pint or more of water, boyl it almost to the height of a sirrup, then put in your Damsins, keeping them with continual scumming and stirring with a silver spoon; let them boyl until they be enough, on a gentle fire; then may you take them up, and keep them all the year.

Another way.

GAther your Damsins in a fair day, and two dayes before you preserve them; let none be bruised, but all full ripe, or else they will not be well coloured; put unto every pound of them, a pound of fine sugar, add to every pound a spoonful of Rose-water; put your Damsins one by one in a fair platter, then put them on a Chafin-dish with Embers, not too hot, cast on them so much sugar as the Rose-water will melt, before you set them on the fire; and when your platter is warm, cast on half your sugar; let your platter be but as hot as you may suffer your hands on it, turn them not, until there be as much sirrup as will bear them up, and then turn them, but let them not seeth when you so do, then cast on the rest of your sugar, and they will
break

break on both fides, but let them lye in firrup a little while, then turn the broken fides downwards again, and let them feeth foftly a little while, then turn them as often as you will; let them feeth until you think they are enough, but not boyl too long, for it will make them tough and fpoyl their colour; fcum them very clean, and when they are cold, put them up in glaffes; putting into it four or five Cloves, with as many fticks of Cinamon an inch long; thus may you do with any kind of Plumbs; but you muft put no Cloves or Cinamon to your white Plumbs.

To preferve Grapes.

TAke them very green, ftone and cut them into little bunches; then take the like quantity of refined fugar finely beaten, and ftrow a row thereof in your preferving-pan, and a laying of Grapes upon it; lay more fugar on them; put to them four or five fpoonfulls of fair water, and boyl them up as faft as you can.

Another way.

TAke your Grapes when they are almoft ripe, cut off their ftalks, and as you ftone them put on fugar; take three quarters of a pound of fugar, to every pound of Grapes; alfo take fome Grapes that are not full ripe, ftamp and ftrain their juice out of them, and put two fpoonfuls thereof to a pound of Grapes; fet them on the fire, but fhake them in your pan, that they burn not to the bottom; when the fugar is melted, let them boyl very faft; you fhall know when they are enough, by the clearnefs of your Grapes, and the thicknefs of your firrup.

To preferve Cherries.

TAke of the beft and faireft Cherries about two pound, and clip off the ftalks by the middle

with

with a pair of sheets; wash them clean, beware of bruising them; then take of fine *Barberry* sugar, set it over the fire in a quart of fair water, in the broadest vessel you can get, and let it seeth till it be somewhat thick, then put in your Cherries, and stir them together with a spoon, so let them boyl, scumming and turning them very gently, that the one side may be like the other, until they are enough; which to know, you must take up some of the sirrup with one Cherry; so let it cool, and if it will scarce run out, it is enough; thus being cold, you may put them up, and keep them for your use.

Another way.

TAke your Cherries in the morning before they are too ripe; pull off the stalks, and lay them in a pan, with a little *S*ugar under them; to a pound of Cherries, add a pound of *S*ugar beat fine; as your Cherries boyl up, cast sugar on them; scum it not, till it be ready to seeth over, boyl them with a quick fire, for the sooner they are boyled, the sourer they will be, fear not their breaking, for they will close again, seeth not above two pound at once, the fewer the better; boyl them not overmuch, but rather too little; when they are boyled, put them into a fair platter; if no water comes from them they are enough; but if it doth, boyl them a little more; use a silver spoon that is imployed about nothing else, take no ladle or knife that have been used about flesh, that will cause mites to bread in it; this is the best and approvedst way to preserve Cherries.

Another way.

HAve a pound of the smallest Cherries, but let them be well coloured, boyl them tender in a pint of fair water, then strain away the liquor, and
take

take two pound of other Cherries, ſtone, and put them into your preſerving-pan, with a laying of Cherries, and another of ſugar, and pour the ſirrup of the other ſtrained Cherries over them, and with a blazing fire, let them boyl as faſt as may be, that the ſirrup may boyl over them, and when it is of a good colour, ſomthing thick, and jelly, ſet them a cooling; and when they are cold, pot them and keep them all the year for your uſe.

To preſerve Barberries.

TAke your Barberries, very fair and well coloured, pick out every ſtone of them, weigh them, and to every ounce of Barberries, you muſt add three ounces of loaf-ſugar, with half an ounce of the pulp of Barberries, and an ounce of red-Roſe-water; you muſt firſt diſſolve your ſugar, then boyl it to a ſirrup, then put in your Barberries, and let them boyl a quarter of an hour; then take them up, and as ſoon as they begin to wax cool, put them up, and they will keep their colour all the year.

To preſerve Raſpberries.

TAke thoſe which are fair and ripe, but not over-ripe, pick them from the ſtalks, add to them weight for weight of double refined ſugar, and the juice of Raſpberries; to a pint of Raſpberries, take a quarter of a pint of Raſpberry-juice, and as much of fair water, boyl up the ſugar and liquor, and make the ſirrup, ſcum it, and put in the Raſpberries, ſtir them into the ſirrup, but boyl them not too much; being preſerved, take them up and boyl the ſirrup by it ſelf, not too long, it will keep the colour, being cold, pot, and keep them. Thus may you alſo preſerve Strawberries.

Another way.

HAve the faireſt and beſt coloured Raſpberries, pick off their ſtalks and waſh them very clean, but in any caſe bruiſe them not; weigh them, and to every pound add ſix ounces of hard ſugar, as much ſugar-Candy, clarifie it with half a pint of fair water, and four ounces of juice of Raſpberries, being clarified boyl it to a weak ſirrup, then put in your Raſpberries, ſtirring them up and down; let them ſo boyl until they are enough; uſing them as your Cherries, you may keep them all the year.

To preſerve your Pomcitrons.

TAke and grate off the upper skin, cut them in pieces as you judge requiſite, let them lye in water twenty four hours, then ſet a poſnet on the fire with fair water, when it boyls put in your Pomcitrons, and ſhift them until you find the water not bitter; take them up, and to each pound add a pound and a quarter of ſugar, then take a pint and a quarter of the laſt water, and ſet it on the fire with the ſugar, and take two whites of eggs, and beat them with a little fair water; and when your ſirrup begins to boyl, caſt in that which riſeth from the eggs, and let it boyl together, then ſtrain it through a fine cloth into a fine Poſnet, ſet it on the fire, and when it begins to boyl, put in your Pomcitrons, let them boyl ſoftly three or four hours, until your ſirrup be thick enough, keep them (never turned) alwayes under the ſirrup; put them into Gallypots or Glaſſes, when they are cold, cover them.

To preſerve Oranges and Lemons.

TAke them large and well-coloured, and take a Raſp of Steel, and take the outward rhine from them, and lay them in water three dayes and three nights,

nights, then boyl them tender, and shift them in their boyling, to take away their bitterness, and when they be boyled tenderly, take two pound of sugar, clarified with a pint of fair water: when your sirrup is made, and betwixt hot and cold, put in your Lemons and Oranges, and there let them be infused all night; in the morning, let them boyl two or three walms in your sirrup, let them not boyl too long in the sugar, because the rhines will be tough; take your Lemons out, and boyl your sirrup thicker; when it is cold, put them up and keep them for your use.

To preserve Saterion Roots.

TAke of the fairest you can get, wash and boyl them upon a gentle fire, as tender as a Codling; then take them off, and pare away the blackest skin from them; as you do them, put them into fair water, and let them stand therein one night, then take them out, and add to every pound of roots, eleven ounces of sugar finely clarified, then boyl it almost to the height of a sirrup, then put in your roots, let them not boyl too long, for then they will grow hard and tough, when they are enough, set them a cooling until they be through cold, and keep them close covered for your use.

To preserve red Rose-leaves.

TAke the leaves of the fairest buds, half a pound, sifted clean from seeds; then take a quart of fair water in an earthen pipkin, and set it over the fire until it be scalding hot, and then take a good many of other red Rose-leaves, & put them into the scalding water until they begin to look white, then strain them, and thus do until the water look very red; then take a pound of refined sugar beaten fine, put it into the liquor with half a pound of Rose-leaves, and let them seeth together until they be enough; which to know, is by taking some of them up in a spoon, as you do your Cherries, and so when they be through cold, put them up and keep them very close for your use.

To preserve Enula Campana Roots.

TAke the Roots, wash and scrape them very clean, cut them thin unto the pith the length of your little finger; as you cut them, put them into water, and let them lye therein thirty dayes, shifting them twice every day, to take away their bitterness; weigh them, and to every pound of roots, you must add twelve ounces of clarified sugar; first boyling your roots as tender as a Chicken, and then put them into your sugar aforesaid, and let them boyl upon a gentle fire, until they be enough, so let them stand off the fire a good while, and betwixt hot and cold, put them up for your use.

To preserve Currans.

TAke your Currans and part them in the top, then have your preserving-pan, put therein a laying of Currans, and a laying of sugar; boyl them pretty fast, scum them, but put not in your spoon, let them boyl until the sirrup be indifferent thick; then take them off, and let them stand until the sirrup be cold, and put it up for your use.

To preserve Mulberries.

TAke the like weight of sugar, as there are of your mulberries, wet your sugar with some of the juice thereof, stir it together, put in your mulberries, and let them boyl until they are enough; then take out your mulberries, but let your sirrup boyl a while after, then take it off, and put it into your mulberries, and let them stand till they be cold for your use.

To preserve Eringo Roots

Take of them fair but not knotty, one pound, wash them clean; so done, set them on the fire, and boyl them very tender; peel off their outermost skin, but break them not; and as you pare them, put them into cold water, let them remain there until all be finished; you must add to every pound of roots, three quarters of a pound of clarified sugar, and boyl it almost to the height of a sirrup, then put in your roots; but look they boyl very gently together, with as little stirring as may be, for fear of breaking, until they be enough; when they are cold, put them up, and keep them for your use.

To preserve green Walnuts.

Boyl them till the water be bitter, then take them off the fire, and put them into cold water; then peel the bark off them, and weigh them, add to them their weight in sugar, with a little more water than will wet the sugar, set them again on the fire, and when they boyl up, take them off; let them stand two dayes, and then boyl them again, so keep them for your use.

To preserve Angelica Roots.

Take, wash and slice them very thin, then lay them in water three or four dayes, and let the water be changed every day; then take them and put them into a pot of water, and let it stand in embers a whole night; then add to every pound of Roots, two pound of sugar and a pottle of water, boyl it and scum it clean, put in the Roots, then take them out, but let the sirrup boyl a little after, so keep it for your use.

The time to preserve green Fruits, according to other Authors.

Gooseberries muſt be taken about *Whitſuntide*, as you ſee them in bigneſs, the long will be ſooner than the red; the white Plumb, which is ever ripe in wheat-harveſt, muſt be taken in the midſt of *July*; the Pear-plumb in the midſt of *Auguſt*; the Peach and Pippin about *Bartholomew-tide*, or a little before; the Grape in the firſt week of *September*; you muſt obſerve, that to all the green fruits in general that you will preſerve in ſirrup, you muſt add, to every pound of green fruit, a pound and two ounces of ſugar, and a grain of musk; your Plumb, Pippin and Peach, will have three quarters of an hours boyling, and that very ſoftly; keep the fruit as whole as you can: Grapes and Gooſ-berries muſt boyl half an hour ſomthing faſt, and they will be the fuller; obſerve, that to all your Conſerves, you muſt add the full weight of ſugar; then take two skillets of water, and when they are ſcalding hot, put your fruit firſt into one, when that grows cold, put them into the other, changing them until they are ready to peel; then peel them, afterwards ſettle them in the ſame water till they look green, then put them into your ſugar ſirrup, and let them gently boyl till they come to a Jelly; let them ſo ſtand for a quarter of an hour, then put them into Gally-pots or Glaſſes, and keep them for your uſe all the year.

Here

Here begins your Conserves.

Conserve of Barberries.

HAve them which are very red and ripe, pick them from the stalks, and wash them, put to them a pretty quantity of fair water, set them on the fire in a earthen pan, and so scald them; when they are throughly scalded, pulp them through a fine searse, to every pound of pulp, add a pound of powder Sugar; boyl them till it be enough, which you may know, when it cuts like Marmalade.

Another way.

TAke of the fairest branches you can get, pick and wash them clean, dry them on a cloth, then take more Barberries, and boyl them in Claret-Wine till they are soft, strain them through a strainer, bruising them so, that the substance may go through, boyl it till it comes to be very thick and sweet, then take it off the fire, and let it stand till it be cold; then put your branches of Barberries into your Pots or Glasses, filling them up with the cold sirrup; so shall you have both sirrup, and conserved Barberries for your use.

To make Conserve of Violets.

HAve of your Violet-Flowers, and pick out all the blew ones from them; Keep and weigh them, add to every ounce of flowers, three ounces of refined sugar; beat them in an Alablaster Morter, till they be very fine, then take them up and put them into an earthen pipkin, and set them on the fire until they are throughly

throughly hot, then take them off, put them up, and keep them for your use.

To make a Marmalade of Quinces.

TAke and boyl them tender, pare them and cut them to the core, then draw the Pulp, that is, the Quince, through a hair searse, and to a pound of Pulp add a pound of clarified Sugar, and boyl them together until they come unto a perfect colour; adding to them in the boyling a little Oyl of Cinamon; and when it is boyled enough, that it will not stick to the pan, put it into your Marmalade boxes; but your Conserve must not be boyled so high in any case, for then it will not be good.

To make Conserve of Borage flowers.

TAke of the flowers well coloured, pick the blacks from them, then weigh them, and to every ounce of flowers, you must add three ounces of sugar, and beat them together in an Alabaster Morter with a wooden Pestle, until they be very fine, so that you cannot discern any sugar in lumps, then take them out and put the Conserve in a pipkin and heat it through hot; and having thus done, put them up, and keep them all the year for your use.

To make Conserve of Rosemary flowers.

TAke them fresh and good, pick them from the green tusk, and weigh them, then add to every ounce of flowers, three ounces of Sugar-candy; beat them very fine together, using them in every degree as you did your other Conserves.

To make Conserve of Buglofs-flowers.

TAke and pick them as you did your Borage flowers, weigh them, and to every ounce, add two ounces
of

of loaf-sugar, and one of sugar-candy; beat them together until they become very fine; then set it on the fire to dissolve the sugar, and when it is so done, and the Conserve hot, put it into your Glasses or Gally-pots, for your use all the year.

To make Pectoral rolls for the Cough.

TAke one ounce of your Liquorish powder finely searsed, of the spices of Diadragaganthum Frigdium two drams, Dragagant in fine powder, and Gum-Arabick of each a dram, white starch half a dram, Anniseeds in fine powder one ounce, mingle it with the rest; then take of sugar six ounces, of Pennets an ounce and half, sugar-candy powdered, and mingled with the afore-mentioned powder, then take Gum-dragagant steeped in Rose-water, beat it into a Paste, make them into long rolls, dry them, and keep them for your use.

To make Conserve of Strawberries.

SEeth them in water, then strain them, casting away the water; boyl them again in white-Wine, (keeping them stirring) to a good stiffness; when they are almost boyled, add to them a convenient quantity of sugar, stirring them all well together, then put them up into your pots for your use.

To make Conserve of Prunes or Damsins.

TAke of your Damsins one pottle, prick them and put them into a pint of Rose-water, or Wine, into a pot, cover them, and let them be well boyled, stirring them well together; when they are done tender, let them cool, and strain them with their liquor; then take the Pulp and set it over the fire, adding to it a sufficient quantity of sugar; then boyl them until they are enough; so may you put them up in your Gally-pots or Glasses for your use.

To make Conserve of Red and Damask Roses.

HAve of them the best coloured buds that can be gotten, clip off their whites, and to each pound of leaves, you must add three pounds of the best clarified sugar; beat them together till they are very fine; then with a wooden Spatter take it up, and set it on the fire till it be through hot, and soon after put it up; and it will be of an excellent colour.

To Conserve Couslips, Marigolds, Violets, Scabions, Sage and Roses, &c.

HAve of the flowers of either of these, being picked clean from those which are withered, and to every ounce of flowers, add three ounces of Sugar; but first let them be stamped very small without the sugar by themselves; as they grow dry, put to them Rose-water, or the juice of Lemons, and when they are beaten small enough, put to them your sugar, and beat them again together untill they are well mingled; after which, you may put them up for your use.

To make a Pomander.

TAke of Beazon a dram and an half, Storax half an ounce, Lignum Aloes in fine powder half a scruple, of Labdanum half an ounce, powder all these very fine, and searce them through Launes; then take of Musk one ounce, Ambergrease and Civet of each half a scruple, and dissolve them in a hot Morter, with a litle Rose-water, so make them into a Pomander, adding to it six grains of Civet.

Another way to Conserve Strawberries.

TAke and strain them when they are full ripe, boyl them in wine with a quantity of sugar, untill it be

stiff

stiff enough; so may you put them up for your use in a Glass or Gally-pot.

To make Conserve of Cichory-flowers.

TAke them new gathered, for if you let them lye but one hour or two at the most, they lose their colour, and will do you but small service; your way is, as soon as they are taken, to weigh them immediately, and to every ounce of them, you must take three ounces of double refined sugar; beat them together in an Alablaster Morter, with a wooden Pestle, until they are throughly beaten, for the better they are so done, the better will your Conserve be: Let this be your general rule; that being very well brayed, you may take them up, and put it into a Chafer clean scoured, and set it on the fire until it be throughly hot, then take it off, put it up as you have formerly heard, so may you keep it for your use all the year.

Here follows the Sirrups.

To make sirrup of Pomcitrons.

TAke them and cut them in halves, juice them, but beware you wring them not too hard lest it be slymy; add to every pint of juice, three quarters of a pound of the best white Sugar; boyl them in an earthen pipkin until it comes to the height of sirrup; but take heed you boyl it not over too hot a fire, for fear it burn; and when you see it is enough, you may put it up, and keep it for your use all the year.

To make sirrup of Liquorish.

Take of Liquorish scraped well and bruised, eight ounces; add to it of Maiden-hair one ounce, Annifeeds and Fennel, of each half an ounce; let them steep together in a pottle of Rain-water for six or seven hours, then set them on the fire, and let them there remain until it be boyled half away; so done, boyl that liquor with a pound and half of the best clarified sugar, until it comes to a sirrup; so glass it up, and keep it for your use.

To make sirrup of Hore-hound.

Take thereof two handfuls, Colts-foot one handful, Calamint, Time and Penny-royal, of each two drams, Liquorish one ounce and half, Figgs and Raisins of the Sun, of each two ounces, Pyony-kernels, Fennel and Annifeeds, of each a quarter of an ounce; boyl all these in a gallon of fair water until it comes to a pottle, or three pints, then strain it; so done, take three pound of white sugar, with three eggs, and clarifie that liquor, so let it boyl to a sirrup, and keep it all the year for your use.

To make sirrup of Hyssop.

Take thereof one handful, of Dates, Raisins, and Figs one ounce, French Barley the like, half a handful of Calamint; boyl them in three pints of fair water until it comes to a quart, then strain and clarifie it with the whites of two eggs, add to it two pounds of white sugar, boyl it to a sirrup, when it is enough, let it stand till it be cool; and put it up in Glasses, which may serve for your use all the year.

To make firrup of Violets.

PIck the flowers and weigh them, put them into a quart of water, and steep them on hot embers, until such time as the flowers are turned white, and the water as blew as any Violet; then add to that quart of infusion, four pounds of refined sugar, and boyl it until it comes to a sirrup, being boyled and scummed on a gentle fire, left it turn its colour; so done, put it up, and keep it for your use.

Another rare way.

TAke and cut away the white of your flowers, then scruise out the juice of them, and add to every spoonful of juice, three of fair water; put it into an Alabaster Morter with stamped leaves, strain them dry through a cloath, then add to it as much of fine beaten sugar as you judge convenient; let it stand about twelve hours in a clean earthen pan, then take the clearest thereof into a glass, with a few drops of the juice of Lemons; it will be very clear and of a Violet colour; this is the best and most excellent way to make sirrup of Violets.

To make firrup of Mulberries.

TAke of those which are very ripe, press the juice from them through a linnen cloth between two sticks, and then to every pint of juice, take a pound of Sugar; boyl it to the height of a sirrup, so may you keep it all the year long: if it wax any thing thinner in a moneths time after you put it up, boyl it again; so put it up.

To make firrup of Clove-Gillyflowers.

TAke a peck of the flowers, cut off the whites, sift away the seeds and bruise them a little, then take a pint

pint of water: when it hath boyled, let it cool a little, and then put in your flowers; let them be kept close covered for a day and a night: it is best to put on but half your flowers at once, for it will make it the stronger: then add to it a pound and half of clarified sugar, and let it stand for one night, the next day put it into a Gally-pot, and lay your pot in a pot of fair water, and let it boyl therein until your sugar be totally melted, and your sirrup indifferently thick, then take it forth, and let it stand until it be cold, so may you Glass it for your use.

To make sirrup of Roses solutive.

TAke your Damask Roses and pull them, then have ready a gallon of fair water, when it is hot, put therein a good many Damask-Rose-leaves: when they look white, take them out, do this ten times together, which will make your water look red, then to every pint of that liquor, add the white of an egg and a pound of sugar, clarifie it and boyl it to a sirrup: so may you keep it all the year; the thicker the sirrup is, the better it will keep.

Another way to make sirrup of Damask-Roses.

YOu may take as much water as you think fit, let it be luke-warm, then put into it a good quantity of Damask-Rose-leaves, the whites of them being first cut away: let them lye in your water until they look pale, then take them out and crush them gently: then put in more fresh leaves, as aforesaid, continuing it so until your water turn to a deep red colour, and very bitter, which will be done in less than twenty changes of the leaves: if you would have it strong, do it as often more as you think fit, adding to every quart of water two pound of sugar, and seeth it with a soft fire until it be as thick as Honey, and of the colour your mind is to have it.

To keep your liquor of Roses all the year.

FOr preventing the ufe of much Sugar, you may preferve fo much of this liquor as you pleafe before you boyl it: you muft let it fettle, fo done, pour out the cleareft into a long necked glafs, to the neck thereof; then put in as much fweet oyl as will fill it up, and let it ftand in the Sun for certain dayes; this will keep good all the year; fo that if you want any firrup, you may feeth this liquor with fugar, if not you may fpare fo much fugar.

To make firrup of Cowflips.

TAke your diftilled water of Cowflips, and put therein your Cowflip-flowers picked clean, but the green in the bottom cut away; fo boyl your firrup in fugar, as you do other firrups.

To make firrup of Lemons.

TAke them and cut them in halves, and between your fingers juice them, and the liquor that runs from them will be very clear; add to every pint of juice a pound and half of loaf-fugar, being very white, fo boyl it to a firrup, and it will keep rarely well.

To make firrup of Maiden-hair.

TAke thereof fix ounces, Liquorifh fcraped and fliced one ounce; fteep them twenty four hours together, in four pints of Conduit-water, then fet it on the fire and boyl it to a quart; then take that liquor, and add to it two pound of clarified fugar, and let it boyl upon a gentle fire of Char-coles, until it comes to a firrup, being fcummed very often, that it may be the clearer; the more it is fo, the better it is; thus being boyled enough, put it up for your ufe.

To make firrup of dry Rofes.

Take of your beſt red Roſes dryed four ounces, infuſe them in a quart of fair water, on hot embers, until the Roſes have loſt their colour; then have a pound and half of ſugar; ſo clarifie your liquor and ſugar with two eggs; then boyl it to the height of a ſirrup, but have a ſpecial care that you ſet not your ſirrup on too hot a fire, for then it will loſe its colour, and be nothing worth.

To keep Cherries all the year, and to have them at Chriſtmaſs.

Take of the faireſt of them you can get, but beware that they be not bruiſed, rub them with a linnen cloth, ſo put them into a barrel of hay; firſt place in the bottom of your barrel a laying of hay, then one of Cherries, ſo do until your Veſſel be ful; then muſt you ſtop them up that no air may come to them, and lay them under a Feather-bed where one doth conſtantly lye, for the warmer they are, the better will they keep: and ſo doing, you may have Cherries any time of the year.

Candying.

To Candy Violet-Flowers.

Take of them which are very good and new, being very well coloured, weigh them, and to every ounce of Flowers you muſt add four ounces of refined ſugar, which is very white and fair-grained, and diſſolve it in two ounces of fair running water, ſo boyl it until it comes to a ſugar again;

again; you muſt ſcum it often, left it be not clear enough, and when it is boyled to ſugar again, take it off, and let it cool, then put in your Violet-Flowers, ſtirring them together until the ſugar grow hard to the pan; this done, put them in a box, and keep them for your uſe.

To Candy Pears, Plumbs, Apricocks, to look clear, &c.

TAke them and give them a cut in the ſide, but your Plumbs or Apricocks muſt be cut in the notch to the ſtone, then caſt ſugar on them, and bake them in an Oven as hot as for Manchet-bread, let your Oven be cloſe ſtopt, but bake them in an earthen pan, or broad platter, which is beſt, where they may lye one by one; let them ſtand but half an hour, then take them out of the platter, and lay them one by one on Glaſs-plates, ſo dry them, if you can get Glaſſes made like Marmalade-boxes to put over them, they will Candy the ſooner; after this manner you may Candy any ſuch fruits.

To Candy Borage-Flowers.

TAke your flowers and pick them very clean, weigh, and uſe them in every reſpect as you do your Roſemary-Flowers, ſave this, that when they be Candied, you muſt ſet them in a ſtill, ſo to keep them in a ſheet of white paper, putting a Chafin-diſh of coals every day into your ſtill; and it will be Candied very excellently, and that in a very ſhort time.

To Candy Roſemary-Flowers.

TAke of them ready picked and weighed, to every ounce of Flowers, you muſt add two ounces of loaf ſugar, and one ounce of Sugar-Candy, diſſolved in Roſemary-Flower-Water; boyl them until they come to ſugar again; which done, put in your roſemary flowers when your sugar is almost cold, so stir them together until they be enough; then take them out, being put in a box, keep them for your use.

To Candy all sorts of flowers after the Spanish way.

TAke of your double refined sugar, put it in a Posnet with as much Rose-water as will melt it, then pot it into the Pulp of half a roasted Apple, with one grain of Musk, let them boyl till they come to the height of a Candy, then put your flowers in, being pickt clean, so let them boyl; then cast them on a fine plate, and cut them in wayes with your knif: spot it with Gold, and keep it for your use.

To make Manus Christi.

TAke half a pound of refined sugar, with some Rose-water, boyl them together till it come to a sugar again, then stir it about till it be somewhat cold; so done, take your leaf-gold and mingle with it; then cast it according to art, that is, in round goblets, so keep them.

To Candy Goos-berries.

TAke your fairest green Goos-berries, and with a linnen cloth wipe them clean, the stalks being picked from them: add to every ounce of Goos-berries two ounces of sugar and an ounce of sugar-Candy: dissolve them in an ounce or two of Rose-water, and so boyl them up to the height of *Manus Christi*, and when it comes to its perfect height, let it cool, then put in your Goos-berries, for if you put them in hot, they will shrink, so stir them together with a wooded Spatter, till they be Candyed, thus put them up and keep them.

To

To dry Apricocks.

TAke them and stone them when they are ripe, then take their rhindes off, when they are weighed, you must add to them half their weight in sugar finely beaten, then take a silver or earthen dish, and lay first a laying of sugar, then of the fruit, and let them stand a whole night together, in the morning the sugar will be melted; then put them into a skillet, boyl them apace, and scum them well, when they grow tender, take them from the fire, and let them stand in the sirrup two dayes, then take them forth and dry them on plates in the stove for your use.

To Candy Enula-Campana.

TAke of your fairest Enula-Campana-roots, take them clean from the sirrup, wash the sugar off, and dry them again with a linnen cloth, weigh them, and to every pound of roots you must add a pound and three quarters of sugar; clarifie it well, and boyl it to the height of *Manus Christi*; when it is so done, pip in your roots, three or four at once, and they will candy very well, so stove them and keep them all the year for your use.

To Candy Eringo-roots.

TAke them and boyl them pretty tender, pill, pith, and lay them together; take their weight in sugar, and put it in as much water as will melt it; then put in your roots, and let them boyl softly, until such time as the sugar is consumed into the roots, then take them and turn them, and shake them until the sugar be dryed up; then lay them to dry on a Lattice of Wier till they be cold; after this manner you may Candy any other roots.

Another way.

TAke them, when they are ready to be preserved, weigh them, and to every pound of your roots, you must take two pounds of the purest sugar you can get, and clarifie it with the whites of Eggs exceeding well, that it may be as clear as Chrystal, for then it will be very commendable; so done, you must boyl it to the height of *Manus Christi*, and then dip in your roots two or three at once, until they be all Candied, so put them in a stove, and keep them all the year for your use.

To dry Pippins.

TAke half a pound of fine sugar, boyl it in a pint of water until it comes to a sirrup, clarifie it with the white of an Egg, and strain it through a linnen cloth: then set it on the fire again in another skillet, then take eight Pippins, being cut in halves and cored, and put in each half into the sirrup as you pare them; let them boyl until the sirrup be almost wasted away, but take the scum off still as it riseth, then take out your Pippins, lay them on plates, and dry them in your stove.

To candy Rose-leaves as natural, as if they grew on trees.

TAke of your fairest Rose-leaves, Red or Damask, and on a sun-shine day sprinkle them with Rose-water, lay them one by one on a fair paper, then take some double refined sugar beaten very fine, put it in a fine laune searse; when you have laid abroad all the Rose leaves in the hottest of the sun, searse sugar thinly all over them, and anon the sun will Candie the sugar: then turn the leaves and searse sugar on the other side, and turn them often in the sun, sometimes sprinkling Rose-water, and sometimes searsing sugar on them,

untill

Rare Receipts in Candying.

until they be enough, and come to your liking, and being thus done, you may keep them.

To Candy all sorts of Flowers, Fruits and Spices, the clear Rock-Candy.

TAke two pound of *Barbery* sugar great grained, clarified with the whites of two Eggs: boyl it almost so high as for *Manus Christi*, then put it into a pipkin that is not very rough, then put in your Flowers, Fruits, and spices, so put your pipkin into a still, and make a small fire with small-coals under it, and in the space of twelve dayes it will be Rock-candyed.

To Candy Marigolds in Wedges, the Spanish Fashion.

TAke of the fair yellow Flowers two ounces, shred and dry them before the fire: then take four ounces of sugar, and boyl it to the height of *Manus Christi*, then pour it upon a wet pye-plate, and betwixt hot and cold cut it into wedges, then lay them on a sheet of white paper, and put them in a stove.

To Candy all manner of Flowers in their Natural colours.

Take the Flowers with the stalks, and wash them over with a little Rose-water, wherein Gum-Arabick is dissolved; then take fine searsed sugar, and dust over them, and set them a drying on the bottom of a sieve in an Oven, and they will glister as if it were sugar-candy.

To Candy Ginger.

Take your very fair large Ginger, pair it, and lay it in water a day and a night, then take your double refined sugar, and boyl it to the height of sugar again: and when that beginneth to be cold, take your Ginger and stir it well about, while your sugar is hard to to the pan, then take it out Race by Race, and lay it by the fire for four hours; then take a pot, warm it, and put the Ginger therein, then tye it very clofe, and every fecond morning ftir it about roundly, and it will be Rock-Candyed in a very fhort fpace.

PASTES.

To make Pafte of Pippins the Genova *fafhion, fome with leaves, fome like Plumbs with ftalks, and ftones in them.*

YOur Pippins being pared, cut them in quarters and boyl them in fair water till they be tender, then ftrain them and dry the pulp upon a Chafin-difh of Coals, then weigh them, and boyl it to *Manus Chrifti*, and put them together; then fafhion them upon a pye-plate, and put them in an Oven, being very flightly heat, the next morning you may turn them, and put them off the plates, upon fheets of Paper on a hurdle, and fo put them into an Oven, like heat, and there let them remain four or five dayes, putting every day a Chafin-difh of Coals into the Oven, and when they be very dry, you may box them, and keep them for your ufe all the year.

To make Pafte of Orenges and Lemons.

TAke of your Oranges and Lemons, and boyl them in two feveral veffels of water; fhift the water fo often, untill the bitternefs be taken away, and they begin to grow tender, then cut them through in the middle, and take out the kernels, wring the water from them, and beat them in a clean ftone Morter, with the pulp of three or four Pippins; then ftrain them through a ftrainer, and take the weight of the pap in fugar, and

boyl

boyl it to the height of a Candy, with as much Rosewater as will melt the sugar, then put into the hot sirrup, the pap of your Oranges and Lemons, and let them seeth softly, being often stirred; and when you find it stiff enough, you may put it into what fashion you please on a sheet of glass, and so set it in a stove or oven: when it is dry, box it up for your use.

To make Paste of Goos-berries.

TAke Goos-berries, cut them one by one, and wring away the juice till you have got enough for your turn, boyl your juice alone to make it somwhat thicker; then take as much fine sugar as your juice will sharpen, dry it, and when it is so, beat it again, then take as much Gum-Dragon steeped in Rose-water as will serve: then beat it into a Paste, in a Marble Morter: then take it up and print it in your Moulds, so dry it in your stove: when it is dry, you may box it up for your use all the year.

Certain old useful Traditions OF CARVING, and SEWING &c.

Terms of a Carver.

Break that Deer; Leach that Brawn; Rear that Goose; Lift that swan; sawce that Capon; spoyl that Hen; Trush that Chicken; Unbrace that Mallard; Unlace that Cony; Dismember that Heron; Display that Crane; Disfigure that Peacock; unjoynt that Bittern; unthach that Curlew; Allay that Pheasant; Wing that Partridge; with that Quail; Mince that Plover; Thigh that Pigeon; border that Pasty; Thigh that Woodcock, also all manner of small fowl; Timber the Fire; Tire the Egg; Chine that Salmon; string that Lampry; splat the Pike; sauce that Place; sauce that Tench; splay that Bream; side that Haddock: tusk that Barbel; culpon that Trout; fin that Chevine: Transon that Eele; tranch that Sturgeon: undertench that Porpas: Tame that Crab; Barb that Lobster.

The Office of the Butler, Pantler, Yeoman of the Seller, and Ewry.

First you must have three Pantry knives, one knife to square Trencher loaves, another to be a chipper, the third shall be sharp, for to make smooth Trenchers: then chip your Lord's bread hot, and all other bread let

Traditions of Carving and Sewing. 269

let it be a day old, houſhold bread three days old: then look your ſalt be white and dry, the powder made of Ivory two inches broad and three long, and look that your ſaltſeller lid touch not your ſalt, let your Table-Clothes, Towels, and Napkins be fair folded in a Cheſt, or hanged on a Perch, then ſee your Table Knives be fair poliſhed, and your Spoons clean: and look you have two Tarriots, a greater and a leſs, and Wine Cannels of Box made according, and a ſharp Gimlet and Fauſets: and when you ſet a Pipe on broach do thus, ſet it four fingers broad above the neather Chine upward aſtaunt, and then ſhall the Lees never riſe; alſo look you have according to the ſeaſons, Butter, Cheeſe, Apples, Pears, Nuts, Plumbs, Grapes, Dates, Figgs, Raiſins, Compoſt, green Ginger, Chard and Quince: ſerve faſting, Butter, Plumbs, Damſons, Cherries and Grapes: after meat, Pears, Nuts, Strawberries, Hurtleberries, and hard Cheeſe: alſo Blanderles or Pippins, with Carrawaies in Confects; after ſupper, roaſted Apples and Pears, with blanched Powder and hard Cheeſe, beware of Cow-cream, and of Strawberries, Hurtleberries, Juncate for Cheeſe will make your Lord ſick, therefore let him eat hard Cheeſe: Hard Cheeſe hath this operation, it will keep the Stomach open. Butter is wholeſome firſt and laſt, for it purgeth away all poiſons. Milk, Cream, and Juncate, they will cloſe the Maw, ſo doth a Poſſet; beware of green Sallets and raw fruits, for they will make your Lord ſick. Set not much by ſuch meats as will ſet the teeth on edge; therefore eat an Almond and hard Cheeſe: Alſo of divers drinks, if their fumoſities have diſpleaſed your Lord, let him eat a raw Apple, and the fumoſities will ceaſe.

Take good heed of your Wines every night with a candle, both red Wine and ſweet Wine, and look they reboyl nor leak not, and waſh the Pipe head every night with

with cold water, and have a Clenching-iron, Adds, and linnen cloths if need be; if they reboyl you will know the hissing, therefore keep an empty pipe with the Lees, of coloured Rose, and draw the reboyled Wine to the Lees, and it will help it; and if your sweet Wine be pale, draw it into a romney vessel for Leesing; also let your compost be fair and clean, and your Ale five dayes old e're men drink it. Then keep your Office clean, and be courteous to answer to each person, and look you give no person paled drink, for it will breed the scab. And when you lay the cloth, wipe the board clean, then lay your cloth (a Couch it is called) let your fellow take the one end, and hold you the other, and draw the cloth straight, the bought on the outer side; take the outer parts and hand it even, then take the third cloth, and lay the bought on the inner side, and lay estate both the upper part half a foot broad, then cover the Cupboard and the Ewry with a Towel of Diaper, then take a Towel about your neck, and lay the one side of your Towel upon your left arm, and thereon lay your Lords Napkin, and lay on your arm seven loaves of bread, with three or four trencher-loaves, with the end of the Towel in your left hand, as the manner is; then take the Salt-seller in your left hand, and take the end of the Towel in your right hand to bear in spoons and knives, then set your Salt on the right side where your Lord shall sit, on the left side your Salt, set your Trenchers, then lay your knives, and set your bread, one loaf by another, and your spoons, and your Napkin fair folded beside your bread, then cover your bread, trenchers, spoons and knives, and at every side of the Table set a Salt-seller with two Trencher-loaves, and if you will wrap your Lords bread stately, you must square and proportion it, and see that no loaf be more than another, and then shall you make your Wrapper handsomly, then take a Towel of Reins of two yards and

Traditions of Carving and Sewing. 271

and half, and take it by the ends double, lay it on the Table, then take the end of the bought, a handful in your hand, wrap it hard, then lay the end so wrapped between two Towels, upon the end so wrapped, this being done, lay your bread bottom to bottom, six or seven loaves, then set your bread in good form: And when your Lords Table is thus arrayed, cover all other boards with salts, trenchers, and cups, also see the Ewry be arrayed with Basons and Ewrs, and water hot and cold; and see you have Napkins, Cups and Spoons, and see your pots for Wine and Ale be made clean, and to the Jurnape make the curtesie, with a cloth under a fair double Napry; then take the Towels end next you, and the outer end of the cloth on the outer side of the Table, and hold these three ends at once, and fold them at once, that a pleat pass not a foot broad, then lay it even where it should lye, and after meat wash with that, that is, at the right end of the Table you must give it out, and the Marshal must convey it, and look to each cloth the right side be outward and drawn straight, then must you raise the upper part of the Towel, and lay it without any groaning, and at every end of the Towel you must convey half a yard, that the Sewer may take estate reverently, and when your Lord hath washed, draw the Jurnape even, and bear it to the midst of the board, then take it up before your Lord, and bear it into the Ewry again; and when your Lord is set, look your Towel be about your neck, then make your Obeysance, then uncover your bread and lay it by the salt, and lay your Napkin, Knife and spoon afore him; and look you set at the ends of the Table four loaves at a Mess; see that every person have a Napkin and a spoon and observe the Sewer, how many dishes be covered, and so many cups cover you; then serve you fore the Table decently, that every man may speak of your courtesy.

Of

Of the Sewing of Fish.

THe Sewer muſt ſew, and from the board convey all manner of Pottages, Meats and ſauſes; and every day commune with the Cook, and underſtand and know how many diſhes ſhall be; and ſpeak with the Pantlers and Officers of the ſpicery, for fruits that ſhall be eaten faſting; then go to the board of ſewing, and ſee you have Officers ready to convey, and ſervants to bear your diſhes; alſo if the marſhal, ſquires and ſerjeants of Arms be there, then you may ſerve your Lord without blame.

Service.

FIrſt Muſtard and Brawn, Pottage, Beef, Mutton, ſtewed Pheaſants, Swan, Capon, Pigg, Veniſon, Hake, Cuſtard, Leach, and Lumbard, Fruiter-Vaunt with a ſubtilty, two Pottages blanched, Manger and Jelly; for ſtandard, Veniſon, roaſt Kid, Fawn, and Cony, Buſtard, ſtork, Crane, Peacock with his tail, Heron-ſhew, Bittern, Woodcock, Partridge, Plover, Rabbits, great Birds, Larks, Doucets, Pampuff, Whiteleach, Amber, Jelly, Cream of Almonds, Curlew, Brew, ſnite, Quail, ſparrow, Martinet, Pearch in Jelly, petty Pervis, Quinced, baked-Leach, Dewgard, Fruter, Fage, Blandrels, or Pippins, with Carrawais in Confects, Wafers and Ipocraſs, they be agreeable; this feaſt being done, voide that Table.

Of Carving of Fleſh.

THE Carver muſt know the Carving, and the fair handling of a Knife; and how he ſhall fetch all manner of fowl, your knife muſt be fair, and your hands clean, and paſs but two fingers and a thum upon your knife, in the midſt of your hand ſet the haft ſure, unlaſing the mincing with two fingers and a thumb,

carving

Traditions of Carving and Sewing.

carving of bread, laying and voiding of crums with two fingers and a thumb, look that you set never on fish, flesh, beast, nor fowl, more than two fingers and a thumb, then take your loaf into your left hand, and hold your knife sure, foul not the Table-cloth, but wipe upon your Napkin; then take your Trencher loaf in your left hand, and with the edge of your Table knife, take up the Trenchers as near the point as you may; then lay four Trenchers to your Lord one by another, and lay thereon other four Trenchers, or else two, then take a loaf in your left hand and pare it round, and cut the upper crust to your Lord, and cut the neather crust and void the paring, and touch the loaf no more after it is served; then cleanse the Table, that the Sewer may serve your Lord.

You must know the fumositives of fish, flesh, and fowls, and all manner of sauces according to their appetites; these are fumositives, salt, four, rusty, fat, fryed, sinews, skins, bony croups, young feathers, heads, Pidgeons bones, and all manner of legs of beasts and fowls, lay to the other side; for these be fumositives, lay them never to your Lord.

Service.

TAke your knife in your hand, and cut Brawn in the dish as it lyeth, and lay on your Lords Trencher, and see there be Mustard.

Venison with Frumenty is good for your Lord, touch not the Venison with your hand, but with your knife, cut it out into the Furmity; do in the same wise with Pease and Bacon, Beef, Hen, and Mutton, and lay to your Lord; beware of fumositives, salt, sinew, fat and raw in sirrup; Pheasant, Partridge, Stock, Dove, Chickens, in the left hand take them by the Pinion, and with the fore part of your knife lift up your wings; then mince it into the sirrup,

Traditions of Carving and Sewing.

beware of skin, raw and sinew; Goose, Teal, Mallard and Swan, raise the legs, then the wings, lay the body in the midst, or in any other platter, the wings in the midst, the legs after, lay the Brawn between the legs, and the wings in the platter; Capon, or Hen, or Geese, lift the legs, then the wings, and cast on Wine or Ale, then mince the wing, and give your Lord; Pheasant, Partridge, Plover, or Lapwing, raise the wings, after the legs; Woodcock, Bittern, Egrit, Snite, Curlew and Heron-sew, unlace them, break off the pinions, and break the neck, then raise the legs, and let the Feet be on still, with the Wings; a Crane, raise the wings first, and beware of the Trump in his breast, Peacock, Stock, Bustard, and Shovillard, unlace them as a Crane, and let the feet be on still; Quail, Lark, Sparrow, Martinet, Pidgeon, Swallow, and Thrush, the legs first, then the wings: Fawn, Kid, and Lamb, lay the kidny to your Lord, then lift up the shoulder, and give to your Lord a rib: Venison roasted cut it into the dish, and lay it to your Lord; a Coney, lay him on the back, cut away the vents between the hinder legs; break the kernel bone, then raise the sides, lay the Coney on the womb on each side the Chine, the two sides parted from the Chine, then lay the bulk, chine, and sides in the dish; also you must mince four Lesses to one morsel of meat, that your Lord may take it in the sauce: All baked meats that be hot, open them above the Coffin, and all that be cold, open them in the mid-way. Custard, cheek them inch-square; that your Lord may eat Doucets, pare away the sides and the bottom; beware of fumositives, Fruiter, Vaunt, Fruiters they say be good; better is Fruiter pouch; Apple-fruiters be good hot, all cold touch not; Tansey is good hot; Worts of Grewel, of Beef, or of Mutton is good; Jelley, Mortrus, Cream of Almonds, blanch Manger, Jussel and Claret; Cabbage

and

and Umbles of the Deer be good, and all other pottage beware of.

Sauce for many sorts of Fowls and Flesh.

MUstard is good with Brawn, Beef, Chine of Bacon and Mutton; Verjuice is good to boyled Chickens and Capons; Swan with Chaldrons; Ribs of Beef with Garlick, Mustard, Pepper, Verjuice, Ginger; sawce of Lamb, Pig, or Fawn; mustard and sugar to Pheasant, Partridge and Cony; sauce Gamlin to Heron-sew, Egript, Plover, and Crane; Brew and Curlew, salt, sugar, and water of Camet; Bustard, Shovillard and Bittern sauce, Gamlin, Woodcock, Lapwing, Lark, Quail, Martinet, Venison, and snite, with white salt; Sparrows and Throsles, with salt and cinamon; thus with all meats, salt shall have the operation.

Of the Feasts and Service from Easter *unto* Whitsuntide.

ON *Easter*-day, and so forth to *Pentecost*, after the serving Table, there must be set bread, trenchers and spoons, after the estimation of them that sit there: And thus you shall serve your Lord, lay trenchers, and if he be of a high degree or estate lay five trenchers, and of a lower degree four, if lower three, then cut bread for your Lord according to his conditions, whether it be cut in the midst, or pared; or else to be cut in small peices; also you must understand how the meat shall be served before your Lord; aud namely on *Easter*-Day after the manner and service of that Country where you were born: First, on that day you shall serve a Calf sodden, and sodden Eggs with green sauce, and set them before the most principle estate: And that Lord, because of his high estate, shall part them all about him; then serve Pottage, as worts, roots or brewis, with beef, mutton, or veal and capons, to be coloured with faffron, and baked; meats, and the fecond Courfe, Juffel with Mamony, and roafted, endowered and Pidgeons, with baked meats, as Tarts, Chewets, and Flaunes, and other after the difpofition of the Cooks; and at fupper-time divers fauces of mutton, or Veal in broth, after the direction of the Steward; and then Chickens with Bacon, Veal, roafted Pidgeons, or tamed, and Kid roafted, with the head and purtenance of Lamb, and Pigs-feet with Vinegar and Parflee thereon; and Tanfy fryed, and other baked meats; ye fhall underftand this manner of fervice dureth to Pentecoft, fave fifh-days.

Alfo take heed how you do array thefe things before your Lord: firft ye fhall fee there be green fauce of forrel, or of Vines; that is, hold a fauce for the firft Courfe, and ye fhall begin to raife the Capon.

General Directions for the Carving up of Fowl.

Lift that Swan.

THe manner of cutting up a Swan, muft be to flit her right down in the middle of the breft, and fo clean through the back, from the neck to the Rump; fo part her in two halves, but you muft do it cleanly and handfomly, that you break not nor tear the meat; then lay the two halves in a fair Charger, with the flit fides downwards, throw falt about it, and fet it again to the Table; Let your fauce be Chaldron for a Swan, and ferve it in faucers.

Rear that Goofe.

YOu muft break a Goofe up contrary to this fafhion, take a Goofe being roafted, and take off both the legs fair like fhoulders of Lamb, take them quite from the body, then cut off the belly-piece round

round close to the end of the breast, then lace her down with your knife clean through the breast, on each side a thumbs breadth from the bone in the middle of the breast, then take off the pinion of each side, and the flesh you first laced with your knife, raise it up clean from the bone and take it off clean from the carkafs with the pinion; then cut up the bone which lyeth before in the breast commonly called the Merry-thought, the skin and the flesh being upon it, then cut from the breast-bone another slice of flesh clean through, and take it clean from the bone, then turn your carkafs and cut it asunder, the back bone above the loyn bones, then take the rump end of the back-bone and lay it in a fair dish with the skinny side upward, lay at the four-end of it the Merry-thought, with the skinny side upwards and before that the Apron of the Goose, then lay your pinions, on each side contrary, set your legs on each side contrary behind them, that the bone ends of the legs may stand up crofs in the middle of the dish, and the wing-pinions may come in the outside of them, put under the wing pinions on each side, the long slices of flesh, which you cut from the breast-bone, and let the ends meet under the leg bones, and let the other ends lie cut in the dish betwixt the leg and the pinion, then pour in your sauce into the dish under your meat, and throw on salt, and set it on the Table.

To cut up a Turkey or Bustard.

YOu must raise up the leg very fair, and open the joynt with the point of your knife, but take not off the leg, then lace down the breast with your knife on both sides, and open the breast pinion with your knife, but take it not off, then raise up the merry-thought, betwixt the breast-bone and the top thereof, then lace down the Flesh on both sides the breast bone,

bone, and raife up the flefh called the brawn, and turn it outward upon both fides, but break it not, nor cut it off, then cut off the wing pinions at the joynt next the body, and ftick in each fide the pinion in the place you turned out the brawn, but cut off the fharp end of the pinion, and take the middle piece, and that will fit juft in the place: You may cut up a Capon or Pheafant the fame way, but of your Capon cut not off the pinion; but in the place where you put the pinion of your Turkey, you muft put the Gizard of your Capon, on each fide half.

Difmember that Heron.

YOu muft take off both the legs, lace it down to the breaft with your knife on both fides, and raife up the flefh, and take it clean off with the pinion, then you muft ftick the head in the breaft, and fet the pinion, on the contrary fide of the Carkafs, and the leg on the other fide of the Carkafs, fo that the bone ends may meet crofs over the Carkafs, and the other wing crofs over upon the top of the Carkafs.

Unbrace that Mallard.

RAife up the pinion and legs, but take them not off, and raife the Merry-thought from the breaft, and lace it down each fide of the breaft, with your knife, bending to and fro like waves.

Unlace that Coney.

TUrn the back downward, and cut the belly flaps clean off from the Kidney, but take heed you cut not the Kidney, nor the flefh, then put in the point of your knife between the Kidneys, and loofen the flefh from the bone on each fide of the bone, then turn up the back of the Rabbet, and cut it crofs between the wings, then lace it down clofe by the bone with your
knife

knife on both ſides, then open the fleſh of the Rabbet from the bone with the point of your knife againſt the Kidney, and pull the leg open ſoftly with your hand, but pull it not off, then thruſt in your knife betwixt the ribs and the Kidney, and ſlit it out, then lay the legs cloſe together.

Sauce the Capon.

TAke up a Capon, and lift up the right leg, and right wing, and ſo array forth, and lay him in the platter, as he ſhould fly, and ſerve your Lord; and know well, that Capons or Chickens, be arrayed after one ſauce, the Chickens ſhall be ſauced with green ſauce or Verjuice.

Allay that Pheaſant.

TAke a Pheaſant, raiſe his legs and his wings, as it were a Hen, and no ſauce, only ſalt.

Wing that Partridge.

TAke a Partridge and raiſe his Legs and Wing as a Hen, if ye mince him, ſauce him with Wine, powder of Ginger, and ſalt, then ſet him upon a Chafindiſh of coals to warm, and ſerve it.

Wing that Quail.

TAke a Quail, and raiſe his legs and wings as a Hen; uſe no ſauce, but ſalt.

Diſplay that Crane.

TAke a Crane and unfold his legs, and cut off his wings by the joynts, then take up his wings and his legs, and ſauce them with powder of Ginger, Muſtard, Vinegar and ſalt.

Dismember that Heron.

TAke a Heron and raise his legs and his wings, as a Crane, and sauce him with Vinegar, Mustard, powder of Ginger and salt.

Unjoynt that Bittern.

TAke a Bittern and raise his legs and wings, as a Heron, and no sauce but salt.

Break that Egript.

TAke an Egript and raise his Legs and wings, as a Heron, and no sauce but salt.

Untach that Curlew.

TAke a Curlew and raise his legs and wings, as a Hen, no sauce but salt.

Untach that Brew.

TAke a Brew and raise him up as before, no sauce but salt, and serve it.

Break that Sarcel.

TAke a Sarcel or Teal, and raise his wings and legs, and no sauce but salt.

Mince that Plover.

TAke a Plover, raise him as a Hen, no sauce but salt.

A Snite.

RAise him as you did the Plover, no sauce but salt.

Thigh

Thigh that Woodcock.

TAke a Woodcock, raise his legs and wings as a Hen, this done, dight him the brain.

From the Feast of Whitsuntide *unto* Midsummer.

IN the second course for the meats aforesaid, you must take for your sauces, Ale, Wine-Vinegar, and Powders after meat, but Ginger a Canel from *Petecost* to the Feast of Saint *John Baptist*.

The first course shall be Beef and Mutton, with boyled Capons, or roasted; but if the Capon be boyled, dress him in the manner aforesaid, and when he is roasted, you must cast on Salt, with Wine or Ale, then take the Capon by the leg, and cast on the sauce, and break him out, and lay him in a dish as he should lie; first ye shall cut the right leg, and right shoulder, and between the four members lay the brawn of the Capon, with the croup in the end between the legs, as it were possible to be joyned together; and other baked meats after: And in the second course Pottage shall be Jussel, Charlet, or Motrus, with young Gheese, Veal, Pork, Pigeons, or Chickens roasted with pam puff, Fretters, and other baked meat, after the direction of the Cook: Also the Goose ought to be cut member to member, beginning at the right leg, and so forth under the right wing, and not upon the joynt above, and it ought to be eaten with Sorrel, or tender Vines, or Verjuice in Summer season, after the pleasure of your Lord; also you must understand, that all manner of fowls that have whole feet, should be raised under the wing, and not above.

From

From the Feaſt of Saint John the Baptiſt, unto Michaelmas.

IN the firſt courſe; Pottage, Worts, Gruel and Frumenty; with Veniſon, and Mortrus, and legs of Pork with green ſauce, roaſted Capon, Swan with Chaldron: In the ſecond courſe Pottage, after the direction of the Cooks, with roaſted Mutton, Veal, Pork, Chickens, or endoured Pidgeons, Heron-ſews, Fritters, or baked meats; take heed of a Pheaſant, for he muſt be baked in the manner of a Capon, but it muſt be done dry without any moiſture, and he muſt be eaten with ſalt and powder of Ginger; and the Heron-ſue muſt be dreſt in the ſame manner, without any moiſture, and he ſhould be eaten with ſalt and powder of Ginger; alſo you muſt underſtand that all ſort of Fowls, having open claws, as a Capon, ſhall be dreſſed and ſet forth as a Capon, or ſuch like.

From the Feaſt of Saint Michaelmas, unto the Feaſt of Chriſtmaſs.

IN the firſt Courſe, Pottage, Beef, Mutton, Bacon, legs of Pork, or with Gooſe, Capon, Mallard, Swan or Pheſant, as it is before ſaid, with Tarts, or baked Meats, or Chines of Pork: In the ſecond Courſe, Pottage, Morrus, or Conies, or Sew, the roaſted fleſh, Mutton, Pork, Veal, Pullets, Pidgeons, Teals, Widgeons, Mallards, Partridge, Woodcocks, Plovers, Bittern, Curlew, Heron-ſew, Veniſon roaſted, ſtreat birds, ſnites, Feldfares, Thruſhes, Fritters, Chewets, Beef with ſauce, and other baked meats, as is aforeſaid: And if you carve before your Lord or your Lady, any boyled Fleſh, carve away the skin above, then carve not too much of the fleſh for your Lord and Lady, and eſpecially for Ladies, for they will ſoon be angry, for
their

Traditions of Carving and Sewing

their thoughts are soon changed, and some Lords will be soon pleased, and some not, as they be of complexion: The Goose and Swan may be cut as you do other Fowls, that have whole feet, or else as your Lord and Lady would have it: Also a swan with a chaldron, capon, or Pheasant, ought to be dressed as it is aforementioned; but the skin must be taken away, and when they are, then carve before your Lord or your Lady; for generally, all manner of whole-fotted Fowls that have their living on the water, their skins be wholsom and clean, for cleanness of water and fish is their living, and if they eat any stinking thing, it is made so clean with the water, that all the corruption is clean gon away from it: But the skin of a Capon, Hen or Chicken, is not so clean, for they eat foul things in the streets, and therefore their skins is not so wholsome; for it is not their kind to enter into the River to make their meat void of filth: Mallard, Goose, or swan, they eat upon the Land foul meat, but after their kind they go to the River, and there they cleanse them of their foul stinck; the skin of a pheasant, as is aforesaid, is not wholsome; then take away the heads of all field and wood-birds, as Pheasant, Peacock, Partridge, Woodcock, Curlew, for they eat in their degree foul things, as worms, toads, and other the like.

Sewing of Fish.

First Course.

TO go to the sewing Fish, Muscalade, Minnews in few, of Porpas, of Salmon, baked Herring with sugar, Green-fish, Pike, Lamprey, Salens, Porpas roasted, baked Gurnard, and Lamprey baked.

Second Course.

JElly white and red, Dates in Confect, Conger, Salmon, Dorey, Brit, Turbet, Halibut for standard, Base, Trout, Mullet, Chevine, Sole, Eeles, and Lamprey roasted, Tench in jelly.

Third Course.

FResh Sturgeon, Bream, Pearch in jelly, a Joll of Salmon, Sturgeon, Welks, Apples, and Pears roasted with Sugar-candy, Figgs of Malike, and Raisins, Dates Capt, with minced Ginger, Wafers, and Ipocras, they be agreeable; this being accomplished, void the Table.

Of Carving of Fish.

THe Carver of fish must see to Peason and Frumenty, the Tayl and Liver; ye must look if there be a salt Porpas, or Sole, Turrentine, and do after the form of Venison, baked Herring, and lay it whole upon your Lords trencher, white Herring in a dish, open it by the back, pick out the bones and the roe, and see there be Mustard: Of salt-fish, green-fish, salt Salmon, and Conger, pare away the skin, salt-fish, stock-fish, Marlin, Mackrel, and Hake with Butter, take away the bones, and the skins; a Pike, lay the womb upon his Trencher, with sauce enough, a salt Lamprey cut in seven or eight pieces, and lay it to your Lord; a Plaice, put out the water, then cross him with your knife, cast on Salt, Wine, or Ale, Gurnard, Rochet, Bream, Chevin, Base, Mullet, Roch, Pearch, Sole Mackrel, Whiteings, Haddock, and Codling, raise them by the back, and pick out the bones, and cleanse the rest in the belly; Carp, Bream, Sole, and Trout, back and belly together: Salmon, Conger, Sturgeon, Turbuthirbol, Thornback, Houndfish, and Halibut, cut them in the dishes; the Porpos about, Tench in his sauce; cut two Eeles, and Lampreys roasted,

pull

pull off the skin, and pick out the bones, put thereto Vinegar and Powder: A Crab, break him afunder in a difh, and clean the fhell, fo put in the ftuff again, temper it with Vinegar, and Powder them, cover it with bread, and heat it, then fet it to your Lord, and lay them in a difh: A Crevis, drefs him thus, part him afunder, flit his belly, and take out the fifh, pare away the red skin, and mince it thin, put Vinegar in the difh, and fet it on the Table without heating: A Joll of Sturgeon, cut it in thin morfels, and lay it round your difh: French Lamprey baked, open the Paftie, then take white bread, and cut it thin, and lay it in a difh, and with a fpoon take of Gallentine, and lay it on the bread with red wine, and Powder of Cinamon; then cut a piece of the Lamprey, and mince in thin, and lay it in the Gallentine, then fet it on the fire to heat; Frefh Herring with falt and wine, Shrimps well picked, Flounders, Gudgeons, Minews, Musfles, and Lampreys; Sprats is good in few Mufculado in Worts, Oyfters in few, Oyfters in gravie, Minews in Porpos, Salmon in Feel, Jelly white and red: Cream of Almonds, Dates in Confects, Pears, and Quinfes in Sirrup, with Parfley roots, Mortrus of Houndfifh raife ftanding.

Sauces of all Fifh.

MUftard is good for falt Herrings, falt Fifh, falt Conger, Salmon, Spatling, falt Eele, & Ling! Vinegar is good with falt Porpos, Turrentine, falt Sturgeon, falt Thrilpole, and falt Whale, Lamprey with Gallentine; Verjuice to Roach, Dace, Bream, Mullet, Flounder, falt Crab, and Chevin, with powder of Cinamon: To Thornback, Herring, Houndifh, Haddock, Whiting, and Cod, Vinegar, powder of Cinamon and Ginger; Green fauce is good with Green-fifh, and Hallibut, Cottel, and frefh Turbet; put not your Green fauce away, for it is good with Muftard.

An

An excellent way for making Ipocras.

TAke of Grains half a dram, of Cinamon four ounces, of Ginger two ounces, Nutmegs half an ounce, Cloves and Mace of each half an ounce, bruise these well in a Morter, and infuse them in a Gallon of White-wine four or five dayes, the vessel being close stopt, adde to them a pound and a half of sugar, when it is dissolved, put to it half a pint of Rose-water, and as much Milk; let it stand one night, then run it through an Ipocras bag, then may you put it into a fine new Runlet if you purpose to keep it, if you presently spend it, you may put it into certain pots.

An approved Receipt for a Consumption, that hath long remained.

TAke nine, or twelve white Snailes, and break away their shells from them, then put them into a bowl of water for twelve hours, to cleanse them from their slime, then change the water, and let them remain in the like bowl of running-water for the like space, then take them out, and put them into half a pint of white-wine, & keep them in it twelve hours; then take the Snails out of the wine, & put them into a quart of red Cows-milk, and boyl it until it comes to a pint, then add to it one ounce of Candied sugar, and give the Party diseased to drink every morning, and at four in the afternoon; but you must not let the Party eat or drink any thing for two hours space after the taking of it: And there is no question by Gods blessing (if rightly prepared, and taken according as is here prescribed) it will recover the Patient; although he hath a long time lyen very weak and lingering under that Disease: Many there are, who when Doctors have left them off for lost, have been raised up again by this Receipt. And whosover
please

pleafe to make ufe of what I have here inferted, will find what I fay to be true.

To coller Flounders.

TAke your Flounders, garinge five, and flea them, and fcotch them, wafh them, put them into a pipkin or skillet, let them be covered with white or claret-wine, put in two or three Anchovies, fome Lemmon fliced, two or three blades of large Mace, fome whole Pepper, a little falt, the duft of manchet, let thefe ftew together half an hour, difh your fifh; for fauce, take fome of the fame liquor with a Lemon minced, a little gravie of Mutton Mingled together, beaten butter, pour it on your Fifh, duft your difh fide, and garnifh it with Lemmon.

To roaft a fhoulder of Mutton in Blood.

TAke grated bread, fome fweet herbs picked, wafhed and minced with a little rind of Lemmon, Beef-fuet, alfo with Pepper, Nutmeg and falt, let your fheep be ready to kill, prepare your Blood, being cold, the bread and herbs with the blood mingled like a Pudding, fearfe the fhoulder, being cut off as hot as you can, fo having your Caul hot from your fheep, pouring the reft of the fearfe with the fame blood on the meat, and prick it up clofe in your warm call, when it is cold, fpit it and roaft it throughly, fauce it with Gravie, two or three anchovies diffolved, and fome minced Lemmon.

To make a Portugal Pie.

TAke two Capons roafted, and being cold, bone and skin them; mince them very fmall with half a pound of Almonds blanched, feafon it with falt and nutmeg, fugar, rofe-water, the juice of two Lemmons, work thefe up with a pound of fweet Butter like a pafte,

then

then make a piece of cold Butter Paste rich, and roul it into a sheet, then two or three sweet-breads of Veal, some sliced Lemmon, then lay on them half of your minced meat, then put on that the marrow of two or three marrow bones, then lay the rest of your meat, put in the yolks of hard eggs, make it up Pastie fashion, garnish it to your fancie, indore it with melted Butter and Rose-water, scrape on a little sugar; a pretty quick Oven, three quarters of an hour will bake it, stick it with Almonds quartered, and send it up.

To stew a carp.

Take a Carp, scale and blood him in the tail, garing him in a vessel, put to him a quart of Claret-wine, a little vinegar and salt, put him into a Pipkin with that liquor, with some Oysters with the liquor, five or six blades of large mace, whole pepper and cloves, the tops of time, three or four Anchovies, an Onion minced, and fryed in Brown Butter, some grated bread, let all these stew together half an hour, with some Lemmon sliced, till it come to a body to your mind; with sippets, dish and garnish it as you please.

To make a Bacon Tart.

Take three pound of Lard, or thick fat Bacon, scrape it as you do Butter for a dish, put it in water a little warm, to draw out the salt, then take it into a dry cloath, and dry up the moisture, put it into a stone morter, and beat it well together with the yolks of eight eggs, when well beaten into a dish, set it over a slow fire keep it continually stirring till you have brought it like Cream, then press it through a strainer, season it with sugar, three or four grains of Amber-greece, or musk, close it betwixt two sheets of Paste in a Patiepan, or else indore it with melted Butter, and bake it quick, and send it up hot.

To

Rare Receipts.

To make Vever Ollie, or Cheese-Pottage.

TAke a pottle of strong Broth, or fair water in a Skillet or Pipken, set it on a clear fire to boyl, put to it half a penny Manchet grated, a little quantity of grated Cheese, season it with Pepper and a blade of Mace; let them boyl together half an hour, having half a pound of Parmisant or well relished Cheese, let it have one walm, remember some Parslee, Penny-royal and Beets, small minced put in at the first, and when you are ready to take it off, put to it the yolks of six eggs, with a quarter of a pound of sweet Butter beaten well together, dish them with sippets, and send it up with grated Cheese about the dish.

Reader,

I Have here presented to thee the order of a Feast, and a Bill of Fare, which was taken out of the Records of the Tower; I have done it the rather, that thou maist see what Liberality and Hospitality there was in Antient times amongst our Progenitors: like this to Solomons Royal House-keeping, yet he was one that was endued with wisdom from above; by which Liberality his Subjects were made rich, so that silver was as plenty as stones in the Streets of Jerusalem, and there was Peace in all his dayes; according to his judgement from his inspired Wisdome, so was his Practice, and so was his Declaration: for food and raiment, is all the Portion that man hath in this life.

Thus hoping to see Liberality flourish amongst us once more, as in old time,

I Remain thine,

W. R.

A

A great FEAST *made by* George Nevil *Chancellor of* England, *and Arch-Bishop of* York, *in the days of* EDWARD *the* FOURTH, 1468.

0300	Quarters of wheat	9400	Heronshaws.
0300	Tun of Ale.	0200	Pheasants.
0100	Tunne of Wine.	0500	Partridges.
0001	Pipe of Ipocras.	0400	Woodcocks.
0104	Oxen.	0100	Curlews.
0006	Wild Bulls.	1000	Egrites.
1000	Muttons.	0504	Stags, Bucks & Roes
0304	Veals.	0103	Pasties of Venison cold.
0304	Porks.	0508	Pikes and Breams.
0400	Swines.	6000	Dishes of Jelly.
3000	Geese.	0103	Cold Tarts.
1000	Capons.	3000	Cold Custards.
3000	Piggs.	1500	Hot venison pasties.
0400	Plovers.	3000	Hot Custards.
0100	Dozen of Quails.	0013	Porrosses and Seals.
0200	Dozen of Fowls called Rees.		Besides abundance of Sweet-meats.
0400	Peacocks.		
0400	Mallards and Teals.		
0204	Cranes.		
0204	Kidds.		
3000	Chickens.		
4000	Pidgeons.		
4000	Coneys.		
0200	Bullers.		

The great Offices.

Earl of *Warwick* Steward.
Earl of *Northumberland* Treasurer.
Lord *Hastings* Cup-bearer

Lord

To the Reader.

Lord *Willowby* Carver.
Lord *John* of *Buckingham* Controuler.
Sir *Richard Stranwig* Surveyer.
Sir *William Worlly* Marshall of the Hall.
Eight Knights of the Hall.
Eighty Esquires of the Hall
Two other Surveyers of the Hall.
Sir *John Malbiury* Pantler

Two Esquires Keepers of the Cubbard.
Sir *John Brakenock* Supervisor of the Hall.

Estates sitting in the Hall.

At the High-Table.

The Archbishop in his State On his Right hand, the Bishops of *London*, *Durham* and *Blie*.
On his left hand, the Duke of *Suffolk*, the Earls of *Oxford* and *Worcester*.

At the second Table.

The Abbots of Saint *Maries*.
The Doctors of *Halls* of *Rivones*.

The Querefters of *Rivones*.
The Prownes of *Durham*, of *Girglen*, and of *Berlenton*, of *Giserow*, & others, the number of eighteen.

At the third Table,

The Deans of *York*, the Lords of *Cornwell*, *York*, *Durham*, with forty eight Knights.

At the fourth Table.

The Deans of *Durham* and of Saint *Ambroses*, all the Prebends of the *Minster*.

At the fifth Table.

The Maoyrs of *York* and *Calice*, and all the Aldermen.

At the sixth Table.

The Judges of the Land, four Barons of *Exchequer*, and twenty six Counsellors.

At the last Table

Sixty nine Knights, wearing the

To the Reader.

the Kings badges and his Arms.

Estates fitting in the chief Chamber.

At the first Table.
The Duke of *Glocester* the Kings Brother, and upon his right hand the Duke of *Suffolk*, and upon his let hand the Countess of *Westmorland* and *Northumberland*, and two of the Earl of *Warwicks* Daughters.

At the second Table.
The Barons of *Greystock*, with three other Barons.

At the third Table.

Eighteen Gentlemen of the said Lands.

Estates fitting in the second Chamber.

At the first Table.

The elder Dutchess of *Suffolk*, the Countess of *Warwick* and *Oxford*, the Ladies *Hastings* and *Barwick*.

At the second Table.

The Earls of *Northumberland* and *Westmorland*, the Lords of *Fitshugh* only with two Barons.

At the third Table.

Fourteen Gentlemen, and fourteen Gentlewomen of quality.

In the low Hall.

Four hundred and twelve of the Nobility, with double service.

In the Gallery.
0200 Noble-mens servants, with their servants.
1100 Inferiour Officers, with their servants.
1500 Other meaner servants of all Offices.
0062 Cooks.
} 2862

FINIS.

GLOSSARY

The books consulted in the preparation of this glossary include those of previous Prospect Books facsimiles and editions: Hannah Glasse, *The Art of Cookery Made Plain and Easy*; Robert May, *The Accomplisht Cook* (both compiled by Alan Davidson); Richard Bradley, *The Country Housewife and Lady's Director* (compiled by Caroline Davidson); *John Evelyn, Cook* and John Evelyn's *Acetaria*; William Ellis, *The Country Housewife's Family Companion*; Hannah Woolley's *The Gentlewomans Companion*; and *The Closet of Sir Kenelme Digbie Kt. Opened* (compiled by Peter Davidson and Jane Stevenson). Many of these glossaries have been combined into a single text on the Prospect Books website (www.prospectbooks.co.uk). I have also used Alan Davidson, *The Oxford Companion to Food*; Jancis Robinson, *The Oxford Companion to Wine*; the glossary by Elizabeth David to the facsimile edition of John Nott, *Cooks and Confectioners Dictionary* (1726); the admirably detailed commentary to *Martha Washington's Booke of Cookery* by Karen Hess; *The Englishman's Flora*, Geoffrey Grigson; *Sugar-Plums and Sherbet* by Laura Mason (1998); Gilly Lehmann, *The British Housewife* (2003); *Encyclopaedia Britannica*, 11th edition; *A Dictionary of the English Language*, Samuel Johnson; *The Oxford English Dictionary*, 2nd edition. I am also very grateful to Mr David Potter for sight of his working notes on words and their meaning in seventeenth- and eighteenth-century cookery texts.

I have included words which are archaic or whose meaning is now obscure; words that have been spelled aberrantly or eccentrically (although by no means every single variation); references to foodstuffs that are no longer in common use; some comment on categories of foods, for example breads, where Rabisha saw fit to distinguish between certain varieties; and some remarks on cooking equipment. In his last section, where Rabisha recycled the *Traditions of Carving, and Sewing*, which was of fifteenth-century origin (although reprinted and reworked up to John Murrell's *Two bookes of cookerie and carving* of 1631, which formed the basis of Rabisha's text), there are many archaic terms deployed. I have explored these with less enthusiasm than those in the main body of the book. A contributory reason is that neither the printers nor the editor (Rabisha himself?) had much acquaintance with the old words and therefore spelled them haphazardly and, in some instances, quite unrecognizably.

All page references, and I have given at least one reference for most items to show their context, are to the modern pagination of the text, that within square brackets at the foot of the page.

Tom Jaine

ALBUM is possibly a misprint for alum, here used in combination with cochineal to make a coloured jelly. The combination is seen again in Rabisha's dyeing of a collar of beef red. [272]

ALEXANDER-BUDS are from *Smyrnium olusatrum*, the herb known as alexanders, horse-parsley, or black lovage. [75]

ALLUM is an astringent salt, a double sulphate of aluminium and potassium, used in pickling and bread baking, as well as in fabric dyeing.

ALMONDS, JORDAN. Rabisha rarely specifies his almonds, the implication being that the sweet, not bitter nut was the general requirement. Jordan almonds had nothing to do with the country of that name, Jordan being a corruption of *jardin*, the Spanish word for garden.

AMBERGREESE, AMBERGREECE, a substance produced in the sperm whale and harvested from the sea or beach in pieces that can weigh up to 200 lb. 'Greece' is a natural description of its texture, which is waxy, though the term refers to its greyish colour (*'gris'*, grey in French). Evidently it imparted a scent rather than a flavour to the food it was prepared with.

ANDOLIANS are an anglicized version of the French word *andouilles*, meaning sausages made of chitterlings. [151]

ANGELICA ROOTS. Although the stalks and leaves are the most commonly consumed parts of the plant, the roots were also made into preserves. [315]

APPLES. A few sorts of apples are defined by Rabisha. BLANDERLES [335] is a variant spelling, found in the early *Traditions of Carving, and Sewing*, for the apple variety Blandurel, first introduced into England by Eleanor of Castile, queen of Edward I (see Joan Morgan and Alison Richards, *The Book of Apples*). CODLINGS OR CODLINS [104] were terms originally used for any small immature apple. In Elizabethan times it was used for a green, somewhat conical, apple which if parboiled (or coddled) would retain its form and could be served as 'Codlins and Cream'. Parkinson (1629) wrote: 'The Kentish Codlin is a fair great greenish Apple, very good to eat when it is ripe, but the best to coddle of all the other Apples.' However, Karen Hess makes clear that the etymology of the two words is different. The apple word derived from a Middle English term meaning 'hard'; the cookery descriptor came from the Norman-French *caudeler*, to heat gently – the same root, she points out, as the word 'caudle', and coddle as in coddled eggs. PEARMAINS [110] were an apple of French origin, known since 1200, pear shaped and well-coloured. They were a tall, five-faceted, dual-purpose fruit. PIPPINS [302] were sweet apples, raised from imported European stock. The skin was usually flecked with gold. The Red Kentish Pippin was first mentioned by the botanist John Ray in 1665. Generically, the term refers to fruit of any tree grown from seed. Golden pippins were recorded as a variety as early as 1629 by Parkinson in *Paradisus in Sole Paradisus Terrestris*, as possibly originating from Parham Park near Arundel. Rabisha refers on one occasion to preserving under-ripe green pippins which he would have you boil softly until they are 'as tender as Codlings'.

ARDER, TO. Rabisha suggests that once you have boned and rolled your collar of veal, you should dip strips of bacon in egg and arder them over the joint before tying it up for cooking. *OED* recognizes the word arder, but ascribes it meanings relating only to the act of ploughing (deriving from the OG), more specifically ploughing in preparation for a field lying fallow. Is it possible that this is a misprint for 'order'? [79]

ASHEN KEYS are ash key, the seed of the ash, usually pickled.

AUGENOTTE is a misspelling of Huguenot. In his table of contents, Rabisha is closer to reality, he writes 'A la Hugenota'. [286]

BARB, TO is the act of trimming, here concerning mushrooms. Had you been Sir Francis Drake, it would have been the King of Spain who was barbed.

BARBERRIES OR BARBARIES are *Berberis vulgaris,* described by Richard Bradley, the eighteenth-century botanist and cookery writer, as 'a pleasant Shrub, bearing beautiful Branches of yellow Flowers in the Spring, and no less delightful Clusters of red Berries towards the Autumn: The Fruit is of a sharp Taste when it is ripe, and seldom us'd any other way than in sauces.'

BARLEY. Rabisha defines two sorts, pearl and French. Pearl barley [295] (which has been husked and milled) is still an article of commerce. French barley [123, 322] is a term often used in seventeenth- and eighteenth-century cookery books. Recipes for Barley Cream, for example, bid one 'take your French barley, and add cream', suggesting that French barley was simply a plump variety and that it too came in husked form. But Margaret Saville (1682) has a recipe for French Barley Cream which says: 'Tye your ffrench barley in a cloth, and dippe itt in water, then beet itt till ye huskes bee clean off...' So perhaps the French variety could be had either husked or unhusked. *OED* quotes the *Family Herbal* of 1789 which defines French barley as being skinned, with the ends ground off. Pearl barley is a further refinement of the grain. Elinor Fettiplace describes in her receipts the preparation of French barley by soaking barley corn, beating it with a beetle in a sack, then rubbing, winnowing and wetting it again before drying the grains in the oven.

BARTHOLOMEW-TIDE was 24 August, Saint Bartholomew's Day. [316]

BASE is a variant spelling of bass, for sea-bass.

BATTALIA PIE, BATTLELY PIES, for meats and fish are repeatedly described by Rabisha. The *OED* derives the name, via the French *béatilles*, from the Latin *beatillae*, meaning small blessed objects; and explains that a battalia pie is therefore a pie containing tidbits such as cockscombs and sweetbreads. In the eighteenth century, John Nott gives two recipes, one for Battalia Pye and the other for Battalia Pye of Fish. The latter incorporates battlements and towers in the pie-case, which might have suggested an alternative origin for the name, if the true one had not been established. Nott's first pie has sweetbreads, but his fish version lacks tidbits of the sort suggested by the *OED*. Rabisha's pies are indeed full of battlements and crenellations and he states, when describing his 'bastard bisk pye', that it may be made 'in the fashion of a Battalia, or a round Pye very large'. When detailing 'a Battlely, or Bisk Pyes in the Spring', he says 'you may make your Coffin round, or Castle fashion'. Although these giant pies had every sort of meat or fish, or in the case of an orangado pie, every sort of sweetmeat, they did not necessarily concentrate on offering offal. The description, therefore, seems to be of the form, not the contents. [228, 240, 241]

BEAT, TO is to stamp or grind, e.g. 'beat mustard seed'. [188]

BEAZON is probably a misspelling of bezoar, a stone-like concretion found in the stomachs or intestines of certain ruminant animals, especially the wild goat of Persia. It was supposed to have medicinal qualities, though this was much disputed by Quincy in his *English Dispensatory*. [320]

BISK. The place of the bisk or bisque as one of the grand assemblages of early-modern English cookery is well described by Gilly Lehmann. Rabisha gives many instances and applications. He even refers to a 'bastard bisk pie' as an interesting variation. [241, 257]

BLANDERLES see apples.

BOG-BERRIES refers to the fruits of one or other of the cranberry family (*Vaccinium*). [73]

BOLTER is a strainer, a cloth through which ground corn was sifted to produce different grades of flour. It might also be a cloth used to strain other foods, such as fruit for jellies. [249]

BRAMBLE-FRUIT usually refers to blackberries although Rabisha here intends services or hips. [73]

BRAWN is flesh suitable for roasting, usually the better bits, a citation in *OED* using the word to distinguish the breast of fowl from its leg. Evelyn refers to the 'brawne of an hen', Rabisha mentions 'brawn of a capon'. Its restriction to meat from a pig was not then universal. Rabisha does, however, use it to refer to preserved and collared joints much as we do. [76]

BRAY, TO means to beat small or pound, usually in a mortar (*OED*).

BREAD. Rabisha refers to several sorts of bread. There is trencher bread, described in the early *Traditions of Carving, and Sewing*. In the same section there is also reference to household bread, i.e. a semi-refined loaf. This is not so fine as a manchet, which usually describes the smaller loaf of white flour used for the master's family. It was cooked in a slightly cooler oven than was household bread (Rabisha sometimes defines the heat of the oven as when it is prepared for manchets). When talking of manchet, Rabisha sometimes appears to mean a bread type, at other times a loaf shape (for instance when he mentions a 'manchet of French bread' [143]). French bread [117] is made from dough enriched with eggs and milk. Loaves were usually small, indeed, he often refers to French rolls [108]. There are some mentions of penny loaves and once of a two-penny loaf [296]. This must refer to a size determined by the Assize of Bread. In a long and intelligent discussion of this point, Karen Hess postulates that a penny loaf of white flour might have weighed between 12 and 16 ounces (*Martha Washington's Booke of Cookery*). Finally, Rabisha mentions 'muskefied bisket bread' [143] which can only describe a flavoured loaf or perhaps a variation on Naples bisket. Robert May refers to this as muskedine.

BRIT OR BRET is a name for either turbot or brill or similar fish. Brit might also refer to the young of herring or sprats. [350]

BROACHES are wooden skewers used to spit foods such as oysters. [189]

BROOK-LIME, *Veronica beccabunga*, a salad plant often found with and eaten with watercress. Culpeper (1653) described it as a 'hot and biting martial plant' and assumes in all his recommendations that it will be used in conjunction with watercress. He says that it may be called water-pimpernel (although it is closer, botanically, to the blue birds-eye or speedwell than to the scarlet pimpernel).

BROOM-BUDS were usually pickled, and used in place of capers. [73]

BURDOCK-ROOT, *Arctium lappa* and allied species, was used for medicinal purposes. The dried roots were supposed to be good for gout. The roots of *A. lappa*, the great burdock, are eaten as a vegetable in Japan. [71]

BUSHEL is a dry measure equivalent to four pecks or eight gallons (of wheat).

BUTTER SQUIRT. Rabisha suggests that a collection of different jellies might be presented together in a variety of moulds: cockleshells, eggshells, an emptied half of a lemon and so forth. Then, he goes on, they might be 'moulded out of a butter squirt'. Elizabeth David describes the butter squirt in her glossary to John Nott as a syringe out of which the cook could extrude butter in ribbons and other shapes. The tool was also known in the making of syllabub. Ideally, the milk was teased directly from the cow on to alcohol and/or acids. If you lacked a cow, you could replicate the effect as Sir Kenelm Digby advises: 'Take a reasonable quantity (as about half a Porrenger full) of the Syrup, that hath served in the making of dryed plums; and into a large Syllabub-pot milk or squirt, or let fall from high a sufficient quantity of Milk or Cream.' To achieve the 'squirt', an instrument was available. It was called a wooden cow. In one of John Nott's recipes for syllabub he recommends you to 'squirt them into the Pot with a wooden Cow made for the Purpose, which you may buy at the Turners.' The same device was suggested by John Evelyn as an aid to making buttermilk curds. [273]

BUTTER is not usually prescribed in much detail by Rabisha. He mentions sweet butter or salt butter very occasionally, but the most regular definition is of drawn butter, an important element in his sauces and finishings. He has instructions to draw butter, where it is melted and emulsified with strong broth so that it will not oil. [122, 293]

CABBAGE LETTUCE see lettuce.
CAGGS is a variant spelling of kegs or barrels. [86]
CALAMINT is *Calamintha officinalis* (common calamint) or *C. Nepeta* (lesser calamint) or *C. sylvatica* (wood calamint). [322]
CANDLEMAS is 2 February, the date of the feast of the purification of the Virgin Mary (or presentation of Christ in the Temple), celebrated with many candles.
CAP-PAPER, see paper.
CAPERS are mentioned regularly, but on one occasion specified as 'French'. Pierre Pomet remarked that 'all the Capers eaten in Europe, except those from Majorca, come from Toulon'. In the early eighteenth century, Richard Bradley attempted unsuccessfully to naturalize the plant here. [260]
CAPONETS are small capons. [141]
CARBOLION is court-bouillon. [283]
CARBONADO is a way of broiling meat. It is usually deeply scored and grilled on a high heat. [160]
CARRAWAY-COMFITS are carraway seeds coated many times with boiling sugar to produce small white 'comfits'. Coriander seeds and aniseeds were similarly treated. Hannah Glasse writes of 'rough' carraway-comfits, by which were meant ones which had been repeatedly coated with sugar boiled to a greater height than for smooth comfits.
CASE, TO, means to skin (specifically of a hare or leveret). [187]
CAVEER is caviare.
CAWDLE OR CAUDLE is a general term for a kind of thick drink. This was generally made from ale, sweetened and spiced, and thickened with egg yolk and often breadcrumbs or oatmeal or something similar. A caudle could also be made with water, milk, or wine. It was used as a hot drink for invalids and was drunk out of a squat, round vessel which usually had two handles and a lid, called a caudle-cup. A hot caudle could be added to a pie, e.g. a wine caudle to a sweet meat pie.
CHAFER in the use made in this text refers to a cooking pot (it was described as 'clean scoured'). It sometimes meant the chafing-dish,

which was more properly the portable brazier in which were contained the charcoals. [321]

CHAFFINDISH is chafing-dish, a portable brazier to hold burning coals or charcoal and designed to be set on a metal stand. Dishes of food could be finished or reheated over this, away from the fierce heat of the hearth; 'A portable grate for coals' (Johnson's *Dictionary*). 'The "chafing dish of coals" ultimately became the elegant silverplated chafing dish set over a spirit lamp and used for the table cookery of Edwardian dishes' (E. David). By then the 'dish' was the dish of food to be cooked or heated, not the dish containing the fire. [286]

CHAINIE OR CHAINNY may possibly refer to the China root, *Smilax china*, an Asian plant which is closely related to plants of North and Central America which are the source of sarsaparilla. The spelling chainy is found describing china, the ware from that country first brought to Europe by the Portuguese. Robert May has a couple of recipes using China root, they are broths. Rabisha uses chainie or chainney in a broth and in a jelly. In a third instance of the word, he suggests baking dowsets (q.v.) in 'little cups of Chainy' which, presumably, is the ware itself. [99, 117, 289]

CHALDRON is chawdron or entrails. This referred to any animal, although it was more and more limited to the guts of a calf. The sauce for a swan was also made from its chaldron. [342]

CHAMPIGNIONS are mushrooms.

CHARD AND QUINCE as printed in the *Traditions of Carving, and Sewing* must be a misapprehension of the term 'chare de quince', i.e. the pulp of the quince made into a preserve. [335]

CHARLET is a kind of custard found in medieval cookery. [347]

CHARNEL is currently a bit of a mystery. It seems unlikely that it is a misspelling of charmele or carmele, which is the heath-pea or wild licorice, or that it has any relation to the unidentified herb carneol, named by Littleton in 1678 but by no-one else (*OED*). [72]

CHEVINE is the fish chub. [334]

CHEWIT OR CHEWET was a small round pie, containing meat or fish. In one instance Rabisha refers to 'chewit meat', i.e. a preparation that might go into a chewit. [205, 220]

CHINE is 'the whole or part of the backbone of an animal, with the adjoining flesh' (*OED*). Animal, in this instance, may mean fish or beast. The chine (of a barrel) was the protecting rim at the heads of casks formed by the ends of the staves (*OED*). [335]

CHIPT, CHIPPED refers to the act (usually) of chipping the crusts off a loaf to expose the crumb. [108]

CHURCENELA, CUTCHENELE are two variant spellings of cochineal, the red colouring from the dried and pulverised bodies of the insect *Coccus cacti*, a parasite of cacti in Central America. After the European colonization of America this product was adopted as a better source of red colouring than the 'sanders' (sandalwood) used in medieval cookery. [272]

CITRON is green citron, *Citrus medica*. It has very thick peel and so was mostly used candied. [285]

CITTERN is a variant spelling (also used by R. May) of citron. [103]

CIVET is a strongly scented substance produced by the African civet cat. Imported into England in powdered form, it was used, like musk, to give an exotic touch to food. [320]

CLARRET, CLARET, WINE. Although the usage that invariably linked claret to the wines of Bordeaux was current from about the year 1600 (*OED*), the earlier meaning, which distinguished wines of a claret colour (orange or light red, i.e. the French *clairet*) from white or fully red wines, was still found. Hess has a useful discussion of this point. [122]

CLARY, *Salvia sclarea*, was used as a remedy for eye complaints (*claws* being the Latin word for clear), but also had culinary uses. It is slightly bitter and was used to add flavour to wine. Clary fritters, i.e. clary leaves fried in batter, were featured regularly. [171]

CLOVE GILLY-FLOWERS are clove-pinks or carnations.

COCKS TREADS are the opaque speck on the yolk of a fertilized egg, usually removed by straining. [285]

CODDLE, TO, means to boil or stew gently. The word survives in 'coddled eggs', but its general use (as in Sterne's pleasant phrase 'whilst dinner is coddling') has ceased. [104]

CODLINGS see apples.

COFFINS are moulds or cases of raised hot-water paste, used as containers for any number of dishes, from meat pies to cheesecakes. Where they were made of coarse pastry, it is not inevitable that they would have been eaten. They were more a way of getting food through the baking process that anything else. Rabisha has many details of coffins and their construction. A venison pie, for instance, was baked in a hot raised rye paste, either square or round but sufficiently large to contain a haunch, with sides a full twelve inches high. It was baked for six hours and would keep a full year. Smaller, more decorative coffins, in heart or diamond shapes, are also described. [89]

COLLER OR COLLAR was a length of meat or fish rolled up on itself and bound tight with tapes. The flesh of a single pig could be trussed up in this way to make a very large collar; or smaller pieces of the animal could be so treated. Collaring was the first stage in preparing meat or fish for pickling and sousing. Rabisha also uses the word figuratively when describing a galantine of turkey or capon (he calls it 'congealed') which was double-boiled in a tall, cylindrical pot. When the pot was broken out, after cooling, the jellied meat was collar-shaped. [76]

COLLOPS are thin slices of meat. Often collops are 'hacked' which usually means cut into smaller pieces. It almost seems as if the escalopes (note the phonetic, perhaps even philological, connection between the two words) have been cut further to become scaloppini. Compare with Hess's remarks on this word. Collops is still current usage in Scotland. The word is of obscure derivation, says the *OED*. From early times it had the primary meaning of a rasher of salt bacon, to be fried, often with eggs; 'a peculiarly British fashion of eating bacon, not known elsewhere in Europe'. Rabisha's recipe for this dish is on page 178 of the present text. Later, the term came to have the more general meaning of a slice of meat. In the eighteenth century, there was some confusion between the nouns collup (or collop) and scollop (or scallop). Indeed there still is. It is compounded by the circumstance that the French word for a slice of meat is *escalope*; and by the formation of a verb 'to scallop' which sometimes is and sometimes isn't connected with scallop shells. Hannah Glasse's recipe for making Collups of Oysters, seems to be an early and pure example of the flowering of this confusion. It has nothing at all to do with collops, but requires the oysters to be put into scallop shells. [129]

COMPOST derives from compôte, a stew of various meats or fruits. [335]

CORRAL was the sea coral used in early medicine, as Rabisha uses it here in a hartshorn jelly which was restringent and good for the back. [100]

CRAFISH, CREVIS are crayfish, but it is rarely clear whether Rabisha is talking of the large spiny lobster, *Palinurus vulgaris*, or the smaller freshwater species. Often he mentions them in conjunction with pranes (prawns) which might imply the latter. In the description of cutting up a 'crevis' in *Traditions of Carving, and Sewing*, the sea creature is intended.

CUTCHENELE see churcenela.

DIADRAGAGANTHUM FRIGDIUM is a composition of gum tragacanth. The prefix dia- merely indicates, a composition of… *Frigdium* is a misprint for *frigidium*, cold. [319]

DIAPER, TOWEL OF, was a fabric woven with raised threads in a diamond pattern – and sometimes further elaboration. [336]

DOWCET is a small, sweet dish. The word may also indicate the stones or testicles of a stag. [251]

DRAGAGANT is gum tragacanth, q.v.

ELL was a measure of length. The English ell was of 45 inches. [147]

ENDIFF, CURLED, is *Cichorium intybus*, known as endive in Britain. The leaves can be blanched by keeping out the light. (The Belgian witloof endive, now perhaps the best known blanched variety, was not produced until about 1850.) [137]

ENULA CAMPANA is elecampane or elicampane (*Inula helenium*), an important medicinal root. Ellis advises it against the itch or scabies. Others recommend it against coughs and snake venom, convulsions, contusions and bad sight. It was also deemed effective against elves. [314]

ERINGO ROOTS are sea holly, *Eryngium maritimum*. The roots were candied with sugar and orange-flower-water, and believed to be aphrodisiac (cf. Shakespeare having Falstaff say 'Rain me eringoes…'). [315]

EWRY was the office, apartment or sideboard where the ewers of water, the table linen and napkins were held in medieval and early-modern halls. [336]

FARCE OR FORCE means to stuff, or the ingredient that has been prepared in a manner fit for stuffing (e.g. forcemeat). [186, 187]

FIRKIN was a small barrel, whose size depended on the commodity stored. The ale firkin was 8 gallons: half a kilderkin, or a quarter of a barrel.

FLAWNE is a flan.

FLEA OR FLAY, TO, means to skin. [88,267]

FLECK, FLACK, FLARE AND FLEED are all related words that describe the leaf of fat or lard around the pig's kidneys. [147, 298]

FLORENDINE was a covered tart or pie, often of meat, made with puff paste, which was itself often connected by seventeenth-century cooks with the town of Florence. Karen Hess observes that many early florentines, even those of meat, contained a custard filling. The French equivalent is a *tourte*; the Italian, a *torta*. [110]

FLOWERDELUCE is a variant on *fleur de lys*. [253]

FRIGACY, FRIGASIES, FRIGGESES are fricassees. [163, 164]

FUMOSITIES are vaporous humours that rise from the stomach to the head: not to be encouraged in early-modern diners. [335]

GALLENDINE is the same word as galantine, but with a meaning different from the modern usage. As May's recipes show, seventeenth-century galantine in England was a dark-coloured sauce made with vinegar, breadcrumbs, cinnamon and sometimes other spices. Earlier, in medieval times, a galantine had been a jellied dish of fish or fowl or meat; and it was this version, which lingered longer in France and eventually crossed in a somewhat new form to England at the beginning of the eighteenth century, which evolved into our present galantine. See C. Anne Wilson (1980). [232]

GALLY-POT is a small earthen glazed pot, mostly used by apothecaries for storing drugs and ointments, but also serving in the kitchen, e.g. to stew preserves. [303]

GARINGE may mean to spit or impale. [353]

GEESE, BRAND, BRAN are Brent or barnacle geese, the two being often confused (*OED*). Stubble geese are the normal farmyard animal fattened on the autumn stubble. [83, 267]

GOBBETS are small lumps or morsels. [80]

GODWEATHS are godwits, marsh birds of the genus *Limosa*, not unlike the curlew. They had a high reputation as table fare. Sir Thomas Browne observed that they 'were accounted the daintiest dish in England and I think, for the bigness, of the biggest price'. [125]

GOOS-BERRIES, GASCOYN are described by Rabisha as 'the largest sort'. Normally, he does not specify any particular variety although he embraces this comparatively recent discovery (early sixteenth century) of the fruit garden with enthusiasm. F.A. Roach, in *Cultivated Fruits of Britain* (1985), does not mention the Gascon as an early variety. For the most part, particular types in the seventeenth century showed their connections to Holland and northern Europe, not to the south. Abercrombie and Mawe, the eighteenth-century gardeners, do list a Gascoyne among their much longer tally of fruits. It was a green gooseberry. [307]

GROAT was a coin, last issued for circulation in 1662, valued at four pence. [109]

GUM ARABICK was a viscid secretion exuded by certain species of the genus *Acacia*. It dries hard, but is soluble in water and has for long been used in making confectionery. It is the best of the natural gums for stabilizing, thickening and emulsifying, and was a standard ingredient. [319]

GUM DRAGON OR GUM DRAGAGANT OR GUM TRAGACANTH is obtained from the shrub *Astralagus* and used to stabilize, thicken and emulsify. It was thought inferior to gum arabic, and used for laundry work in the eighteenth century. [333]

HARTS-HORN was the shavings of a stag's antler, used to set a jelly. Isinglass eventually superseded hartshorn in most cookery operations.

HOG-HAWS are the fruit of the hawthorn. In dialect dictionaries for Hampshire and Gloucestershire there are references to words such as 'hag' and 'haigh' meaning 'haw' (*OED*). [73]

HOGO means *haut-goût*, high gusto. When applied to foods, it means properly, even strongly, seasoned, and is often found next to, or in relation to, discussion of French or foreign dishes. Already, by the end of the seventeenth century, it was being used to denote 'high' in the sense that game is high (*OED*). [118]

HORE-HOUND is probably *Marrubium vulgare*, white horehound, used against coughs. [322]

HUMBLES are innards – usually referring to deer, but often the entrails of other species. [274]

INDORE, TO, means to gild or wash, usually with the yolk of egg, before roasting or baking.

IPOCRAS is hippocras, a sweetened and spiced (red) wine, for consumption after a meal. 'Hippocras took its name from the bag through which it was strained, said to resemble Hippocrates' sleeve, and more probably shaped like the gown-sleeve of a medieval medical man' (C. Anne Wilson). [350]

IZENGLASS OR ISINGLASS was a pure form of commercial gelatine obtained from the swimming bladder or sound of several species of fish, notably the sturgeon. It is well described by Elizabeth David in her glossary to John Nott. The usual manner of its sale, she asserts, was in fine shreds, easily dissolved in water. She suggests that an ounce of isinglass will make a pint and a quarter of water a 'tremulous jelly'. [80]

JACK is a young pike. [195]

JAGGING-IRON was an instrument for ornamenting pastry etc., usually made in the form of a wheel with teeth, set in a handle. The verb to jag was the act of finishing pastry with a denticulated border. In its first use, the word referred particularly to slashing fabrics to make a dagged edge. [237]

JEGGET OR JIGGET are variant spellings of gigot. It is defined by Rabisha as the leg of mutton with half the loin cut to it, a definition also entertained by Markham (*OED*). [183]

JOLL OR JOUL are variants of jowl or jole, that is the head and shoulders of a fish (either porpoise, salmon, sturgeon or ling). [205]

JURNAPE is a misspelling of surnape in Rabisha's recycling of *Traditions of Carving, and Sewing*. The surnape was the towel used for drying the hands before the feast. [337]

JUSSEL is a hodge-podge composed of a variety of meats. [340]

KETTLE is an open metal pot used to boil food. [147]

KICK-SHAWS is a word derived from the French *quelque chose* and meant a fancy dish, a 'little something'. The term denoted an 'elegant, dainty dish' in the sixteenth century, but later was often used in a derogatory sense (thus Addison, writing in the *Tatler* in 1709, referred to 'That Substantial English Dish banished in so ignominious a Manner, to make way for French Kick-shaws'). Rabisha's usage is not dismissive at all, his kick-shaws are merely pleasing ornaments. [269]

KNOTS are *Calidris ranutus*, also called red sandpiper (or 'grey plover' when in its winter plumage), a bird of the snipe family. It breeds within the Arctic Circle, but is common on British coasts in late summer and autumn. [125]

KNOTS OF EGGS. Rabisha writes of cooking 'knots of eggs' together with artichoke bottoms, hard-boiled egg yolks, sweetbreads, cocks combs and stones, lambstones and young chicken and pigeons. Is he adding beaten egg that has already been fried and sliced into lumps? [143]

LABDANUM is ladanum, a resin exuded from shrubs of the genus *Cistus*, used in perfumery. Herrick wrote, 'How can I choose but love, and follow her, Whose shadow smels like milder Pomander! How can I chuse but kisse her, whence do's come The *Storax, Spiknard, Myrrhe* and *Ladanum*.' Rabisha's pomander also contained storax (q.v.). [320]

LAMB STONES are lambs' testicles.

LARD, TO, means to add strips of fat or lard which were threaded into pieces of meat to keep them from drying out when spit-roasted. The threading was done with a kind of needle, the 'larding prick'. Even something as small as an oyster would be larded. [188]

LAUNE SEARCE is a fine sieve, made of lawn, a linen. [330]

LEACH, as a verb, means to cut in slices, e.g. 'leach your brawn'. The word was also a noun, referring to a wide variety of dishes consisting of sliced-up material, from almond jelly to gingerbread. A leach was a cream or other mixture set hard enough to be sliced, the word leach itself originally meaning slice. White leaches were usually made with almonds, but there were some recipes that omitted this ingredient. See Hess for some useful observations.

LEAR shares the same derivation as the French *lier*, to bind, and refers to a thickened sauce.

LETTUCE. Cabbage lettuce is the sort of lettuce most often specified by Rabisha. It is the standard headed lettuce, as opposed to the Cos or Romaine. In the first instance, the word cabbage described the tender, unexpanded heart of the cole, the original brassica. Thus when Rabisha refers to the cabbage as a part of the lettuce, he is intending the denote the heart, not the outer leaves. [224, 233]

LIGNUM ALOES is the wood of the aloes tree, used in perfumery and medicine. [320]

LOZENGES. The place of lozenges in early sweet-making is explained by Laura Mason in her *Sugar-Plums and Sherbet* (1998). [150]

LUMBER, LUMBARD PIE. The name may be a corruption of Lombard. It was a savoury pie made of meat (or fish) and eggs. Robert May's two versions called for a filling consisting of separate little puddings or forcemeat balls, but the longer recipe given by Rabisha did not have this requirement. [230]

LUMPS is the lumpfish, *Cyclopterus rumpus*. Sir Thomas Browne recorded that it was 'esteemed by some as a festival dish, though it affords but a glutinous jelly ...' In fact there is a great difference between the flesh of a male (which is palatable) and that of the female (which at some seasons is quite inedible). In the Scandinavian countries, where this fish is eaten, there is a different name for each. [88]

MAIDEN-HAIR is the fern of that name, either *Adiantum Capillusveneris*, or *Asplenium Trichomanes*, or *Asplenium Rutamuraria*, used much in medicine. [322]

MAIDS are defined by *OED* as young skate or thornback or, less commonly, the twait shad – which is called *pucelle* in French. Elizabeth David, in her glossary to John Nott, suggests they are the cuckoo wrasse, *Labrus mixtus* – in French the *demoiselle*. [208]

MAJESTY OF PEARL is, more correctly, magistery of pearl: an alchemical term denoting the residue obtained from precipitation in an acid solution. [100]

MALLAGATOONS, MELLACATOONS are now spelled melocoton, a kind of peach. [75]

MAMONY is the medieval dish mawmeny. [342]

MANUS CHRISTI is a confection, a small round sweetmeat (see Karen Hess and Laura Mason). Rabisha's recipe is almost verbatim that given in *A Closet for Ladies and Gentlewomen* of 1608. Manus Christi height was also a point on the scale of sugar boiling. Laura Mason suggests it is somewhere between 110 and 120 degrees Celsius. [328]

MARROW invariably refers to bone marrow.

MERRY THOUGHT is the wishbone and attached meat of a fowl. [225]

MILT is the soft roe of a (male) fish. [193]

MINCE, TO, means to chop.

MORTERS OR MORTARS are often identified by type by Rabisha: either alabaster, stone, brass or marble. He also sometimes prescribes a wooden pestle. [317]

MORTRUS is mortress, a soup or pottage current in medieval cookery. [340]

MUSCADINE is wine made from the muscatel grape, for example Frontignac in France, but also throughout the Mediterranean and Italy. Gooseberry wine was considered the 'English Frontignac'. When Rabisha writes of 'white and red' muskadines, he presumably is referring to the grapes themselves. [177, 285]

MUSCALADE is musculade or, as we would know it, *mouclade*, a sauce or dish made of mussels. [349]

MUSCOVIA-DUCKS are Muscovy ducks. However, they do not come from Russia but rather from America, and were more correctly called Musk ducks. [267]

MUSK is the perfume extracted from a gland (the size of an orange) in the male musk-deer, filled with a dark brown or chocolate-coloured secretion which is the consistence of 'moist gingerbread' when fresh, but dries to a granular texture after keeping (*Encyclopaedia Britannica*, 11th edition). Much used in cookery, although Karen Hess argues that by the later seventeenth century both musk and ambergris were out of fashion and more honoured in the breach than the observance of the recipes wherein they figured.

NAPLES BISKET is what we now term sponge fingers. In John Evelyn's collection of recipes (*John Evelyn, Cook*) the compiler refers to 'a role of napell bisket' cut in thin slices. This may imply that 'Naples biscuit' sometimes described the sponge mixture, made into whatever shape was most convenient, rather than the fingers themselves as we now buy or make. Although *A Queens Delight* (1655) suggests that Naples biscuit is the same as macaroon mixture, with the addition of pine kernels, there is a recipe in John Nott that may fairly be said to represent the norm: 'take a Pound and half of fine Flour, and as much double-refin'd Sugar, twelve Eggs, three Spoonfuls of Rose-water, and an Ounce and half of Carraway-seeds finely pownded, mix them all well together with Water; then put them into Tin-plates, and bake them in a moderate Oven, dissolve some Sugar in Water, and glaze them over.' As support for the view of *A Queens Delight*, however, John Evelyn also mentions how the cook should 'grate in two or three maqueroons or Naples biscuits without seeds' when preparing a pudding of entrails.

NEATS-TONGUE is ox-tongue.

OLIVE OR OLUE of fish or meat (and in one instance of veal) refer to two distinct types of dish. The olive of veal is escalopes of veal rolled round a farce, as we would also use the term in beef olives. The other olives (or olues) are more properly olios, those grand assemblages, like bisks, that were the centrepieces of seventeenth-century haute cuisine (see Gilly Lehmann). [126, 197]

ORANGADO is candied orange peel, a familiar ingredient of the time and still current in the eighteenth century.

PACKTHRED OR PACKTHREAD was one of the essentials of the seventeenth- and eighteenth-century kitchen. If bundles were not tied with tapes, flags or ribbons, then it was packthread that was deployed. [189]

PALED (of drink) means spoiled by oxidization. [336]

PALLET OR PALATE, not to be confused with the tongue, is the roof of the mouth. The softer parts, to the rear, were those used in cookery.

PAM PUFF is pastry. [347]

PAPER is referred to several times in the text, usually with respect to baking. Cap-paper [227] was a type of paper used to place pastry (and possibly other baked items) on. Rabisha has it as the underlining (well floured) to a venison pasty in the oven. The *OED* has many citations, the earliest describing a strong brown paper such as was used to wrap groceries or goods. Rabisha also used a finer white paper [250]. In one instance, he buttered white paper and placed small puffs thereon before slipping them into the oven. In another place, he refers to beating collops of veal until they are as large as half a sheet of white paper, thus implying that there was a standard known to all. [294]

PARMYZANT, PARMIZANT is Parmesan cheese. [181]

PASTY-PEEL is a broad, flat blade on the end of a long handle which would be used for handing in, or removing, pasties from the oven. [253]

PATIE-PAN OR PATTEE PAN is a small tin pan or shape for baking small pies or pasties. [250, 354]

PEARMANE see apples.

PEASE are the eggs or spawn of fishes. [196]

PECK, two gallons of wheat make a peck, four pecks a bushel. As a dry measure, it was 14 pounds.

PECTORAL ROLLS are liquorice cough sweets. The recipe is taken by Rabisha from *A Closet for Ladies and Gentlewomen* of 1608. (See Laura Mason.) [319]

PEDNYROAL is pennyroyal.

PEEPER is a name for very young birds, especially pigeons and chickens. [141]

PEN-KNIFE. Rabisha likes to use his penknife, for instance to carve ornaments for his pastry cases, or for slipping out the backbone from a salmon. Presumably he refers to a fine-bladed knife, more delicate than the hackers and cleavers of the kitchen. [96]

PENNETS were little sugar sticks, the ancestors of humbugs. (See Laura Mason.) [319]

PESTLE see morter.

PETETES, PETTEETS OR PETEETS appear to refer to small pastry coffins filled with meat or fish. The words have nothing to do with pettitoes. [126, 217, 295]

PHRAISE was more usually spelled fraise. It meant a kind of pancake or omelette, often containing slices of bacon, although Rabisha's is a sweet dish of candied citrus peel. [172]

PILL is peel.

PINDENTS are not identified in *OED*. The recipe would imply that they are some form of Scotch pancake or fritter. [290]

PINE-APPLES are pine kernels.

PIPE is a large barrel, usually deemed the equivalent of four barrels, up to 105 imperial gallons. [335]

PIPKIN was the standard earthenware cooking pot in the English kitchen. At various points, Rabisha mentions that it should be well-glazed on the inside, that it should not be too rough on the inside, that it should be broad-mouthed and that it might contain two quarts. Pipkins might be very large indeed. [268, 282, 331]

PIPPINS see apples.

PISTATIOUS are pistachio nuts.

PLATE, FRENCH. In his instructions for dressing eggs Portugal fashion, Rabisha specifies that they should be put up 'on a French plate, in a clean dish'. What this means is not clear. [285]

POMANDER is a ball of aromatic substances, usually worn as a preventative. The orange stuck with cloves is a simple descendant of the form. [320]

POMCITRON is a citron (pom here means 'fruit of'). [312]

POSNET is a three-legged metal cooking pot. [312]

POSSET is a hot drink made of milk curdled by the addition of an acid (wine, ale, citrus juice) and often spiced. Ordinary eating posset was made by adding breadcrumbs to beer or ale posset. Rich eating posset for the gentry was made with cream and sack or brandy with eggs, beaten almonds and grated Naples biscuit. A rich posset of this sort was partly eaten, partly drunk. Hence posset pots or cups with spouts; there was always a thin whey at the bottom of the posset, and this could be drunk through the little spout. [104]

POTTLE is a measure of two quarts.

POWDER, TO, is to sprinkle, with salt or other preservative. Powdered meat was salted, preserved meat, i.e. dry cured. This was done in powdering tubs, a frequent item in inventories of early kitchens. [130]

PRANES are prawns.

PREWENS OR PRUINS are prunes. [249]

PUETT is the lapwing or pewit, *Vanellus vulgaris*. [229]

PURSLAND OR PURSLIN is purslane.

PYONY-KERNELS might be expected to be pine-kernels, but OED would suggest they are the seeds of the peony. The flowers, roots and seeds of this plant were used medicinally, although it was not truly native to Britain. OED cites a 1796 edition of Hannah Glasse which advises the cook to 'stick the cream with piony kernels'. In her first edition, she deploys the roots in one recipe. [322]

RAIL is a bird of the genus *Rallus*, either land-rail or water-rail. [229]

RAISONS OF THE SUN meant simply sun-dried grapes. The phrase had been in use from medieval times to distinguish true raisins from raisins of Corinth, which were currants (and also sun-dried).

RANGE. Rabisha uses this word on two occasions. In the first, he writes that a sauce of drawn gravy will be useful for much of your meat 'especially your Range'. In the second, he describes the assembly of a small bisk of meat, stating 'when your Range is ready, baste up your birds, and dish them into the middle of the dish'. The precise meaning of the word is not clear. OED defines the culinary use of range as the place where cooking was undertaken. It also gives a subsidiary meaning, with one citation, of dripping (the cook's perquisite). But these do not seem to cover the figurative use of the word in Rabisha. [122, 271]

RASPINE is rasping, when the crust was rasped from a loaf.

REA is the fish, the ray.

REINS, TOWEL OF, is a variant spelling of Raines, i.e. Rennes, the Breton source of fine linen. [336]

REVET is rivet, the liver of a fish. [193]

RHINE is rind. [178]

RINGO are eringo roots, q.v.

ROMNEY VESSEL is a rumney vessel. Rumney was a sweet wine (of Greek origin) much liked in the late medieval and early modern periods. [336]

ROTCHET is rochet, the red gurnard, *Aspitrigla cuculus*. [197]

RUFFS are birds of the species *Philomachus pugnax*. The female is known as a reeve. [124]

RUNLET is a cask or barrel. Small runlets contained between a 'pint and a quart and 3 or 4 gallons' (*SOED*). [276]

RUNNET is rennet. [249]

RUSTY is resty, i.e. rancid. [86, 254]

SACK is a generic name for fortified wine from Spain or the Canaries: it might be Malaga, Sherry, Canary or Palma (Majorca). The word (see Robinson) may derive from the Spanish for export (*sacas*), rather than from the French for dry (*sec*).

SALENS is a fish not identified by *OED*. The nearest it can get is to draw a parallel with the *salena*, a fish found in Lake Como. [349]

SAMPIER is rock samphire. [70]

SANDERS is a dye from the red sandalwood tree which was imported from the Orient. [121]

SATERION ROOTS are satyrion. They are roots of the orchid, and they were held to be aphrodisiac. [313]

SCORTCHES are also scotches and are deep scorings across a piece of meat or fish. [96]

SCRAPE describes the act of scraping sugar with a knife off the loaf, which was the form it entered the household and how it would be deployed in the kitchen. No sugar casters for Rabisha.

SCRUSE OR SCRUISE OR SCRUCE, TO, means to squeeze.

SCUMMER is a broad, flat ladle or slotted spoon for lifting scum from the top of liquids.

SEARCE, TO, is to sift or sieve. The searce was the instrument used. According to the *OED* our culinary term sieve was used mainly in agricultural contexts at this time. Rabisha refers at least once to a hair searce. [320, 330]

SERVICE is the sorb, *Pyrus domestica*. [73]

SEW, TO, sewing relates to the service of the sewer, the attendant at banquets and feasts. His description derives from the French *asseoir*, i.e. one who superintends the seating and settling of the guests. His tasks included the formal ceremonies of hand-washing and table-laying as well as transferring food to the table. [334]

SHAMPINNIONS are mushrooms. [74]

SHERDOWNS, SHIRDOWNS OR SHERDOONS are cardoons. [70, 136]

SHOVELLERS are a name probably applicable to several species of wading bird with spoon-shaped bills, more commonly called spoonbills. [267]

SIMBER, SIMBRE, SIMPER, TO, is to simmer. [98]

SIPPETS are slices or small triangles of fried, dried or toasted bread, or sometimes puff pastry, used to ornament a dish. In John Evelyn's collection of receipts they were sometimes of manchet 'roasted crispe by a quick fire'. The word is the diminutive of sop. See Karen Hess for a short discussion.

SIVES are chives.

SKEATE is skate.

SKILLET is a metal cooking pot, often with legs to stand in the fire, cast in one piece.

SKIRRETS are *Sium sisarum*, a sweet rooted plant which used to be cultivated and eaten, but has now lapsed into the wild state and near-oblivion. Elizabeth David, who was still able to find it on sale in London in about 1960, has described it thus: 'In appearance something between salsify and the parsnips we know, but less pronounced in flavour than the latter.' [119]

SLEEP-AT-NOON is goat's beard. [74]

SOWCE OR SOUSE is a pickling liquid, often referred to as a 'sousing drink'. It is also a verb, meaning to pickle or to immerse in a pickle. [77]

SPANISH POTATOES are referred to several times by Rabisha. These are probably sweet potatoes. Whether other mentions of potatoes, without the qualification, are to our more familiar tuber is uncertain. [119, 136]

SPARRAGRASS is asparagus.

SPATTER, WOODEN, is a spatula. [320]

STORAX was the resin from the tree *Styrax officinalis*. It was used much in medicine. [320]

STOVE. When finishing the candying of eringo roots and marigolds, Rabisha places them in a stove. This is presumably a heated cupboard. When drying orange paste, he places it in either a stove or an oven. [330, 331, 333]

SUCCORY is chicory (*Cichorium intybus*). [273]

SUCKETS, from *succade*, are sweetmeats of fruit preserved in candy (dry) or syrup (wet). [146]

SUGAR. Rabisha calls for several different sorts of sugar. The position regarding sugar and its various types in this period is best discussed in Laura Mason's *Sugar-plums and Sherbet* (1998). The types that are mentioned in this text are: Barbary sugar [308], double refined sugar [272], refined sugar [309], hard sugar [312], loaf sugar [311], and sugar candy [312, 332]. In turn, they were as follows. The name Barbary sugar reflects the source of the earliest sugars in England, Morocco. Loaf sugar recalls the conical loaf shapes in which sugar entered the kitchen. Double refined sugar was refined in the country of origin but as this was often insufficient for European taste, so local refineries were established that produced the white loaves of sugar familiar from contemporary still-lifes. Ordinary refined sugar was likely to be yellow. Double-refined sugar, the result of reboiling, recrystallization, and a second refining, was off-white. (Royal sugar, triple-refined, not mentioned by Rabisha, was whitest of all.) Sugar candy was refined sugar clarified and crystallized by slow evaporation. The name candy sugar, from *khanda*, the Sanskrit word for 'a piece', applied and still applies to large crystalline pieces of sugar grown on threads suspended in a saturated solution of refined sugar.

TAFFATY-TARTS. Rabisha's recipe for this dish is akin to a pasty. Its main ingredient was apple, flavoured with citrus peel. John Evelyn's tarts were more like an open apple tart, with the slices laid thin across the surface 'like slateing of houses with round slates'. Quite what relationship these tarts had to taffeta, the fabric, has not yet been elucidated. There was also taffeta cream, but that too has little connection with the tarts. The two coexist in John Nott's *Cooks Dictionary*. Elizabeth David, who compiled the glossary for the 1980 facsimile of that work, suggested the creams were so called because their lustrous surface matched the sheen of taffeta silk. However, she was unable to make the link between a simple egg cream and (in the case of John Nott) a tart of high-flavoured apple purée. The *OED* connects the word in its culinary sense with the figurative usage, for example Shakespeare's 'taffata phrases, silken tearmes precise', when it means bombastic, florid, highly decorated. [238]

TANSEY OR TANZIE was a flat omelette, sometimes thickened with crumbs, and coloured green with juice of vegetables and herbs (tansy). Variations, like apple, also exist. [103, 173]

TAPES were the equipment of choice for tying collars of meat before sousing or cooking.

TARRIOTS are a misprint for tarriers, which were augers used for extracting the bung from a barrel. [335]

TENT was a generic name for dark, red Spanish wine, presumably deriving from *tinto*. [177]

THESSELL is a variant spelling of thistle. [70]

THRILPOLE is thirlepoll, a whale of some sort. [351]

TIFFINEE CLOTH is tiffany, fine silk or lawn used as a mesh for sieving and straining, or as cloth to make up a spice bag. [98]

TIME is thyme.

TRENCHERS are regular in their appearance in this text. In the early *Traditions of Carving, and Sewing*, of course, they are bread trenchers, carved and distributed by the sewer in traditional form. When they are referred to by Rabisha in a contemporary context, however, they were of other materials. He writes of 'trencher plates' in silver or glass; he certainly implies wooden trenchers when describing pressing cream cheese; and he refers to the type in general when advising something to be cut or shaped like a trencher. [102, 273, 288, 334]

TRIED in relation to lard, for example, means rendered or clarified. [177, 178]

TRIVETT was a tripod for resting a pan on before the fire. [178]

TURNSOLE was the plant *Crosophoria tinctoria* whose root gave a violet or blue dye used to colour jellies and foods. [272]

VERJUICE OR VIRJUICE was the acid juice of green or unripe grapes, crab apples, or other sour fruit. In one instance, Rabisha specifies verjuice from grapes. [286]

VEVER OLLIE. This strange name for a cheese pottage, the last recipe in the text, is of uncertain derivation. Does vever have some relation to the chiefly Scottish usage 'vivers' meaning foodstuffs; and does ollie bear a connection with *olla* or *olio*? [355]

WALM is a bubble in boiling; a boiling-up.

WARDENS are winter cooking pears, usually put into pies.

WATER. Rabisha, like his colleagues and contemporaries, will often specify the type of water he thinks best for a particular recipe. Sometimes, it may be no more than 'fair', i.e. pure, but others are pump water, conduit water, rain water, spring water and running water. The source of the water (either the sky or deep below the earth) will affect its hardness, and therefore its suitability for certain tasks. See the comments by Karen Hess. [79, 97, 301, 305, 306, 322]

WESTPHALIE BACON was a notable delicacy in early-modern Britain. It was lightly salted and cold-smoked. [82]

WHOPPERS are the wild or the whistling swan. The recipe where these birds are mentioned is identical to that in Robert May's *The Accomplisht Cook*. [267]

WIER, LATTICE OF is a wire rack. [329]

WIGGENS are widgeons. [82]

WINE CANNELS OF BOX are wooden taps or spigots for barrels. [335]